Delphi in Depth: ClientDataSets

by

Cary Jensen

Published by Jensen Data Systems, Inc., USA.

ISBN-10: 1461008581 (print edition)
ISBN-13: 978-1461008583 (print edition)

Printed copies of this book are available for sale from companies listed at, and linked to from, http://www.JensenDataSystems.com/cdsbook. Any other download or sale outlet is likely to be illegal. This is not a free ebook - do not distribute it.

Project Editor: Loy Anderson
Contributing Technical Editors: Stephen Blas, Nick Hodges, and Jim Tierney
Cover Designer: Loy Anderson

For more information and links for purchasing this book, visit:
http://www.JensenDataSystems.com/cdsbook

Delphi is a trademark of Embarcadero Technologies. Windows 7, Windows Vista, Windows XP, and Visual Studio are trademarks of Microsoft Corporation. Advantage Database Server is a trademark of Sybase, An SAP Company. Other product and company names mentioned herein or in accompanying online material may be the trademarks of their respective owners.

Dedication

This book is dedicated to my wife, business partner, and best friend, Loy Anderson. I know how lucky I have been to find the perfect companion on this journey we call life.

Chapter Titles

Table of Contents

About the Author

Cary Jensen

Cary Jensen is Chief Technology Officer of Jensen Data Systems, Inc., a company that provides software services, software training, documentation, and help system development. Cary is an active developer, providing companies with assistance in data modeling, software architecture, software development, and software migration. He is an award-winning, best-selling author of over 20 books, including Advantage Database Server: A Developer's Guide, 2nd Edition, Building Kylix Applications, Oracle JDeveloper, JBuilder Essentials, Delphi In Depth, and Programming Paradox 5 for Windows. A frequent speaker at conferences, workshops, and seminars throughout much of the world, he is widely regarded for his self-effacing humor and practical approaches to complex issues. Cary is an author and speaker for the 2001-2010 Delphi Developer Days tours in the US and Europe (more recently, Delphi Developer Days 2009-2011 with fellow author and Delphi expert Marco Cantù), the 2003-2006 Advantage Developer Days tours, 2000-2001 Delphi Development Seminars, the 1999-2000 Borland Developer Days, and the 1995-1999 Delphi World Tours. Cary has a Ph.D. from Rice University in Human Factors Psychology, specializing in human-computer interaction.

You can follow Cary on twitter at:
http://twitter.com/caryjensen/

Cary also writes a blog, *Let's Get Technical,* in which he typically posts magazine-length articles on Delphi and other software-related topics:
http://caryjensen.blogspot.com/

For more information about Cary's company, please visit:
http://www.JensenDataSystems.com/

Acknowledgements

Writing is a solitary task, but creating a book takes a team. I want to express my thanks to the many people who contributed directly and indirectly in the publishing of this book. At the top of this list is my wife and business partner, Loy Anderson. Loy played many roles in this book, including project manager, cover designer, indexer, and many more tasks that often go unrecognized. It would be an understatement to say that I could not have written this book without her critical eye and attention to detail.

Next on this list are technical editors, Jim Tierney and Stephen Blas. Jim and Stephen are on the Delphi development team, and I am grateful that they were willing to take their valuable time to review some of the technical passages found within these pages.

Thanks also goes to the people who offered to read and technically review some of the drafts of this book, especially to Nick Hodges of Gateway Ticketing Systems.

I also want to thank everyone in the Delphi community for their support of Delphi, beginning with the Delphi development team. Delphi continues to be a groundbreaking product, and the vision and experience of this team is directly responsible for that. I also want to thank my friends in Embarcadero Developer Relations for their support, including David Intersimone (David I), Anders Ohlsson, Tim Del DelChiaro, and Christine Ellis.

In addition, I want to thank my fellow Delphi authors and friends, Marco Cantù and Bob Swart. Marco is a Delphi expert, the author of the popular Mastering Delphi and Delphi Handbook series of books, and a tireless blogger (www.marcocantu.com). In addition, Marco and I work together with Loy Anderson on the Delphi Developer Days tours, www.DelphiDeveloperDays.com. Bob Swart (Dr. Bob) is the President of the Delphi section of the Software Development Network (www.sdn.nl), a dedicated Delphi evangelist, and prolific content producer (www.drbob42.com).

Finally, I want to thank everyone who uses Delphi to build software, from the hobbyist to the professional developer. Your continued commitment to this amazing tool is one of the reasons why it continues to be a force in software development.

Introduction

Before there was the ClientDataSet, Delphi's Borland Database Engine supported cached updates. When cached updates were enabled, changes to your database tables and editable queries were not written to the underlying database on a record-by-record basis. Instead, updates were delayed, permitting a group of changes to be applied to the underlying database in an all-or-none fashion (or even discarded altogether).

I wrote extensively about cached updates in the early days of Delphi, but over time, cached updates lost their appeal. There were two reasons for this. First, the Borland Database Engine became dated, and it's SQL counterpart, the Borland SQL Links for Windows became deprecated. The second is that cached updates became hopelessly broke, and this happened sometime around the release of Delphi 6.

Fortunately, there was a ready replacement — ClientDataSets. ClientDataSets supported all of the basic features of cached updates and much more. In addition to providing a mechanism for grouping updates, ClientDataSets also introduced in-memory management of data and indexes, the ability to persist data and restore it to its previous state, an intuitive interface for managing the cache, and a convenient mechanism for transferring a ClientDataSet's state between processes.

Originally ClientDataSets were only in the high-end versions of Delphi. Specifically, the Client/Server edition. Furthermore, the license to use a ClientDataSet in a distributed application was separate from Delphi, and was originally very expensive.

With the release of Kylix and subsequently Delphi 6, the ClientDataSet became available in the Professional version of Delphi, and the MIDAS (Multitier Distributed Application Services) license became affordable, and then eventually free. (The technology that was MIDAS is now called DataSnap.)

With ClientDataSets now within reach of all Delphi developers, I became an enthusiastic advocate for their use. Not only did I speak extensively about the virtues of ClientDataSets at developer conferences, I also published an extended series of articles on the Borland Developer Network detailing the use and capabilities of ClientDataSets.

At a recent Delphi conference at which I was presenting a talk on advanced ClientDataSet features, I had a revealing discussion with an attendee. His questions about an issue he was having with ClientDataSets demonstrated a fundamental misunderstanding about how they worked.

When I explained what was happening, he expressed frustration that this information was not more readily available. I directed him to my previous articles and commented, in passing, that maybe I should write a book about ClientDataSets. "I'll be the first one in line to buy it if you write that book" was his reply.

This idea has been with me for some time, and this past winter, I finally pulled myself together and started on this book in earnest.

Initially I thought that I could write this book by starting with some of my previous writings, including both the published series as well as a two-day Delphi course that I wrote and train called *Mastering ClientDataSets*. The trick, I reasoned, would be in the organization, and I had a lot of ideas about how I would go about this.

Projects like these tend to take on a life of their own, and once I was happy with the book's outline, I realized that I was committed to writing new material — a lot of new material. In the end, I estimate that at least 80 percent of this book is completely original, and that material that I salvaged from my previous writings often received extensive revision.

I am really happy about how this book turned out. I hope that you are, too.

This book takes an in-depth look at ClientDataSets. It begins with an overview of what a ClientDataSet is, and describes some of the ways that ClientDataSets can be used in your Delphi applications. It continues with a close examination of one of the more common uses for a ClientDataSet, reading and writing data from an underlying database through its interaction with a DataSetProvider.

Next you learn how to define the structure of a ClientDataSet, a process that can be undertaken both at design time as well as at runtime. The relative roles of FieldDefs and Fields are discussed, and the roles of persistent versus dynamic Fields are considered. How virtual Fields differ from data Fields is also explained.

Chapter 5 introduces indexes, including the difference between persistent and temporary indexes. The relationship between a ClientDataSet's indexes and those of an underlying database are also considered.

In Chapter 6, I take a long look at the change cache, the mechanism responsible for caching updates. Here you learn how to enable and disable the cache, how to detect changes to it, and how to modify the contents of the cache.

Chapters 7 through 9 introduce topics that will be familiar to many Delphi database developers, including how to edit, navigate, search, and filter data. These discussions, however, demonstrate the flexibility that ClientDataSets bring to these features, providing you with capabilities not available in other DataSets.

Chapters 10, 11, and 12 introduce some of the more interesting features found only in ClientDataSets. These features include aggregates, cloned cursors, and nested datasets.

The final three chapters of this book take a close look at DataSnap. These chapters specifically look at DataSnap applications where ClientDataSets in a client application interact with DataSetProviders running in a DataSnap server. Here you will learn to create DataSnap servers and clients using both the classic COM-based DataSnap as well as the newer IP-based DataSnap first introduced in Delphi 2009.

Consistency is important when writing a book. And while I know that there are always some inconsistencies that slip between the cracks, a lot of effort went into using terminology consistently in this book.

One of the areas that was most challenging in this respect was how to refer to objects. By convention, Delphi classes begin with an upper case T, and in most of my Delphi writings, I have carried that convention into the discussion of objects. For example, I might talk about ClientDataSet instances as TClientDataSets.

I did not adopt that convention in this book, however. I did not like how it looked to be talking about TClientDataSets. I though that referring to instances of the TClientDataSet class as ClientDataSets read better and looked more natural. As a result, when I refer to an instance of the class, I omitted the T. In those cases where I refer to the actually class declaration, I used the T.

While this approach worked well, for the most part, there are some places were it made the prose a little more difficult to read. This is especially true in the discussion of Fields, instances of classes that descend from TField. Frankly, those discussions, especially those in Chapter 5 dealing with ClientDataSet structure, were challenging to write clearly, since sometimes I was referring to a field (lower case, and referring to a column of data from a database table), sometimes to a Field (an instance of a TField descendant), and other times referring to a TField (the actual class definition).

There was another significant challenge in this book, besides how to refer to objects, and this was related to the code samples. In short, I felt that it was extremely important to provide code samples that made few assumptions about your Delphi installation, and required little or no additional configuration.

One place where this was especially difficult was in the selection of a database. Many, but not all, uses of a ClientDataSet involve interacting with a database. Where would the database come from, and what data access mechanism should be used to interact with that data?

One solution would have been to include a sample database in the code download. Loy Anderson and I created a sample database that we have used in other books, and we considered making it available for this book. But that would have required you to both install that database, as well as any data access mechanism it required. I considered going with a free solution such as MS SQL Server Developer Edition, InterBase Developer Edition, or even the Advantage Database Server, a remote database about which Loy Anderson and I have written three books.

The main drawback to all of these solutions was that it would require you to not only download the database, but also download a client API (application programming interface). In addition, additional configuration of the data access mechanism, such as an ODBC driver or an OLE DB Provider would be necessary, and all of that would have to be done successfully before you could run the first code example.

In the end, I opted to use the Borland Database Engine (BDE) and the sample Paradox database that is shipped with every copy of Delphi. While the BDE is obsolete, it provides what you need — a pre-configured database that requires no additional files or configuration on your Delphi machine. It also supports SQL, which was one feature in its favor.

When you install Delphi, the Borland Database Engine is installed by default, and a Database alias named DBDEMOS is inserted into the BDE configuration. Assuming that you have performed a typical installation of Delphi, everything should be ready for the code examples.

One aspect of the BDE's obsolescence is that it is not Windows 7 or Vista aware, and the added layers of security and user account control (UAC) might be an issue. This might require you to run Delphi with administrative privileges. Similarly, some of the Delphi executables that you compile from the code samples may also need to run with administrative privileges. If any of your executable's fail with an error related to reading the Paradox configuration file, PDOXUSRS.NET, it is likely an issue of privilege.

One more point about the code samples deserves mention. With the exception of a few of the IP-based DataSnap examples, which require Delphi 2009 or later, most if not all of these sample projects should run in almost any version of Delphi that supports ClientDataSets. The other exception is the DataSnap servers based on COM. Many of the early versions of Delphi had difficulty using the type library created with a different version of Delphi. If you run into that problem, you will need to follow the provided steps to create new versions of those COM servers.

Note: You can download the code samples form this book's web site.
http://www.jensendatasystems.com/cdsbook/

See Appendix A for details.

Chapter 1
Introduction to ClientDataSets

ClientDataSets are Delphi components that provide the services of an in-memory dataset. In-memory datasets are transient, structured, high-performance, self-describing data storage mechanisms that hold their data in memory, as opposed to durable data structures stored primarily on disk, which is typical of a database.

A significant feature of ClientDataSets, and one that is often supported by other types of in-memory datasets, is that they maintain, and can persist, a change cache. The change cache permits you to programmatically determine what changes have been made to the data since some point in time, often that point immediately after the data was first loaded into the ClientDataSet. This information is essential if you need to persist these changes back to an original source, such as a Web service, underlying database, or other persistence mechanism.

Delphi has included ClientDataSets since Delphi 3. However, up through Delphi 5 ClientDataSets were only available in the Client/Server version of Delphi. With the release of Kylix, and subsequently Delphi 6, the ClientDataSet was added to the Professional version, making it a component that nearly all Delphi developers can use in their applications.

This chapter begins with an overview of the features that make ClientDataSets so useful. It continues by examining the different ways that ClientDataSets are used in Delphi applications. Finally, this chapter concludes with a look at an issue affecting ClientDataSet deployment.

While most developers think of ClientDataSets as components used in the presentation layer of database applications, this use represents only a fraction of the possibilities for these powerful data structures. As this chapter will demonstrate, the characteristics of ClientDataSets make them a valuable tool for many different aspects of application development.

The following are the essential features of ClientDataSets:

- High performance

- Self describing

- Change cache managing

- Persistable

Individually, these characteristics provide a compelling argument for using ClientDataSets in your applications. But it is the combination of these features in a single, easy-to-use class that makes them so valuable for a wide range of software features.

The following sections look at each of these features in depth.

High Performance

ClientDataSets store their data entirely in RAM (random access memory). Consequently, operations that they perform on the data they contain, including searches, filters, and sorts, are very fast.

Note: The data managed by a ClientDataSet is always held entirely in memory. Some in-memory datasets support paging, where data is selectively moved into memory from disk, when needed. That the ClientDataSet does not natively support paging means that the amount of data it can work with is limited. This limit may be thousands, hundreds of thousands, or even millions of records, depending on the size of the individual records, your operating system, and the amount of available RAM.

In addition, ClientDataSets support indexes, special structures that represent a custom ordering of the records in a ClientDataSet. Indexes provide additional performance enhancements for features that work with records, such as searches (FindKey), ranges (SetRange), and dynamically linking two or more ClientDataSets (a key feature in supporting nested datasets, a mechanism by which related data from two or more sources can be represented by a single ClientDataSet. Nested datasets are described in detail in Chapter 12, *Using Nested DataSets*).

Self-Describing

ClientDataSets are formally designed around the concept of a database table. Unlike an array or sequence, whose data elements have a data type, and that's about it, each column of a database table has a name, a data type, and sometimes a data size (for example, the size of a text field or precision of a floating point number). In addition, the columns of a database table may have constraints, such as a required field constraint. This information is typically referred to as metadata, which is data about data.

With ClientDataSets, you access the metadata of a dataset using the Fields property of the dataset, which contains a collection of Field instances. Alternatively, if you have a reference to a particular Field, you can use this reference directly. Each Field has a name, a data type, and sometimes a size. Fields are discussed in many different chapters of this book, especially in Chapter 4, *Defining a ClientDataSet's Structure*, and Chapter 7, *Navigating ClientDataSets*.

Change Cache Managing

All ClientDataSets have a change cache. Whether the change cache is enabled or not is controlled by the LogChanges property, which defaults to True. The change cache permits you to manage the unresolved changes that have been posted to the ClientDataSet's data since the change cache became enabled, which normally occurs after the ClientDataSet's data is loaded. This management includes the ability to determined precisely what changes have occurred (which records were inserted, deleted, and field-level modifications), revert changes to their prior state, cancel all changes, or commit those changes permanently, thereby emptying the change cache.

The Delta property of a ClientDataSets holds the change cache. To manage the change cache, you use its methods, such as RevertRecord, UndoLastChange, CancelChanges, and ApplyUpdates. In addition, you can use the RecordStatus, StatusFilter, and Fields properties to examine the change cache contents. Working with the change cache is discussed in detail in Chapter 6, *Managing the ClientDataSet Change Cache.*

Persistable

Of all the features supported by ClientDataSets, its ability to persist itself is arguably the most powerful. Not only do you save a ClientDataSet's data, but you are saving its change cache as well (if the change cache is enabled). For example, it is possible to save the current state of a ClientDataSet to a file, Web service, or memo field of a database, and then to restore that ClientDataSet at a later time. In short, there is absolutely no difference between the original ClientDataSet and its restored version.

Note: Individually, I think that the ClientDataSet's support for a change cache and its support for persistence are a tie, as far as overall value is concerned. However, it is the combination of these two features that provide the synergy to make the combination unbeatable.

Consider the following scenario: After loading data into memory, and making several edits to a ClientDataSet, you can save its data to a file. At some later time, that ClientDataSet can be restored from the file, and the edits that were previously performed can be examined and rejected or accepted.

Furthermore, since the change cache is restored to its prior state, that information can be used to resolve those edits to the underlying database from which the data was originally loaded. No information is lost during the time that the ClientDataSet is in storage, no matter how long.

ClientDataSets work with data, and therefore, can be used in a variety of situations where data manipulation and/or storage are required. In the following sections I will consider some of the ways in which ClientDataSets can be used. In these discussions, I am going to focus on the mechanisms involved. In doing so, I will mention examples of these particular uses. I will not, however, go into details about how to implement these mechanisms. Those discussion are reserved for later chapters of this book.

ClientDataSets and Databases: A Layer of Abstraction

When ClientDataSets were originally introduced in 1997, there was a companion component released at that same time that has become synonymous with ClientDataSets — the DataSetProvider. By employing a DataSetProvider, a ClientDataSet can easily load data from, and resolve data back to, a database. Most often this database is one supported by a remote database server.

This use of a ClientDataSet/DataSetProvider combination provided the cornerstone for DataSnap, a technology that was original called MIDAS (Multi-tier Distributed Application Services). We'll discuss DataSnap in a little more depth in a bit, and in detail in Chapter 13, *ClientDataSets and DataSnap Servers*, but let's begin by focusing on the interaction between a ClientDataSet and its DataSetProvider.

When a ClientDataSet and DataSetProvider work together, the DataSetProvider takes responsibility for reading and writing data from an underlying database. This database might be accessed through a remote database server, such as MS SQL Server, Oracle, or Advantage Database

Server (ADS), or it might be a file server-based database, such as Paradox, dBase, or Advantage Local Server (ALS).

In order to read and write the data, the DataSetProvider must make use of another DataSet. This DataSet could be part of Delphi's Visual Component Library (VCL), such as a SQLDataSet (dbExpress), ADODataSet (dbGo, an ActiveX technology), or Table (a BDE, or Borland Database Engine, technology). Similarly, a DataSetProvider could access data through a third-party DataSet, such as Direct ORACLE Access (DOA, from Allround Automations) or an AdsTable (a part of Advantage Delphi Components from Sybase, an SAP Company). In fact, the DataSetProvider could even get its data from another ClientDataSet.

In other words, a DataSetProvider does not read directly from a database, or through a database's local client API (application programming interface), but rather uses the data accessing capabilities of another data access mechanism, specifically one that implements the TDataSet interface. Similarly, a DataSetProvider uses this same DataSet, or one of its related classes (usually a connection class of some type), to write data back to the underlying database.

When used with a DataSetProvider, a ClientDataSet makes the requests for data of the DataSetProvider, holds the obtained data in memory, maintains the change cache (when enabled), and requests that the DataSetProvider persist the changes in the change cache back to the underlying database. The ClientDataSet and DataSetProvider can also be instructed to interact if errors are encountered during update, such as when a record that was edited in the ClientDataSet is no longer available in the underlying database.

Let's return to DataSnap for a moment. The feature that made DataSnap originally work was that a ClientDataSet and its associated DataSetProvider could appear in completely separate applications, often running on separate computers on a network. The DataSetProvider would exist in the application server, the middle tier in the multi-tier architecture. This DataSetProvider would communicate with a ClientDataSet on one or more clients, often referred to as *thin clients*, since these clients had no direct access to the underlying database themselves. These thin clients represent the second tier. The DataSetProvider would in turn communicate with an underlying database, which when that database is one supported by a remote database server, formed the third tier of the multi-tier architecture.

Other components (such as the RemoteConnection component) and technologies (specifically COM, the component object model) were necessary for DataSnap to work. Since Delphi 2009, DataSnap added support for ClientDataSet-DataSetProvider communication over TCP/IP (transmission control protocol/Internet protocol) and HTTP (hypertext transfer protocol). Nonetheless, the ability of ClientDataSets and DataSetProviders to communicate is an essential component of Delphi's multi-tier implementation.

This interaction between the ClientDataSet and DataSetProvider is depicted in Figure 1-1. In this figure, it is assumed that the DataSetProvider and the ClientDataSet are both part of a common executable.

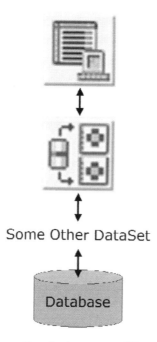

Some Other DataSet

Database

Figure 1-1: The interaction between a ClientDataSet, DataSetProvider, and an underlying database

As is the case with all discussions in this section, this description has been simplified. For example, it is possible for a ClientDataSet to obtain data directly from some DataSet, without the intervention of a DataSetProvider. Doing so, however, would have to be done programmatically. Likewise, whether or not a DataSetProvider was used to load the original data from a database into a ClientDataSet, the ClientDataSet itself could take responsibility for writing changes to the underlying database. Once again, this would require you to write, debug, and maintain custom code.

A Database Application without an External Database

A ClientDataSet can write its data, as well as the change cache, to a file. Similarly, a ClientDataSet can load data that was previously stored in a file into memory, permitting that data to be used within an application. In this regard, the ClientDataSet can act as a standalone database. Delphi refers to ClientDataSets used in this fashion as *MyBase.*

In this scenario, the ClientDataSet does not employ the services of a DataSetProvider. It simply isn't necessary. The ClientDataSet methods are sufficient to perform all of the tasks required. It is even possible for a ClientDataSet to load its data from a stream, as well as write its data to a stream, meaning that the physical storage of the data that is held by the ClientDataSet could be located on another computer on the network, or anywhere on the Internet, for that matter. (Doing this, however, would require you to write additional software, including a communication service capable of receiving, sending, and storing the ClientDataSet's data on the storage end of the network. Communication capabilities on the ClientDataSet side of things would need to be implemented as well.)

There are serious limits to how you can work with data when the ClientDataSet is loading and saving data to a file (including when that file is stored somewhere else on the network). In short, that data can only be used by one client application at a time, where the client application in this discussion is the one using the ClientDataSet to load and save the data. As a result, this type of approach is typically only used in single user or readonly situations.

For example, imagine that you want to write a simple contact management system that an end user could use to save information about their professional contacts, such as phone numbers, addresses, appointments, and the like. So long as the end user does not need to share this data simultaneously with any other users, you can forgo the additional complexity associated with supporting some external database for storage, and do it all with the ClientDataSet alone.

Likewise, if the data is readonly, meaning that the data-managing ClientDataSet will never actually permit changes to the data, MyBase is similarly useful. For example, you might write an application that the users in your company run to lookup other employees for the purpose of discovering their phone extensions, job titles, or office numbers. This application could employ a ClientDataSet that reads from a readonly file on a network share, providing two or more users the ability to load this data on demand, again without the application needing to support the additional complexity of attaching to, and reading from, an external database.

In reality, the use of a ClientDataSet to support a standalone database is limiting, and therefore, limited in utility. Consider the first example, where a ClientDataSet could be used to deploy a simple contact management system. Such a system is considered a single-user system, in that only one user can work with the data at a time (otherwise one user's changes might completely replace another user's changes). Except in the simplest contact management systems, it is often quite useful to permit several users to access, and even make changes to, the data simultaneously. For example, it would be useful if an executive assistant could add an appoint for their executive while that executive is viewing his or her current schedule. That's just not possible with MyBase.

A similar limitation appears in the company directory example. Though many users can access the data simultaneously, what happens when it comes time to update the employee database. Sure, it might work to simply replace the existing file with a new copy, but what if that happens at the same time as someone is trying to read the data? Typically, a client application trying to load a file while it is being written to will raise an exception.

These problems can be easily solved by employing an external database, specifically a multi-user database. And, to be honest, while being more complex, the advantages of an external database are usually worth the extra trouble and (sometimes) expense. For example, remote database servers typically support transactions and stored procedures. These are features that are hard to live without, and MyBase does not support them.

Nonetheless, that a ClientDataSet can be used as a standalone database is important to know, and gives you a valuable tool to use in the right situation.

The use of a ClientDataSet in a standalone application is depicted in Figure 1-2.

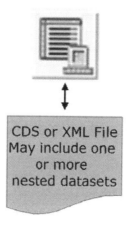

Figure 1-2: A ClientDataSet in a standalone application scenario

The second advantage is associated with situations where there is a large amount of local data that needs to be maintained. Since the ClientDataSet supports indexes, filters, searches, ranges, and other similar features that are well-adapted to large amounts of data, it is far more well-suited for handling these situations compared to the more free-form INI file format.

Both of these advantages also apply, to some extent, when compared to the use of the Windows registry for storing configuration data. The Registry class (found in the Registry unit), cannot be hooked up directly to data-aware controls. On the other hand, the Registry can be searched more quickly than INI files (since it is cached by the operating system), though it still lacks the database-related features of filters and ranges.

The Registry suffers another shortcoming in that most developers try to limit the extent to which their applications store large amounts a data in the Windows registry, since this complicates the process of fully uninstalling an application.

In many respects, the use of a ClientDataSet as a local data storage mechanism closely mimics its use as a standalone database. However, in this use, the use of the ClientDataSet for local storage is independent of the storage of application data. In other words, it is not uncommon for an application to connect to a remote database server (whether or not a ClientDataSet is involved in this operation), yet use a ClientDataSet to manage one or more local files that store information about the specific client installation, such as each user's display preferences, usage history, and the like. Since this usage is single user, by definition, the ClientDataSet provides an acceptable solution.

The use of a ClientDataSet to manage local storage is depicted in Figure 1-3.

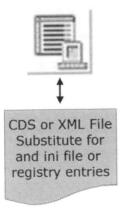

Figure 1-3: Using a ClientDataSet for local storage

Data Carrier

The ClientDataSet's ability to persist itself, either as a file or a file stream, makes it an attractive candidate as a data transport mechanism. Making this feature even more interesting is the ClientDataSet's support for BLOB (Binary Large OBject) fields, such as BlobField and MemoField, which means that you can load any type of binary content imaginable (within size limits) into a ClientDataSet before you send its content across a network.

Here's an example. Imagine that you need a mechanism for programmatically distributing corporate Web site updates to a large number of local offices. For example, updated pages describing new policies on scheduling vacation time, updates to corporate medical insurance coverage, updated cascading style sheets to improve the Web site's appearance, and new logos.

Here is a simplified description of how this can be done. Each record in the ClientDataSet can have three fields. The first might be the file name of the file being transported, the second field might contain the relative folder name, with respect to the root directory of the Web site, where this file needs to be saved, while a third field might indicate whether this file is new or a replacement for an existing file.

After the new and updated files of the Web site have been stored in the ClientDataSet, a socket connection can be made from a workstation at corporate headquarters to each of the local offices, one at a time. Once that connection has been accepted by a server at the local office (a service specifically setup for this type of update), the ClientDataSet is written to a stream and the stream is transferred to the receiving office.

Once the transfer has been received at the local office the service can load this stream into a ClientDataSet. The receiving application can then scan through this ClientDataSet, one record at a time, examining the file name and destination location, saving the BLOB contents to the appropriate file, replacing those files being updated and simply writing the new files that have been made available.

While other mechanisms for the data transfer could have been used, the structured nature of the ClientDataSet, its ability to be easily streamed, and its support for BLOB and memo fields that can be loaded from a file or written to a file in a single statement make the process straightforward.

Another situation where a ClientDataSet can be used as a general data carrier is in a message-based environment, such as SOA (software oriented architecture). The message can be the contents of a ClientDataSet that is passed as a string parameter to a remote procedure call. The object that implements the remote procedure call can load that string into another ClientDataSet, where its contents are then examined to determine what type of message it holds, as well as any additional information required to process the message, such as support documents, files, and configuration information.

Figure 1-4 depicts a ClientDataSet being used as a data carrier.

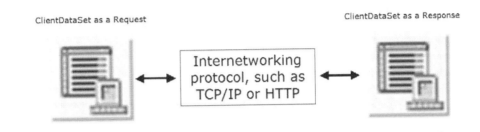

Figure 1-4: Using a ClientDataSet as a data carrier

There is just one more item we need to discuss before continuing on to the remaining chapters of this book where we explorer ClientDataSet features in detail. ClientDataSets require a special set of services that are not required by other Delphi applications. These services are referred to as MIDAS, and you must either ship them with your application or link them directly into your application before it can be successfully deploy.

Two options for deploying MIDAS are discussed in the remaining sections of this chapter.

Using MIDAS.DLL

Under normal circumstances, when you use a ClientDataSet you are relying on an external DLL (dynamic link library) named midas.dll. You can see this in Figure 1-5, which displays Delphi's debugger Modules window. To see the Modules window in Delphi, ensure that the integrated debugger is enabled before running your project from within the IDE (integrated development environment). If you are using Delphi 2005 or later, make sure that you run with the debugger (Delphi 2005 and later support a Run without Debugging feature.)

Once your project is running, select View | Debug Windows | Modules, or press Ctrl-Alt-M. The Modules window displays the various DLLs that your application is using (including in-process COM servers). Notice the inclusion of midas.dll at the bottom of the Modules window shown in Figure 1-5.

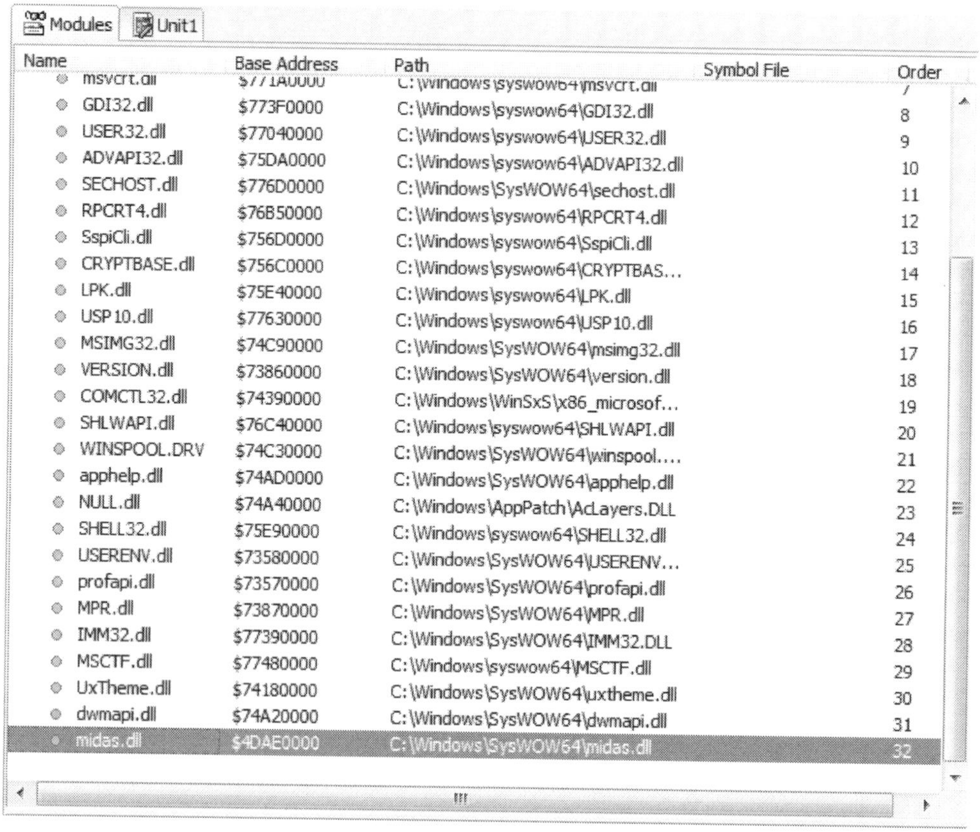

Name	Base Address	Path	Symbol File	Order
msvcrt.dll	$771A0000	C:\Windows\syswow64\msvcrt.dll		7
GDI32.dll	$773F0000	C:\Windows\syswow64\GDI32.dll		8
USER32.dll	$77040000	C:\Windows\syswow64\USER32.dll		9
ADVAPI32.dll	$75DA0000	C:\Windows\syswow64\ADVAPI32.dll		10
SECHOST.dll	$776D0000	C:\Windows\SysWOW64\sechost.dll		11
RPCRT4.dll	$76B50000	C:\Windows\syswow64\RPCRT4.dll		12
SspiCli.dll	$756D0000	C:\Windows\syswow64\SspiCli.dll		13
CRYPTBASE.dll	$756C0000	C:\Windows\syswow64\CRYPTBAS...		14
LPK.dll	$75E40000	C:\Windows\syswow64\LPK.dll		15
USP10.dll	$77630000	C:\Windows\syswow64\USP10.dll		16
MSIMG32.dll	$74C90000	C:\Windows\SysWOW64\msimg32.dll		17
VERSION.dll	$73860000	C:\Windows\SysWOW64\version.dll		18
COMCTL32.dll	$74390000	C:\Windows\WinSxS\x86_microsof...		19
SHLWAPI.dll	$76C40000	C:\Windows\syswow64\SHLWAPI.dll		20
WINSPOOL.DRV	$74C30000	C:\Windows\SysWOW64\winspool....		21
apphelp.dll	$74AD0000	C:\Windows\SysWOW64\apphelp.dll		22
NULL.dll	$74A40000	C:\Windows\AppPatch\AcLayers.DLL		23
SHELL32.dll	$75E90000	C:\Windows\syswow64\SHELL32.dll		24
USERENV.dll	$73580000	C:\Windows\SysWOW64\USERENV...		25
profapi.dll	$73570000	C:\Windows\SysWOW64\profapi.dll		26
MPR.dll	$73870000	C:\Windows\SysWOW64\MPR.dll		27
IMM32.dll	$77390000	C:\Windows\SysWOW64\IMM32.DLL		28
MSCTF.dll	$77480000	C:\Windows\syswow64\MSCTF.dll		29
UxTheme.dll	$74180000	C:\Windows\SysWOW64\uxtheme.dll		30
dwmapi.dll	$74A20000	C:\Windows\SysWOW64\dwmapi.dll		31
midas.dll	$4DAE0000	C:\Windows\SysWOW64\midas.dll		32

Figure 1-5: The external library midas.lib appears in the modules dialog box

The use of midas.dll has implications for any application that uses a ClientDataSet. Specifically, so long as your application is using midas.dll, you must make sure to deploy this DLL to any machine on which your application will run. This DLL can be deployed in the same directory where the application executable resides, or it can be deployed in a directory on the search path (configurable through the PATH environment variable).

If you do deploy midas.dll, I recommend that you place it in the same directory as the application that will use it. If you deploy it on the search path, you risk introducing incompatibilities if you, or someone else, has or will deploy midas.dll also on the search path. This can easily lead to the malady known as *DLL hell*.

Each release of Delphi since Delphi 3 has included a copy of midas.dll that you can distribute with your applications. This file is backwards compatible, in that Delphi applications compiled with an earlier version of Delphi can use the midas.dll that shipped with a later version. However, the reverse is not true. In most cases, an application compiled with one version of Delphi cannot use the midas.dll that shipped with an earlier version. This is yet another reason to deploy midas.dll in the directory where your application is installed.

To learn where midas.dll is located on your computer, use the Path column of the Modules window.

Using MidasLib

Fortunately, there is an alternative to deploying midas.dll. Delphi includes a unit, named MidasLib, which contains the routines found in midas.dll, permitting you to compile this support directly into your applications. To use MidasLib, add this unit name to the uses clause of your project file (.dpr).

An application compiled with the MidasLib unit is about 200K larger than one that uses midas.dll. On the other hand, applications compiled with MidasLib do not require midas.dll. Furthermore, by using MidasLib, you avoid the possibility of DLL incompatibility. Even if two applications compiled with different versions of Delphi have been deployed to a given machine, they will use the MidasLib routines that they were compiled with, rather than attempting load a version of midas.dll that they may or may not be compatible with.

Figure 1-6 shows the Modules window for the same application used to create Figure 1-5, with the exception that this application now includes MidasLib in its project's uses clause.

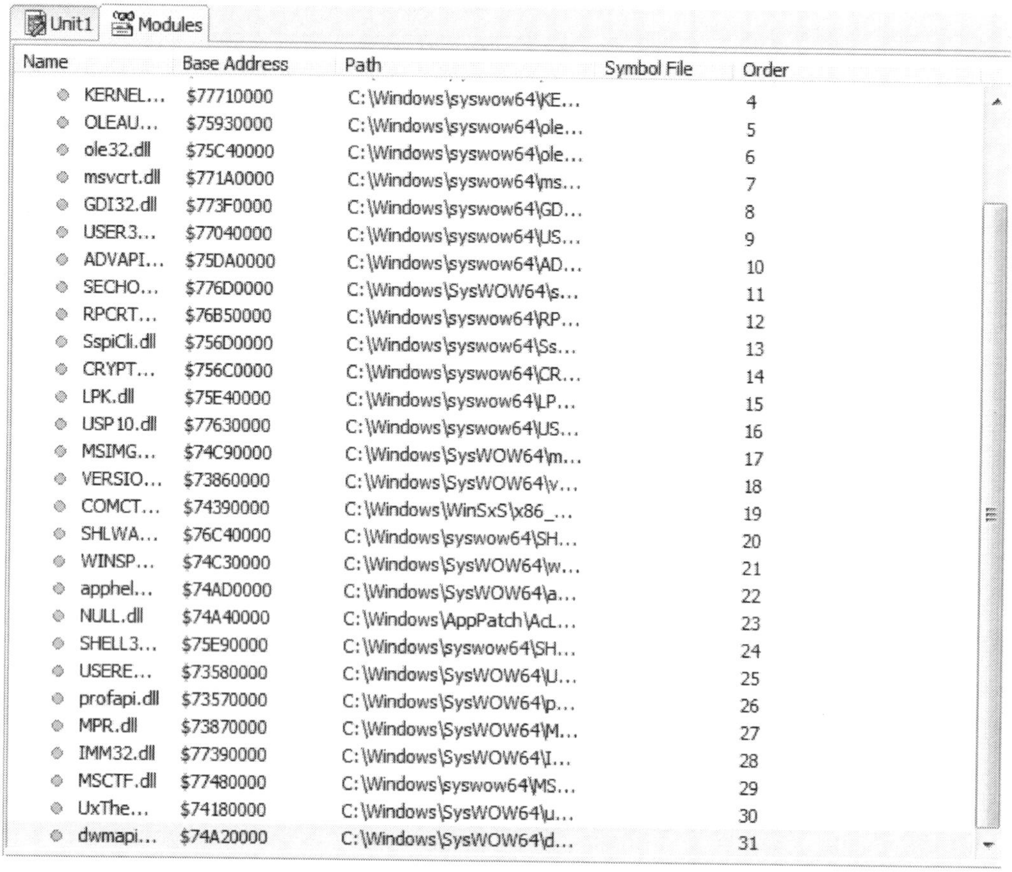

Name	Base Address	Path	Symbol File	Order
KERNEL...	$77710000	C:\Windows\syswow64\KE...		4
OLEAU...	$75930000	C:\Windows\syswow64\ole...		5
ole32.dll	$75C40000	C:\Windows\syswow64\ole...		6
msvcrt.dll	$771A0000	C:\Windows\syswow64\ms...		7
GDI32.dll	$773F0000	C:\Windows\syswow64\GD...		8
USER3...	$77040000	C:\Windows\syswow64\US...		9
ADVAPI...	$75DA0000	C:\Windows\syswow64\AD...		10
SECHO...	$776D0000	C:\Windows\SysWOW64\s...		11
RPCRT...	$76B50000	C:\Windows\syswow64\RP...		12
SspiCli.dll	$756D0000	C:\Windows\syswow64\Ss...		13
CRYPT...	$756C0000	C:\Windows\syswow64\CR...		14
LPK.dll	$75E40000	C:\Windows\syswow64\LP...		15
USP10.dll	$77630000	C:\Windows\syswow64\US...		16
MSIMG...	$74C90000	C:\Windows\SysWOW64\m...		17
VERSIO...	$73860000	C:\Windows\SysWOW64\v...		18
COMCT...	$74390000	C:\Windows\WinSxS\x86_...		19
SHLWA...	$76C40000	C:\Windows\syswow64\SH...		20
WINSP...	$74C30000	C:\Windows\SysWOW64\w...		21
apphel...	$74AD0000	C:\Windows\SysWOW64\a...		22
NULL.dll	$74A40000	C:\Windows\AppPatch\AcL...		23
SHELL3...	$75E90000	C:\Windows\syswow64\SH...		24
USERE...	$73580000	C:\Windows\SysWOW64\U...		25
profapi.dll	$73570000	C:\Windows\SysWOW64\p...		26
MPR.dll	$73870000	C:\Windows\SysWOW64\M...		27
IMM32.dll	$77390000	C:\Windows\SysWOW64\I...		28
MSCTF.dll	$77480000	C:\Windows\syswow64\MS...		29
UxThe...	$74180000	C:\Windows\SysWOW64\u...		30
dwmapi...	$74A20000	C:\Windows\SysWOW64\d...		31

Figure 1-6: When MidasLib is used, midas.dll is not loaded and does not need to be deployed

In Chapter 2, you will learn how to load data from an underlying database into a ClientDataSet using a DataSetProvider.

Chapter 2
Loading Data with ClientDataSets and DataSetProviders

As mentioned in the preceding chapter, there a number of different ways in which you can use a ClientDataSet in your applications. One of the most common is to use a ClientDataSet to hold and/or edit data obtained from an underlying database. Most applications that do this employ a DataSetProvider.

The DataSetProvider is a specialized component that understands how to read data from a DataSet and to package that data up for use by a ClientDataSet. When a ClientDataSet and a DataSetProvider have been properly configured, loading of data into a ClientDataSet can be as simple as calling the ClientDataSet's Open method. Similarly, in most cases, writing the changes held in the ClientDataSet's change cache takes little more than a call to the ClientDataSet's ApplyUpdates method.

But it is not always that simple. For example, under normal conditions, a ClientDataSet will ask a DataSetProvider for all of the data associated with the DataSet from which the data is being loaded, even if there is more data than the ClientDataSet can hold in memory. Fortunately, there are several things you can do to alter this behavior, and these solutions often require custom code. Similarly, some ClientDataSet-DataSetProvider combinations can apply the changes in the change cache automatically, as a result of the call to ApplyUpdates, while other configurations require code to manage the process. This code can get complicated.

This chapter is the first of three that takes an in-depth look at the use of ClientDataSets in conjunction with DataSetProviders. In this chapter, I will look at how a ClientDataSet obtains its data through a DataSetProvider, as well as the options you have for configuring this process. In Chapter 3, *Saving Data with ClientDataSets and DataSetProviders,* you will learn how the changes in the change cache can be applied to the underlying database. Chapter 15, *Remote ClientDataSet-DataSetProvider Interaction*, provides a look at how ClientDataSets and DataSetProviders communicate when they run in separate applications.

It is important to note that once the ClientDataSet has been loaded with data, many of the capabilities that it has have nothing to do with a DataSetProvider. For example, after loading a ClientDataSet with data, you can save that data to a file or stream. Likewise, you can filter, search, define aggregates, create cloned cursors, and the like. None of these operations involve the DataSetProvider in any way.

What I am getting at is that while this chapter and the next one focus on loading and saving data using a ClientDataSet/DataSetProvider combination, the topics covered in later chapters still apply to operations involving the ClientDataSet, including those situations where a DataSetProvider is involved.

In addition, it is possible to use a ClientDataSet to hold and edit data from an underlying database without the use of a DataSetProvider. For example, your code could open a SQLConnection component, and then execute a query through it using a SQLDataSet. You could then navigate each record in the SQLDataSet, inserting a record into a ClientDataSet for each one found in the result set. To apply changes, your code could iterate through the records in a ClientDataSet's change cache, applying each change to the underlying SQLConnection using SQL INSERT, UPDATE, and DELETE statements. Taking this approach, however, is much more involved than when you use the features and power of a DataSetProvider.

You can use a DataSetProvider to load data from a DataSet into the ClientDataSet. Loading a ClientDataSet in this manner produces a number of interesting results. First, if the ClientDataSet does not have persistent fields defined for it, dynamic fields are created for each column in the result set being loaded. These Fields can be used to examine the metadata of the result set being loaded, as well as to read and write data associated with the individual columns of the result set. Second, if the ClientDataSet's IndexName or IndexFieldNames property has been set, the ClientDataSet will now build the necessary index. Third, the change cache is initialized as both empty and enabled (the ClientDataSet's LogChanges property is set to True). Finally, the ClientDataSet becomes active.

At this point, the ClientDataSet is ready to use. If the ClientDataSet is wired to data-aware controls, those controls will display data associated with the first record, so long as the DataSetProvider pointed to a result set that was not empty. If the DataSetProvider was pointing to an empty result set, the data-aware controls will paint themselves consistent with an empty data set.

The ClientDataSet is now ready to receive edits, or any other operation that you need to perform on the data. For example, if the ClientDataSet is not empty, you can navigate to a new record, search for a record, or begin performing edits. If the ClientDataSet is empty, you could start inserting records, after which you could perform other tasks that apply to non-empty DataSets. It does not matter if these operations are performed by a user interacting with data-aware controls in the user interface or are the result of method calls and property manipulation implemented in your code.

Unless you specifically set the LogChanges property to False, the changes to the data once loading is completed will create entries in the change cache (and some operations might actually remove entries from the change cache). Recall, however, that the change cache is initialized after the loading has completed. As a result, the actual records that were loaded are not considered "inserted" records.

At this point, I'm not going to go into much more detail about the change cache, other than describe what happens when you want to resolve changes in the change cache back to the database from which the records were retrieved. For a detailed description of the change cache and how it is manipulated, see Chapter 6, *Managing the ClientDataSet Change Cache.*

In the remainder of this section, I will consider how the DataSetProvider and ClientDataSet interact during the loading process, as well as ways that you can control this process.

Configuring ClientDataSets to Use DataSetProviders

Most Delphi developers use the design-time properties of the ClientDataSet, DataSetProvider, and data access DataSet classes to configure the data loading. At a minimum, there are three properties that you need to set. These are listed in Table 2-1.

ClientDataSet.ProviderName	This is a string property that holds the name of the DataSetProvider instance that should load the data.
DataSetProvider.DataSet	This is a reference to the DataSet from which the DataSetProvider will load the data.
DataSet properties	The DataSet from which the data will be loaded must be configured so that it opens a handle to a database table, executes a SQL SELECT query, or executes a stored procedure that returns a result set. The

	specific properties to do this differ depending on the data access mechanism you are using.

Table 2-1: Properties for Configuring a ClientDataSet to Use a DataSetProvider

While most developers configure these properties at design time, some or all of them can also be defined at runtime. The following is a somewhat simple example taken from the OnCreate event handler of the RuntimeForm, which you will find in the CDSLoadBehavior project:

```
procedure TRuntimeForm.FormCreate(Sender: TObject);
var
  CDS: TClientDataSet;
  DSP: TDataSetProvider;
  Table1: TTable;
begin
  //When configuring a ClientDataSet and
  //DataSetProvider using the ClientDataSet's
  //ProviderName, both must have the same owner,
  //and the DataSetProvider must have a name
  CDS := TClientDataSet.Create(Self);
  DSP := TDataSetProvider.Create(Self);
  Table1 := TTable.Create(Self);
  Table1.DatabaseName := 'DBDEMOS';
  Table1.TableName := 'CUSTOMER';
  DSP.Name := 'DSP1';
  CDS.ProviderName := DSP.Name;
  DSP.DataSet := Table1;
  CDS.Open;
  DataSource1.DataSet := CDS;
  //Disable the menu item used to create this form
  Form1.RuntimeConfiguration1.Enabled := False;
end;
```

Code: The code project CDSLoadBehavior is available from the code download. See Appendix A for details.

These properties are not the only way to configure these components — they are just those that are most commonly used. Alternative approaches to hooking up your ClientDataSet and DataSetProvider are shown later in this chapter.

Initiating Loading

The DataSetProvider, ClientDataSet, and data source DataSet, interact in very specific ways during the loading process, and it is useful to understand these interactions very well. On the code disk associated with this book you will find the CDSLoadBehavior project, which I am going to use to demonstrate these effects.

Once your components have been properly configured, you can initiate the loading of the data by activating the ClientDataSet. You can do this either by setting the ClientDataSet's Active property to True (which you can do at design time, if you want the ClientDataSet to initiate loading once the form or data module on which it appears has been created), or you can call the ClientDataSet's Open method.

With the configuration described here, activating the ClientDataSet triggers a series of events, which I will describe here in simplified form. To begin with, the ClientDataSet requests that the DataSetProvider retrieve data. The DataSetProvider, in return, will look to its DataSet. If the DataSet is already active, the DataSetProvider will begin its process from the current record of that DataSet. If the DataSet is not active, the DataSetProvider will make it active, and then begin processing, starting with the first record in the result set that the DataSet returns.

The processing begins by the DataSetProvider creating an empty variant array, of the type OleVariant (which, as implied by the COM-based name *Ole*, is a reference counted variant array). The DataSetProvider then prepares another variant array, and populates this array with metadata information about the DataSet, including field names, field types, size or precision, and so forth. This metadata variant array is then added to the initial variant array.

The DataSetProvider now systematically navigates through each of the records in the DataSet, creating a new variant array for each record found, populating this array with the columns of the record, and adding the array to the initial variant array. When the final record of the DataSet has been read (that is, when DataSet.Eof returns True after an attempt to read data) and its data has been added to the initial array, the DataSetProvider sets the DataSet's Active property to False. It then assigns the created variant array to the ClientDataSet's Data property, which is also of type OleVariant, after which the DataSetProvider sets it's Data property to nil (thereby reducing the reference count on the variant array by one).

The ClientDataSet now unpacks this variant array, retrieving the metadata and any row data included in the data packet. The ClientDataSet will now create Fields (if necessary) to accommodate the metadata, and will unpack the row data, if present, into an internal memory stored.

Note: In addition to the metadata and individual row data, the data packet may also include additional data of virtually any type. Adding additional data to the data packet is achieved by adding one or more event handlers to the DataSetProvider, and is retrieved by adding corresponding event handlers to the ClientDataSet. In the preceding description, no additional data was included in the data packet. Adding additional data to the data packet is described in more detail in Chapter 15, Remote ClientDataSet-DataSetProvider Interaction.

The ClientDataSet is now active, but it has one more step before is informs any DataSource components that it is active. As mentioned earlier in this section, the ClientDataSet will now build an index if either the IndexName or IndexFieldNames property has been assigned a value. When this step is complete, the ClientDataSet sends a notification to any interested DataSources.

If any of those DataSources are wired to other controls, they will now respond appropriately. For example, if one or more of those DataSources are connected to data-aware controls, then those controls will now re-paint themselves. Similarly, DataSources connected to other objects that need to react, such as a DataSet that is listening for changes through its MasterSource property, will now react according to its prescribed behavior.

The results of this sequence of behaviors can be observed using the CDSLoadBehavior project. The main form of this project is shown in Figure 2-1.

There are two DBGrids on this form. The DBGrid on the right is associated with the component Table1, while the grid on the left is associated with ClientDataSet1. ClientDataSet1 points to DataSetProvider1 through its ProviderName property, and DataSetProvider1 points to Table1 through its DataSet property. Initially, the Active property of Table1 is False.

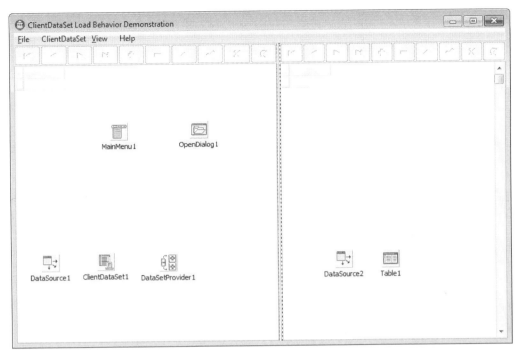

Figure 2-1: The main form of the CDSLoadBehavior project in the designer

ClientDataSet1 is activated (and loaded) by selecting ClientDataSet | Load from the main menu of this project. The event handler on this menu item toggles the caption of this menu item between Load and Close, as well as toggles the ClientDataSet's Active property between True and False. The following is the event handler associated with this menu item:

```
procedure TForm1.Load1Click(Sender: TObject);
begin
  if ClientDataSet1.Active then
  begin
    Load1.Caption := 'Load';
    ClientDataSet1.Close;
  end
  else
  begin
    Load1.Caption := 'Close';
    ClientDataSet1.Open;
  end;
end;
```

When you run this project, and then select ClientDataSet | Load from the main menu, you will see a very interesting behavior. You will see the DBGrid on the right display the contents of Table1, after which it will immediately begin scrolling the grid. This scrolling occurs because the DataSetProvider is navigating Table1. After about a second or two the scrolling ends and the right-hand grid will paint itself the way it does when it is pointing to an inactive table (since the DataSetProvider has now closed Table1).

Immediately after the right-grid becomes inactive, the left grid will display the contents of ClientDataSet1 (the data obtained through DataSetProvider1 from Table1). Your form should now look like that shown in Figure 2-2.

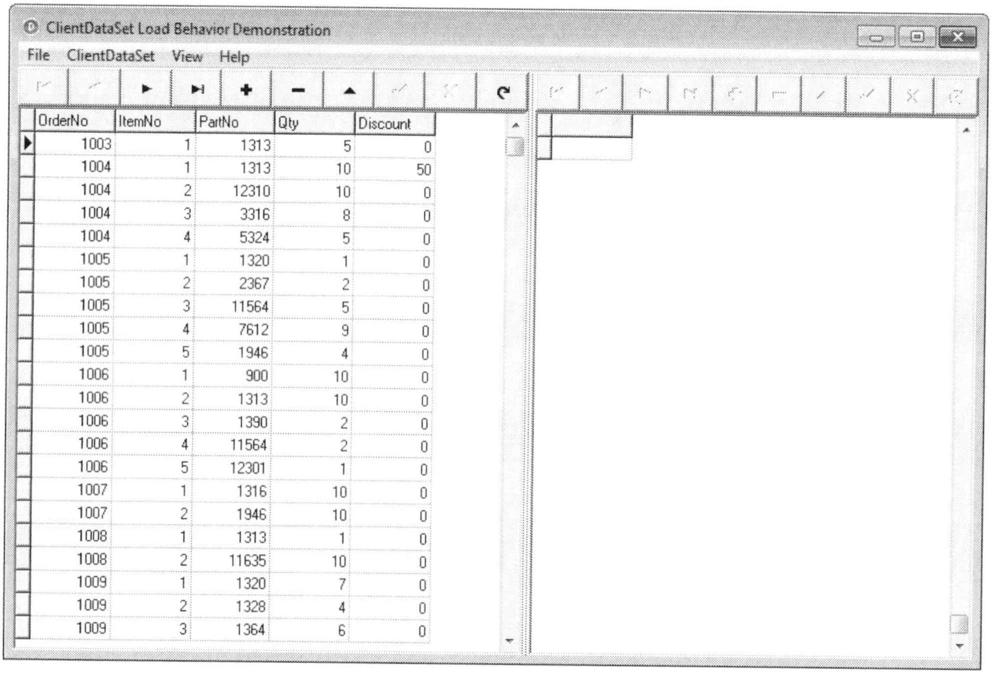

Figure 2-2: The contents of Table1 have been loaded by DataSetProvider1 into ClientDataSet1

If you now select ClientDataSet | Close, the left-hand DBGrid will also display an inactive grid. Calling the Close method of the ClientDataSet causes the Data property (as well as the Delta property, but we haven't talked about that property yet), to be set to nil. This reduces the reference count on the OleVariant to zero, at which time, it is released from memory. Note that calling ClientDataSet.Close (or setting the ClientDataSet's Active property to False) has no effect on either DataSetProvider1 or Table1. Neither of these components is aware of this change.

One of the first things that you might notice when you run this project is that it appears to take quite a while (a second or so) for the DataSetProvider to load the data. And given that the table that this example uses has only about a thousand records (and not very large ones at that), this might portend a serious problem for loading ClientDataSets.

Fortunately, this delay in loading is not caused by either the ClientDataSet or the DataSetProvider (or even the DataSet, technically speaking). It is an artifact of the repaint that is produced each time the current record of Table1 changes. Repainting, especially something as complex as a DBGrid, is a very expensive operation. The loading delay will go away almost completely if we simply do not display the contents of Table1 in a grid while it is being navigated by DataSetProvider1.

The CDSLoadBehavior project exposes a menu item that you can use to suppress the display of Table1 in the right-hand DBGrid. This menu item has an OnClick event handler that executes the Table's DisableControls and EnableControls methods, depending on how the Table is currently communicating with its DataSource. When DisableControls is executed, a DataSet stops informing any listening DataSources about changes to its state, including its current record. Calling EnableControls restores the normal communication that takes place between a DataSet and any interested DataSources.

The following is the event handler that performs this operation:

```
procedure TForm1.TableLoading1Click(Sender: TObject);
begin
  if TableLoading1.Checked then
  begin
    Table1.DisableControls;
    TableLoading1.Checked := False;
  end
  else
  begin
    Table1.EnableControls;
    TableLoading1.Checked := True;
  end;
end;
```

You can easily demonstrate how turning off the right-hand DBGrid repaint affects the speed of loading the ClientDataSet using the following steps:

1. If the project is not already running, run it.

2. Begin by selecting ClientDataSet | Load, and note how long it takes to load the ClientDataSet.

3. Now select ClientDataSet | Close to close the ClientDataSet.

4. Next, select View | View Table Loading to uncheck this menu option.

5.   Once again select ClientDataSet | Load.

This time the ClientDataSet appears to load almost instantaneously. Actually, it does take time (less than 20 milliseconds in my tests), with that time being proportional to the amount of data being loaded. In most cases, a thousand records or so take only a fraction of a second, but a hundred thousand records will take a measurable amount of time (from less than a second to a couple of seconds, depending on the amount of data being loaded, the speed of your computer, and the amount of memory that you have).

Note: In order for a DataSetProvider and a ClientDataSet to interact successfully, they must be owned by the same Component. Components that are defined at design time are owned by the form, data module, or frame on which they have been placed, which is why this example works. When you create ClientDataSets and DataSetProviders at runtime, and you need them to work together to load data, either call their constructors using the same owner, or associate the DataSetProvider to the ClientDataSet by calling the ClientDataSet method SetProvider.

Variations on Loading

While the technique described in the preceding section is how most developers use ClientDataSets and DataSetProviders, the following sections provide you with some of the variations.

Getting a DataSetProvider's Data Directly

Rather than simply activating a ClientDataSet that refers to a DataSetProvider in its ProviderName property, you can simply read the DataSetProvider's Data property, assigning it to the ClientDataSet's Data property. The DataSetProvider's Data property produces a side effect when read, which is to load and return an OleVariant from the DataSet to which its DataSet property refers. Note that the DataSetProvider does not retain a reference to the OleVariant (which means that the Data property causes the DataSet to be scanned each and every time you read the Data property).

The following code segment performs essentially the same effect as that shown in the previous Load1Click event handler, with one difference. There is no persistent relationship between the ClientDataSet and the DataSetProvider (the ClientDataSet's ProviderName property is not set).

```
procedure TForm1.Load1Click(Sender: TObject);
begin
  if ClientDataSet1.Active then
  begin
```

```
    Load1.Caption := 'Load';
    ClientDataSet1.Close;
  end
  else
  begin
    Load1.Caption := 'Close';
    ClientDataSet1.Data := DataSetProvider1.Data;
  end;
end;
```

Loading Some of the DataSet

In the CDSLoadBehavior project, all of the records from Table1 are loaded into ClientDataSet1 when you select ClientDataSet | Load. This happens because the ClientDataSet's PacketRecords property is set to -1.

If you set PacketRecords to a positive integer, that number defines how many records you want to load. For example, if you want to load just the first 20 records from Table1, set PacketRecords to 20.

You can also set PacketRecords to 0, in which case the DataSetProvider reads the metadata from Table1, but includes no records in the OleVariant. In other words, once the ClientDataSet is activated, it will have Fields with the appropriate data types based on the underlying DataSet (Table1 in this case). It will also be editable, in that records can be inserted (and with the change cache enabled, those records would be marked for insertion).

Setting PacketRecords to 0 has another important implication. The underlying DataSet is opened by the DataSetProvider (if it was not already open), just as it is when PacketRecords is set to any other value.

Setting PacketRecords to a value greater than -1, but less than the total number of records in the DataSet (again, Table1 in the current project), has an important impact on how the DataSetProvider reacts to requests for data from the ClientDataSet. Specifically, whether or not the DataSetProvider has to initially activate the DataSet, it does not close the DataSet once the OleVariant has been delivered to the ClientDataSet. Only when the DataSetProvider actually reaches the DataSet's Eof (end of file) marker, does it close the DataSet.

Use the following steps to demonstrate this effect:

1. If the project is running, close it.

2. Select ClientDataSet1, and set its PacketRecords property to 50.

3. Run the project. From the form's main menu, select ClientDataSet | Load.

4. At this point, your form may look something like that shown in Figure 2-3. Notice that the Table is still open (its data is still displayed in the right DBGrid) and that the DBGrid's slider bar is close to the top of the grid, somewhere around the 5 to 10 percent position. Also notice the slider bar on the left side DBGrid. That slider bar is rather wide, indicating that you are looking at a large proportion of the records contained in the ClientDataSet.

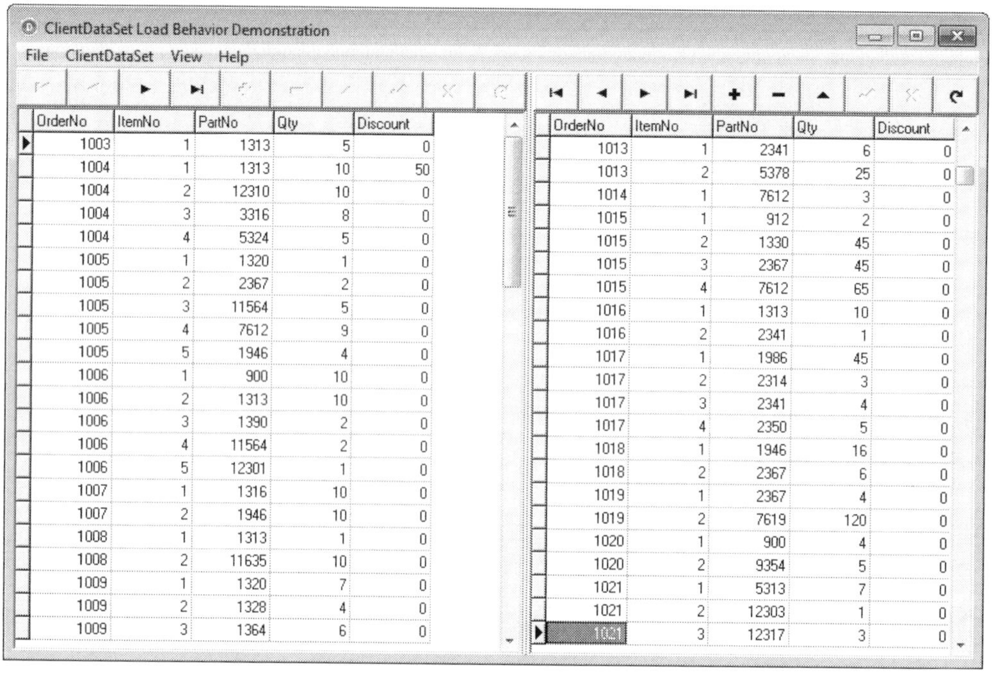

Figure 2-3: A subset of data has been retrieved. The DataSetProvider is keeping the DataSet open for additional data requests

5. Now click on a record in the left DBGrid. Once a record is selected, press the PageDown key a couple of times. Notice that when the slider bar reaches about the bottom of the DBGrid, suddenly a new set of records are read (the right DBGrid scrolls a bit further), and the slider on the left side DBGrid shortens, representing the fact that there are now more records in the ClientDataSet than before.

6. Continue to press PageDown. At some point, after about 1000 records have been read from Table1, Table1 closes (the DataSetProvider closed it), and the ClientDataSet is now fully loaded.

7. Close the running project.

These steps have demonstrated that it's the nature of a DataSetProvider to continue to keep its DataSet open, so long as it still might need to read more records. This is done for performance purposes (since opening and closing a DataSet can be expensive, especially if closing the DataSet also closes its database connection), as well as to maintain a reference to the last record read (the record before the current record in the DataSet). However, this behavior is not obvious, unless you have played with a project like CDSLoadBehavior, where the navigation of the DataSet by the DataSetProvider can be viewed clearly.

Note: This incremental loading behavior only occurs when a ClientDataSet that is associated with a DataSetProvider is activated. It does not occur when you read the Data property of a DataSetProvider. Specifically, reading the Data property of a DataSetProvider always reads to the end of the result set (beginning with the current record if the DataSet is already active), and always results in the DataSetProvider closing the DataSet following the read operation.

Fetching Records on Demand

In step 5 of the preceding example, you observed that the DataSetProvider read additional records, loading them into the requesting ClientDataSet, when you pressed PageDown to move to a record that would otherwise be past the last record already read from the DataSet.

There is a similar effect, which you can observe if you run the project again. Once the ClientDataSet is loaded with the first set of records, if you click the Last button on the ClientDataSet's DBNavigator, you will see that the DBNavigator attempts to move to the end of the ClientDataSet which then causes the DataSetProvider to read all remaining records in the DataSet, after which, as expected, the DataSetProvider closes the DataSet.

These behaviors occur because the ClientDataSet's FetchOnDemand property is set to True by default (and the CDSLoadBehavior project is making use of these default values). If you set FetchOnDemand to False, and you activate a ClientDataSet that is associated with a DataSetProvider, only PacketRecords number of records will be loaded.

Use the following steps to demonstrate this behavior:

1. Select ClientDataSet1 and set its PacketRecords property to 10.

2. Next, set its FetchOnDemand property to False.

3. Run the project and select ClientDataSet | Load. Your screen should look something like that shown in Figure 2-4.

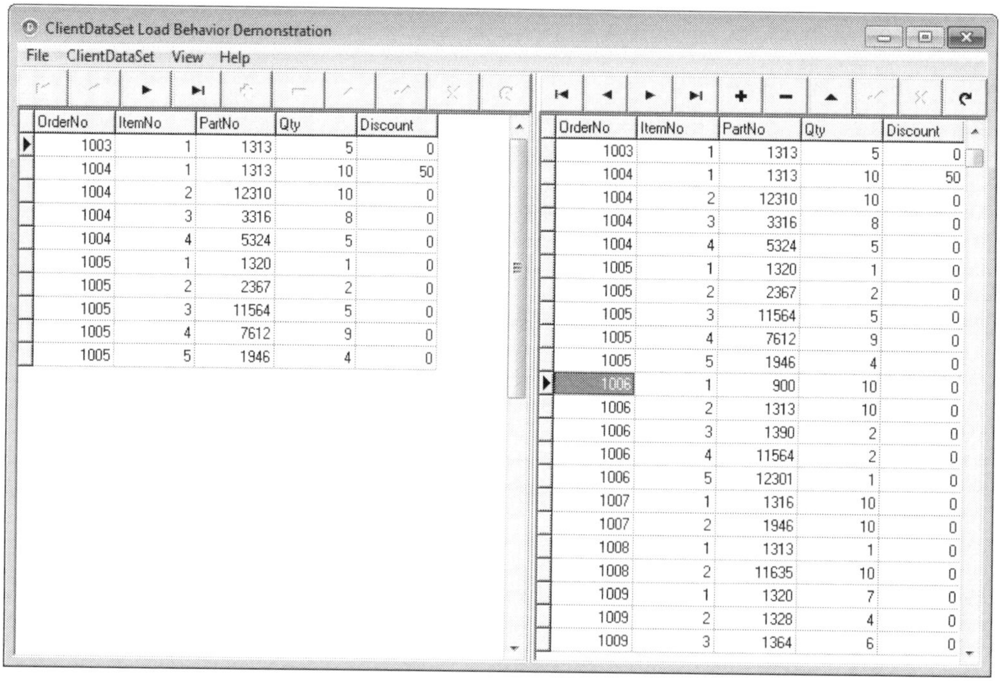

Figure 2-4: When FetchOnDemand is True, and PacketRecords is greater than -1, only some of the DataSet's records are loaded, or none (if PacketRecords is 0)

Like when FetchOnDemand was True and PacketRecord was set to a value less than the total number of records in the DataSet, the DataSetProvider does not close the DataSet from which it loaded its data. However, unlike the situation where FetchOnDemand was True, moving to the end of the ClientDataSet does not initiate any more read operations. And, in this particular situation, where there is nothing to cause the DataSetProvider to read additional records, the DataSetProvider will never reach the Eof marker and the underlying DataSet will remain open.

Manually Requesting Additional Data

When FetchOnDemand is False, you must explicitly request additional data if you want it. You do this by calling the ClientDataSet GetNextPacket method.

Each time you call GetNextPacket, an additional PacketRecords number of records are requested by the ClientDataSet from the DataSetProvider, which causes the DataSetProvider to attempt to retrieve that number of records.

GetNextPacket returns an integer indicating how many records were actually returned. If GetNextPacket returns fewer than the value of PacketRecords, the DataSetProvider encountered the Eof marker, and has also closed the DataSet. If GetNextPacket returns the value of PacketRecords, the DataSet is still open.

It is also interesting to note that when GetNextPacket returns the value of PacketRecords, there actually may be no more records to read in the underlying DataSet. This happens when the remaining number of records in the DataSet is exactly equal to PacketRecords. Since Eof is set to True only when you attempt to read beyond the end of the result set, the DataSetProvider doesn't know it has read the last record. A subsequent call to GetNextPacket from the ClientDataSet will return 0 (no records where returned) and the DataSetProvider will then close the DataSet.

The use of GetNextPacket is demonstrated by the OnClick event handler of a menu item named GetNextPacket1. This menu item, which is located under the ClientDataSet main menu item, is enabled only when FetchOnDemand is set to False and at least one packet of records has already been retrieved. This is done from the AfterOpen event handler of the ClientDataSet, as shown in the following code:

```
procedure TForm1.ClientDataSet1AfterOpen(DataSet: TDataSet);
begin
  GetNextPacket1.Visible := not ClientDataSet1.FetchOnDemand;
end;
```

Similarly, when the ClientDataSet is closed, or the DataSetProvider has closed the DataSet, this menu item is once again made not visible, as seen in this AfterClose event handler, which is assigned to the AfterClose property of both ClientDataSet1 and Table1:

```
procedure TForm1.ClientDataSet1AfterClose(DataSet: TDataSet);
begin
  if GetNextPacket1.Visible then
    GetNextPacket1.Visible := False;
end;
```

The OnClick event handler on the GetNextPacket1 menu item retrieves the next packet of data from the DataSetProvider, comparing the returned integer with that found in the ClientDataSet's PacketRecords property. When the event handler determines that the last packet of records has been read, DataSetProvider1 closes Table1, and the event handler displays a dialog box indicating that the final packet of records has been loaded.

Figure 2-5 depict how your form will look if you run this project, with FetchOnDemand set to False, and have selected ClientDataSet | Get Next Packet enough times to complete the loading of data from Table1.

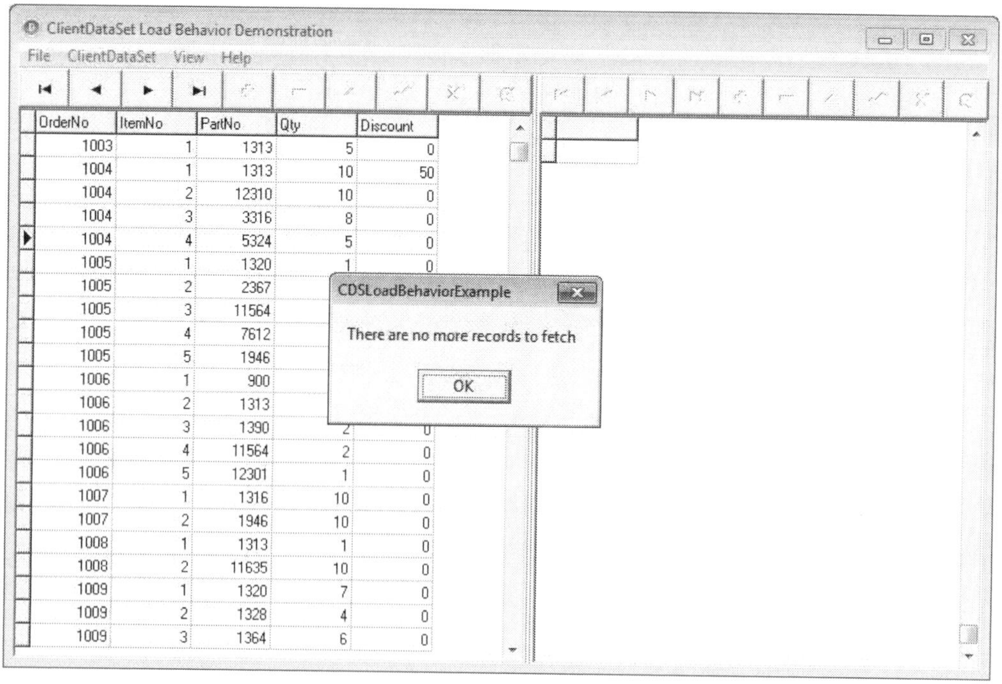

Figure 2-5: The last call to GetNextPacket retrieved the final packet of data from DataSetProvider1, which in turn, closed Table1

Limiting the Data in a Request

FetchOnDemand is a property of the ClientDataSet, and you can use it to limit how many records are returned in a single request, so that the ClientDataSet is not overwhelmed when the result has a large and unknown number of records. The DataSetProvider also supports properties that can influence how much information is returned to the ClientDataSet with each request. These properties are flags of the Options set property.

When the Options property includes the poFetchBlobsOnDemand flag, BLOB field data, including binary, memo, and image fields, are omitted from the OleVariant. When the poFetchBlobsOnDemand flag is set and the ClientDataSet's FetchOnDemand property is set to False, you can optionally call the ClientDataSet's FetchBlobs method to instruct the DataSetProvider to retrieve BLOB data. When FetchOnDemand is set to True, attempting to access a BLOB field will cause that BLOB data to be retrieved automatically.

Similarly, if the poFetchDetailsOnDemand flag is absent from the Options property, the DataSetProvider does not automatically include nested datasets in the data it returns. Nested datasets are complete DataSets that are nested in a single row and column of a ClientDataSet. Nested datasets are an advanced ClientDataSet topic, and they are covered in detail in Chapter 12, *Using Nested DataSets*. But suffice it to say that when a result set includes nested datasets, the size of the returned data packet can be very large indeed.

If you retrieve data from a DataSetProvider where the poFetchDetailsOnDemand flag appears in the Options set, you can specifically retrieve the nested dataset fields by calling FetchDetails. As is the case with optional BLOB fields, if FetchOnDemand is set to True, nested datasets are automatically retrieved when you attempt to access them.

In the next chapter, we'll continue this look at ClientDataSet/DataSetProvider interaction by discussing how data in the change cache can be applied back to the underlying database.

Chapter 3
Saving Data with ClientDataSets and DataSetProviders

When the data held in a ClientDataSet is obtained from a database, typically a remote database server, subsequent changes that are made to that data while in the ClientDataSet often need to be resolved back to the underlying database. The ClientDataSet's change cache makes this possible. Specifically, the information in the change cache is sufficiently detailed to permit the cumulative changes to the data to be applied to the original source.

As you learned in the preceding chapter, most Delphi developers load data into a ClientDataSet by employing a DataSetProvider. Similarly, applying the changes from the ClientDataSet's change cache back to the original database is normally done using a DataSetProvider.

It is not mandatory to use a DataSetProvider to apply a ClientDataSet's change cache back to the underlying database, just as a DataSetProvider is not required to load data from a database into a ClientDataSet. For example, as soon as the changes in a ClientDataSet are ready to be applied to the source database, it would be perfectly reasonable to write code that determines which records have been modified, what types of modifications have been made (deletes verses inserts verses field-level changes), and to use a DataSet, such as a SQLDataSet, to execute queries that apply those changes to the original tables from which the data was loaded.

This code is often necessarily complicated. For example, imagine that your ClientDataSet is used to display data for user editing, and a user then deletes a record. When you are ready to apply the user's edits to the source database, and having detected that a given record had been deleted, it is normally not sufficient to simply execute a SQL DELETE statement against the original table. What if someone else had already deleted that record after the data was loaded into the ClientDataSet, but before your user had completed their edits? What if another user had applied changes to that record before your user had completed their edits?

The issue is even more complicated when you consider that you need to make these decisions about each and every edit performed by your user. What if your user made ten changes to the data, but only five of those could be applied because the other five edits affected records that had been changed by other users since the data was originally loaded into the ClientDataSet?

While programmatically applying the changes in a ClientDataSet's change cache back to the underlying database is not rocket science, it can be complicated, and often involves a lot of code. On the other hand, if you employ a DataSetProvider, it can normally handle most of your concerns through its properties. In the end, applying a ClientDataSet's change cache back to the underlying database using a DataSetProvider involves a call to the DataSetProvider's ApplyUpdates method, and then a little extra code to handle the situations where one or more of the changes could not be applied.

This chapter provides you with a detailed look at applying updates using a DataSetProvider. It begins with a discussion of the default behavior of the DataSetProvider when you call ApplyUpdates, and what you can do when those updates cannot be applied. This chapter continues with a look at the various options for applying those updates that the DataSetProvider exposes, and under what circumstances they should be used.

What Exactly is Being Saved?

The discussions of the change cache, up to this point in this book, have been fairly high level. We know that, when it is enabled, changes made to the data in a ClientDataSet are recorded. There is much more too it than that, and many of those details are discussed in their own chapter, Chapter 6, *Managing the ClientDataSet Change Cache.*

However, since this chapter is specifically concerned with how to apply the changes in the change cache to a database, it is important that we have a better sense of what the change cache actually holds.

The change cache contains the status of records that have been inserted, deleted, and modified since the change cache was initialized (and empty), less those operations that may have occurred while the change cache was disabled. (The ClientDataSet's LogChanges Boolean property is used to disable and enable the change cache.) Also absent from the change cache are changes that have been specifically removed from the change cache.

The change cache also includes information about the order in which the changes where applied, but this is an artifact of how the change cache is managed internally. For example, imagine that you insert a record. That record is now in the change cache, marked as an insertion. If you then delete that same record before applying the updates in the change cache, that record is removed from the change cache.

Note: The preceding description applies when you have loaded your data from a DataSetProvider. However, if your data is loaded from a file, or your ClientDataSet structure is created dynamically, inserted records that are later deleted may result in two distinct records in the change cache (marked as inserted then deleted, but appearing as currently deleted). However, when the change cache is applied (or merged), only the most recent version of that record will represent the record in the update process.

When it is time for the updates to be applied to the underlying database, each entry in the change cache will represent a new record insertion, an existing record deletion, or a modification to an existing record. Technically, modifications to existing records are represented by two records in the change cache — the original record, and a record that represents its current state. This is a detail, however, and really has no impact on this discussion. It is best to simply consider that each existing record that has been modified is represented by data in the change cache that holds information about what has changed.

Note: The code project CDSLoadBehavior is available from the code download. See Appendix A for details.

You can use the CDSLoadBehavior project to view the change cache. This project includes a form that displays the value of a ClientDataSet's Delta property as long as the change cache is not empty. As you can see in the following code segment, which is associated with the menu item used to display the change cache, the Delta property of the ClientDataSet on the main form is assigned to the Data property of the ClientDataSet on the form used to display the change cache:

```
procedure TForm1.Delta1Click(Sender: TObject);
begin
  if not Self.ClientDataSet1.Active then
  begin
    ShowMessage('The ClientDataSet is not active');
    Exit;
  end;
  if Self.ClientDataSet1.ChangeCount = 0 then
  begin
    ShowMessage('Delta is empty');
    Exit;
  end;
```

```
with TForm2.Create(nil) do
begin
  ClientDataSet1.Data := Self.ClientDataSet1.Delta;
  ShowModal;
  Release;
end;
end;
```

Use the following steps to view the change cache:

1. With the CDSLoadBehavior project open in Delphi, click the Run button or press F9.

2. Select ClientDataSet | Load to load the ClientDataSet.

3. Change the PartNo field for the first record to 12310.

4. Delete the second record.

5. Click the insert button on the associated DBNavigator (the button labeled "+") to insert a new record. Set OrderNo to 1003, ItemNo to 2, PartNo to 900, Qty to 5, and Discount to 0. Click the post button (the one with the checkmark) to post this change (or simply navigate off this record to post it automatically).

6. Select ClientDataSet | Delta to view the change cache. Your screen should look something like that shown in Figure 3-1.

7. Close the Change Cache form, and then close the running application. Since you did not specifically select to save the changes, the change cache is discarded and the changes are lost.

Saving ClientDataSet Changes Using a DataSetProvider

When your ClientDataSet data has been obtained from a database, and changes have been made to that data, you can use a DataSetProvider to persist that data to the underlying database. Whether the changes can actually be applied relies on a number of issues.

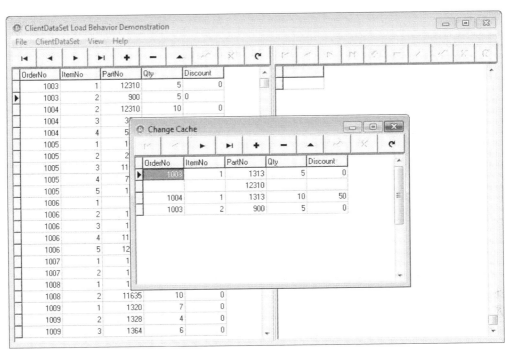

Figure 3-1: The contents of Delta, the change cache

Consider the records in the ClientDataSet's change cache. In fact, to make it easier still, imagine that only one record has been modified since it was loaded into the ClientDataSet (and that no records were either inserted or deleted). Whether or not the changes to that record can be applied depends on two things: The current state of that corresponding record in the underlying database, and any constraints or business rules that the database will apply to that record.

Consider first the state of the corresponding record. So long as a change to that record has not been posted to the database by some other user since it was read into the ClientDataSet, and so long as that record has not been deleted from the underlying database since the time it was loaded into the ClientDataSet, there is a good chance, all other things being equal, that the changes can be applied.

Even if the corresponding record has been modified in the database since the time it was loaded into the ClientDataSet, it still might be possible to apply the updates. For example, imagine that two columns in the underlying record have been changed since that record was loaded into the ClientDataSet. Furthermore, suppose that neither of those fields were modified in the ClientDataSet, and those fields are unrelated to the primary key of the record (a primary key enforces uniqueness amongst the records of a table). In a lot of data models, it should be acceptable to apply the changes from the change cache record, so long as they don't conflict with any other changes. In other words, it should be possible to *merge* the changes in the change cache with those changes in the underlying database. Configuring a DataSetProvider to perform a merge is discussed later in this chapter.

Let's now consider constraints and business rules. If the changes in the change cache are inconsistent with database-level constraints or business rules, it may not be possible to apply the changes. Attempting to do so would raise an exception, and the update would be rejected.

One type of constraint is a primary key constraint. Fortunately, if you loaded your ClientDataSet from a DataSetProvider, the DataSetProvider has probably noted the primary key, and included that information with the data packet's metadata. In other words, if the ClientDataSet knows about the primary key, it will not even accept a change to the change cache that would result in a primary key violation. Honestly, I don't know if this works in all situations, but my experience is that ClientDataSets loaded from DataSetProviders from the remote database servers that I work with all enforce the primary key within the ClientDataSet.

Other types of constraints, such as referential integrity constraints, as well as business rules, are another thing. Unless you specifically take steps to implement, or mirror, those constraints or business rules in your client application, any violations that sneak into your change cache will result in a change that cannot be applied.

Note: You can set the DataSetProvider's Constraints property to False if you do not want the DataSetProvider to attempt to retrieve constraints from the DataSet.

For example, your ClientDataSet may have been loaded through a query on a table that includes an OnUpdate record-level trigger. From within that trigger, business rules are enforced, and updates that violate those rules are rejected.

Unless the rules are so important that you deem it necessary to duplicate those rules in the ClientDataSet (perhaps from the AfterPost event handler of the ClientDataSet), you probably will find it sufficient to simply attempt to post those records, and hope that the exception that is raised contains enough detail that you can display that information to your user and permit them to make adjustments to their edits. Again, the DataSetProvider has provisions for handling these issues, and these are discussed later in this chapter.

There is one final issue that can affect how the change cache is applied to the underlying database. This is related to the original source of the data that was loaded into the ClientDataSet.

Some types of data naturally lend themselves to the cached updates approach that the ClientDataSet supports. For example, records loaded by querying one or more columns from a single table. In these cases, there is a one-to-one relationship between the query result and the records in the underlying table.

On the other hand, queries that pull their data from two or more tables (using joins, unions, subqueries, and the like) do not produce records that have a one-to-one correspondence with an underlying table. Similarly, queries that make use of aggregation, such as those that perform SUM, AVERAGE, and COUNT operations, and those that use GROUP BY, also do not produce records that a have a one-to-one correspondence with an underlying table. The same thing goes for stored procedures, which by their nature have no inherent table affinity.

These types of result sets pose a problem. For queries that draw data from two or more tables, applying updates requires an intimate knowledge of the database's data model. The DataSetProvider cannot possibly determine what data goes where. Likewise, many of the fields in an aggregate query do not actually exist in the underlying database (the value returned by a SUM operation, for instance). And those values that actually do correspond to a table in an underlying database may be found in more than one record. Again, it is not possible for the DataSetProvider to determine what data is updateable and how that update should be achieved. The same thing is true regarding stored procedures.

Once again, however, the DataSetProvider provides solutions to these problems. Specifically, although the DataSetProvider cannot know how changes made to records resulting from queries against two or more tables and queries that employ aggregates are to be applied, they provide hooks so that your code can get involved and perform any necessary updates on behalf of the DataSetProvider. Once more, how to accomplish this is described later in this chapter.

The next section describes how to configure and initiate the application of updates to a ClientDataSet's change cache using a DataSetProvider.

Configuring ClientDataSets to Use DataSetProviders

You configure ClientDataSets and DataSetProviders to apply updates in the same manner that you configure ClientDataSets and DataSetProviders to load data from a database (you might want to refer back to Chapter 2 for a more lengthy discussion of the issues). In most cases, you will associate a DataSetProvider to a ClientDataSet by assigning the ClientDataSet's ProviderName property with the name of the DataSetProvider.

Similarly, you associate the DataSetProvider with the DataSet that is used to load the data by assigning the DataSet to the DataSetProvider's DataSet property. Actually, the DataSetProvider must point to a DataSet that gets its data from the same source (table or query) as the one that produced the records that reside in the ClientDataSet, even if that DataSet was not used to initially load the ClientDataSet.

Of course, that DataSet must be properly configured. For example, it must reference some kind of connection component (SQLConnection for dbExpress, ADOConnection for dbGo, Database for the Borland Database Engine, and so forth). Furthermore, that connection component must be properly configured so that it can attach to the underlying database, meaning that it must have an appropriate connection string or other required configuration parameters.

Let's consider this DataSet a bit further. You might be wondering, why the DataSetProvider does not have to refer to the same DataSet as that from which the ClientDataSet's records were obtained. The simple answer is that that original DataSet may no longer be around.

Consider a briefcase application. In a briefcase application, a DataSet is used to populate a ClientDataSet with data from a database. Once that data is loaded into the ClientDataSet, the ClientDataSet saves it locally. It is now possible to disconnect the machine on which this application is running from the network through which the database is accessed.

While the machine is disconnected, the application accesses the data by loading it from disk, saving it back to disk when done. Since the change cache is also saved when the data is saved to disk, each new session with the data is nothing more than a continuation of the previous one. (Saving a ClientDataSet to disk is discussed in Chapter 6, *Managing the ClientDataSet Change Cache*.)

At some later point in time, which could be hours, days, weeks, or even months later, the application is once again connected to the network over which the underlying database can be accessed. At that time, it is possible to use a DataSetProvider to apply the changes to the underlying database. The original DataSet, however, is unavailable (it was destroyed long ago). But it is not needed. What is needed is a DataSet that the DataSetProvider can use to figure out which single table the data was drawn from. The DataSet doesn't even have to produce the same original set of records. In fact, it doesn't even have to return the same metadata (the ClientDataSet's Delta property already contains that metadata).

For example, the original DataSet used to load data into the ClientDataSet may have executed a query similar to the following, where all records associated with a particular sales consultant are extracted from the ACCOUNTS table:

```
SELECT * FROM ACCOUNTS WHERE SalesConsultantID = 'SC0726'
```

The DataSet used to assist the DataSetProvider in resolving the cached changes back to the underlying database may contain a query that looks like the following:

```
SELECT 1 FROM ACCOUNTS WHERE 1 = 2
```

While the first query obviously selects all of the particular sales consultant's records, the second query will always return an empty result set. Furthermore, the metadata of the second query includes a single integer field. But that doesn't matter. All that is required of the second query is that it queries the same table as did the original query, and the second query accomplishes this just fine. (It must also be configured to use a connection object that can connect to the database where the ACCOUNTS table is located.)

Nonetheless, even though the DataSet used while applying updates does not have to return metadata that matches the original DataSet, it is probably a good idea that the DataSet's metadata match as closely as possible to the original DataSet. Doing so retains the clarity of purpose that makes your code more maintainable.

Note: Under some conditions, such as when you take programmatic control over the application of updates using a DataSetProvider.BeforeUpdateRecord event handler, the DataSet does not even have to query the original table. Writing BeforeUpdateRecord event handlers is discussed later in this chapter.

Initiating Saving

When using a DataSetProvider to apply the updates, you initiate the process by calling the properly configured ClientDataSet's ApplyUpdates method. The following is the signature of ApplyUpdates:

```
function TCustomClientDataSet.ApplyUpdates(MaxErrors: Integer): Integer;
```

ApplyUpdates returns an integer indicating how many records were successfully applied to the underlying database. You use the single integer parameter, MaxErrors, to instruct the ClientDataSet how to request that failures to updated records be handled.

Let's begin by considering what happens when ApplyUpdates is called. We'll return shortly to MaxErrors, and learn how it affects this process. As was done in the description of the loading process provided in Chapter 2, this process has been simplified to cover the essence of this interaction.

When ApplyUpdates is called, the contents of the ClientDataSet's Delta (the change cache) are sent back to the DataSetProvider, along with the value of MaxErrors. (If Delta is empty, ApplyUpdates returns 0 and no action is taken.)

The DataSetProvider begins by examining the DataSet to which it points, determining what object it needs to connect to the database (SQLConnection, ADOConnection, and so forth), and from which table the data originated.

Next, the DataSetProvider creates an instance of a SQLResolver. The SQLResolver is used to create INSERT, UPDATE, and DELETE SQL queries, which can be executed against the table from which the data was originally retrieved.

The DataSetProvider is almost ready to go. It starts by checking whether or not the connection object that the DataSet points to supports transactions. If it does, it begins a transaction.

At this point the DataSetProvider examines the changes in Delta. For each change it finds, it uses the SQL query generated by the SQLResolver to execute an INSERT, UPDATE, or DELETE query, again using the connection object the DataSet is configured to use.

The DataSetProvider will continue to execute SQL statements until each of the entries in Delta has been processed, or the MaxErrors number of errors has been exceeded. If more than MaxErrors errors have been produced, the DataSetProvider stops attempting to apply updates, and rolls back the transaction (if one is active). Otherwise, the transaction is committed.

Note: Recall that the information in your ClientDataSet is always stale. If, following the successful application of updates to the underlying database, you intend to continue to work with the data in the ClientDataSet either by permitting a user to make additional changes or by making those changes programmatically, it is usually beneficial to refresh the ClientDataSet before continuing. This ensures that the data is as up-to-date as possible, thereby reducing the likelihood that future updates will result in failures due to out-of-date data.

The use of ApplyUpdates is demonstrated in the CDSLoadBehavior project first introduced in the preceding chapter. In this project, updates are applied when you select File | Apply Updates. The following is the OnClick event handler for this menu item:

```
procedure TForm1.ApplyUpdates1Click(Sender: TObject);
begin
  ClientDataSet1.ApplyUpdates(-1);
end;
```

You can use the following steps to demonstrate applying updates both when the updates can be applied as well as when they cannot be applied:

1. If you are using Delphi 2005 or later, select Run | Run without debugging from Delphi's main menu to run the project without the debugger. If you are using Delphi 7 or earlier, after making sure that the project has been compiled, use the Windows Explorer to locate the project's executable and run it.

2. Select ClientDataSet | Load from the application's main menu to load the ClientDataSet.

3. Change the PartNo field of the first record from 1313 to 12310. Post this change (either by using the post button on the DBNavigator or by navigating off of the record).

4. Select File | Apply Updates to apply your changes.

5. Now run a second instance of the application (this time you can run with the debugger, so you merely need to select Run | Run from Delphi's main menu).

6. From the second copy of the application, select ClientDataSet | Load. Notice that the loaded data includes the changed value to the first record.

7. Again with the second application, change the value of the PartNo field of the first record to 1313. Then, from this second application, select File | Apply Updates.

8. Return to the first copy of the running application, and change the value of the PartNo field for the first record to 900. Post this change.

9. Now attempt to save this change from the first application. Select File | Apply Updates. This time the change cannot be applied, and an exception is raised, as shown in Figure 3-2.

10. Close the exception dialog box, and then close both running applications.

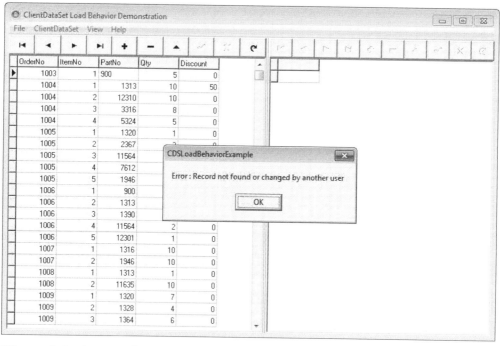

Figure 3-2: Attempting to apply an update to a record that has changed in the underlying database raises an exception

ApplyUpdates and MaxErrors

The MaxErrors parameter controls what will happen if errors are encountered during the update process. When MaxErrors is –1, the DataSetProvider attempts to apply all changes in the change cache. After all updates have been attempted, the applied updates are committed by committing the transaction. Any changes that cannot be applied remain in the change cache following the call to ApplyUpdates.

In addition, if you have written an OnUpdateError event handler, it is executed once for each record that could not be applied. If you do not have an OnUpdateError event handler, the DataSetProvider raises an exception for each error encountered. Any executions of OnUpdateError, or raising of exceptions, occur before the transaction is committed.

Note: If you do not want the user to be confronted with exceptions each time an update fails, create an OnUpdateError event handler for the DataSetProvider and place a comment line in the body of that event handler (to prevent Delphi from deleting this empty event handler). Its execution will be a no op (no operation), but nothing will happen, other than the suppression of the exception.

When you call ApplyUpdates with a MaxErrors value of 0, a single failure causes the DataSetProvider to abort the update process and to roll back the transaction. In this case, the change cache is unchanged. Otherwise, all changes were necessarily successfully applied, the transaction was committed, and the change cache is empty.

Again, if an OnUpdateError event handler has been assigned, it is executed. Otherwise, the DataSetProvider raises an exception.

When MaxErrors is a positive integer, and the number of errors encountered do not exceed MaxErrors, the transaction is committed (all of the successful updates are committed), and the unsuccessful changes remain in the change cache. If the number of errors exceeds MaxErrors the transaction is rolled back and the change cache remains unchanged.

To some, setting MaxErrors to a positive integer seems counter intuitive. Why would you accept errors? Actually, you are not accepting any errors. Only valid data is being applied to the underlying database. Those errors that are encountered remain in the change cache, where they can be reviewed, discarded, or corrected. If the invalid records can be fixed, those changes can then be applied by calling ApplyUpdates again.

The idea behind a positive MaxErrors value is that some number of failures can be tolerated, especially if the change cache includes a large number of updates. At some point, however, too many errors (this is a relative value) is a sign of a more significant problem, in which case the whole update process should be aborted and that problem addressed.

Using ResolveToDataSet

In the DataSetProvider's default behavior, the role played by the DataSet object is to identify the underlying table to which the data must be resolved, as well as to point to the connection object that is connected to the database in which this table resides. In this situation, the DataSet does not even become activated during the process.

However, the DataSetProvider can be configured to use its DataSet directly to update the underlying table. For example, if the DataSetProvider gets its data from a Table, the DataSetProvider can edit the Table directly, inserting, deleting, and editing individual records using the DataSet interface. As must be obvious, in order to use this technique, the DataSet must refer to an editable result set that maps directly to the records in the ClientDataSet's change cache.

Not all DataSets support this feature. For example, the dbExpress components, such as SQLDataSet, return readonly result sets, and therefore, resolving to the DataSet is not an option. Likewise, a Query (BDE) component that returns a result set where CanModify is False cannot be edited, and therefore, resolving to the DataSet is not possible.

You enable the DataSetProvider to use its DataSet directly by setting its ResolveToDataSet property to True. After that, calling ApplyUpdates causes the DataSetProvider to navigate its DataSet to delete and update records in the change cache, and to insert any new records directly into that DataSet. All other aspects of applying updates remains the same, including how MaxErrors is used and the raising of exceptions or the execution of an OnUpdateError event handler.

There are several conditions under which this approach is beneficial or even necessary. For example, if the underlying database does not support SQL, or is somehow incompatible with the SQL generated by the SQLResolver, using ResolveToDataSet may be your next best solution. Consider the ClientDataSet class itself. ClientDataSets don't have any kind of connection component, and therefore there is nothing that a DataSetProvider can attach to in order to issue SQL statements. If your DataSetProvider's DataSet is a ClientDataSet, you cannot use the default behavior. Resolving directly to the ClientDataSet is a good option.

A second benefit is that it permits you to easily implement client-side business rules using the BeforePost, BeforeInsert, and BeforeDelete even handlers of the DataSet. From these event handlers, you can evaluate the data that the DataSetProvider is attempting to apply, raising an exception if you want to reject the data. Note that the DataSetProvider's BeforeUpdateRecord event handler also provides this option, and can also be used in conjunction with the default behavior.

The CDSLoadBehavior project demonstrates resolving to a DataSet. It includes a menu item that allows you to toggle between resolving to a DataSet and back. The following is the code associated with this menu item:

```
procedure TForm1.ResolveToDataSet1Click(Sender: TObject);
begin
  if ResolvetoDataSet1.Checked then
  begin
    ResolvetoDataSet1.Checked := False;
    DataSetProvider1.ResolveToDataSet := False;
  end
  else
  begin
    ResolvetoDataSet1.Checked := True;
    DataSetProvider1.ResolveToDataSet := True;
  end;
end;
```

So that you can detect that resolving to the DataSet is occurring, Table1 has code on its AfterDelete, AfterInsert, and AfterPost, as shown in the following code segment:

```
procedure TForm1.Table1AfterDelete(DataSet: TDataSet);
begin
  ShowMessage('A record has been deleted');
end;

procedure TForm1.Table1AfterInsert(DataSet: TDataSet);
begin
  ShowMessage('A record has been inserted');
end;

procedure TForm1.Table1AfterPost(DataSet: TDataSet);
begin
  ShowMessage('A record has been updated');
end;
```

Use the following steps to see the effects of resolving to the DataSet:

1. Run the project.
2. Select ClientDataSet | Load.
3. Select ClientDataSet | Resolve to DataSet.
4. Change the value of the PartNo field of the first record to 900.
5. Insert a new record. Set OrderNo to 1004, ItemNo to 5, PartNo to 900, Qty to 1, and Discount to 0. Post this record.

6. Select File | Apply Updates. The first dialog box that you'll see will look like that shown in Figure 3-3, noting that a record is being updated. Accept that dialog box and another is displayed indicating that a record is being inserted.

7. Close the application.

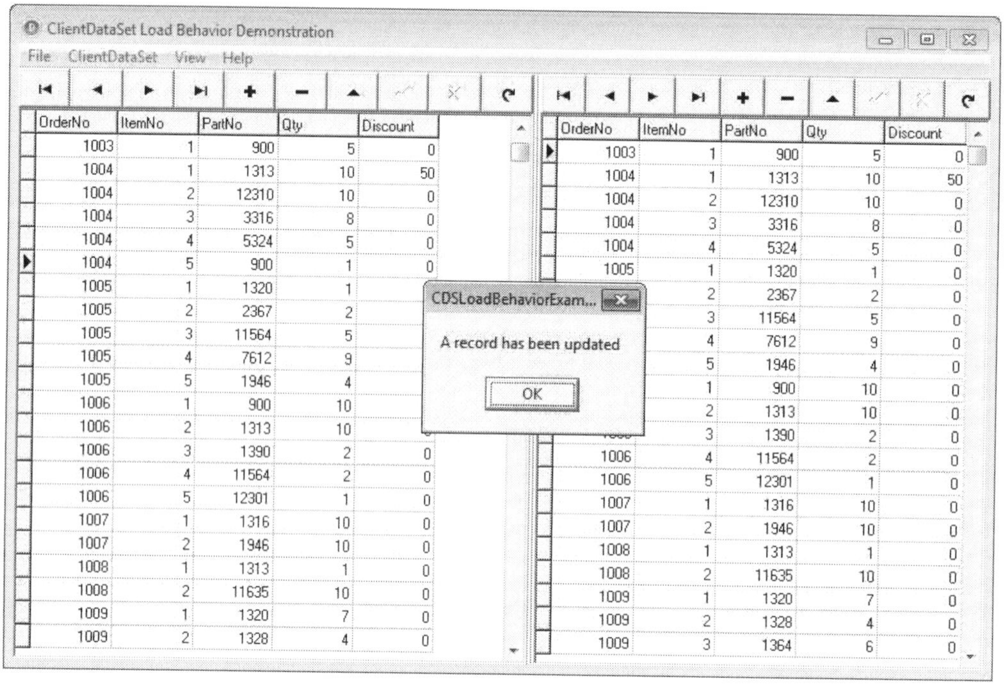

Figure 3-3: When resolving to a DataSet, the DataSet is edited directly, which may cause event handlers to trigger

Handling Update Failures

As you learned earlier in this chapter, if one or more errors occur when ApplyUpdates is invoked, those records that could not be posted remain in the change cache (and if MaxErrors is exceeded, the change cache remains unchanged).

The ClientDataSet surfaces an event handler that you can use to process those records that the DataSetProvider could not update. This event is called OnReconcileError.

Here is how it works. Imagine that you have five updates that need to be applied by the change cache, and due to the circumstances of the data, none of them can be applied (maybe someone delete all of the records from the underlying table). If you attempt to apply these updates with a call to

ApplyUpdates where MaxErrors is two, there will be three failures before the DataSetProvider aborts the update process (and the change cache will be unchanged).

In this situation, if you have an OnReconcileError event handler, it is triggered three times, one for each of the failed updates. The remaining two records are not included in this process, since no attempt was made to update them, and therefore, their potential to fail is unknown.

The OnReconcileError event handler is of the type TReconcileErrorEvent. The following is the declaration of this type:

```
type
  TReconcileErrorEvent = procedure(DataSet: TCustomClientDataSet;
    E: EReconcileError; UpdateKind: TUpdateKind;
    var Action: TReconcileAction) of object;
```

As you can see, when invoked, the OnReconcileError event handler is passed four parameters. The first parameter is the ClientDataSet attempting to apply its updates. The second parameter is an exception that describes the reason for the failure. The third parameter, UpdateKind, describes what kind of update failed, and the forth parameter, Action, permits you to specify what to do with the corresponding record in the change cache. Action is of the type TReconcileAction. The following is the TReconcileAction type declaration:

```
type
  TReconcileAction = (raSkip, raAbort, raMerge,
    raCorrect, raCancel, raRefresh);
```

Table 3-1 describes the effect of each of these reconcile actions.

raAbort	Stop reconciling errors. This will prevent OnReconcileError from executing any of the remaining failures for this particular call to ApplyUpdates.
raCancel	Undo the changes to the record. This has the effect of removing the record from the change cache.
raCorrect	Attempt to update the record again. This is normally done after the record that failed has been corrected.
raMerge	Attempt to merge the changes in the record with that current version of the record in the underlying database.
raRefresh	Cancel the changes to the record from the change cache and re-read the record from the underlying database.

raSkip	Ignore the error and leave the modified record in the change cache

Table 3-1: The Effects of the Various Reconcile Actions

Writing OnReconcileError event handlers can be complicated. Fortunately, Delphi includes a special dialog box in the Object Repository that permits you to handle most types of errors. This dialog box, called the Reconcile Error Dialog, can be found on the Delphi Files tab of the Object Repository. (In early versions of Delphi, this dialog box can be found in the Dialog tab.) The Reconcile Error Dialog box is shown in Figure 3-4.

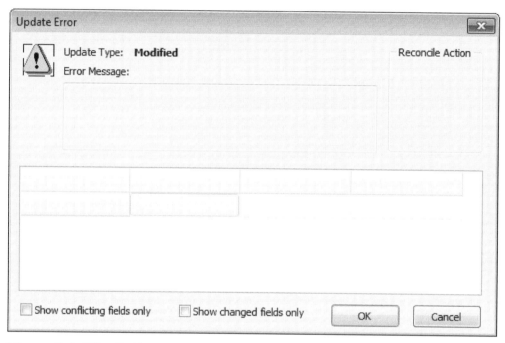

Figure 3-4: The OnReconcileError dialog box

To use this dialog box, copy or inherit it to your project from the Object Repository. Next, add the dialog box's unit to the unit that contains your OnReconcileError event handler. Finally, invoke the dialog box unit's HandleReconcileError function, which appears in its interface section. Pass to this function the TCustomClientDataSet, the EReconcileError, and the TUpdateKind parameters that are passed to your OnReconcileError event handler. The HandleReconcileError function returns a TReconcileAction result, which you assign to the Action parameter of your OnReconcileError event handler. The invocation of this function is shown in the following OnReconcileError event handler:

```
procedure TForm1.ClientDataSet1ReconcileError(DataSet:
  TCustomClientDataSet; E: EReconcileError;
  UpdateKind: TUpdateKind; var Action: TReconcileAction);
begin
  if UseOnReconcileErrorDialogBox1.Checked then
    Action := HandleReconcileError(DataSet, UpdateKind, E)
  else
    ShowMessage('Error : ' + e.Message);
end;
```

In this event handler, located in the CDSLoadBehavior project, the call to HandleReconcileError is made conditionally, depending on whether or not you have enabled using this dialog box by selecting the UseOnReconcileError menu item. In most applications, this event handler looks like this:

```
procedure TForm1.ClientDataSet1ReconcileError(DataSet:
  TCustomClientDataSet; E: EReconcileError;
  UpdateKind: TUpdateKind; var Action: TReconcileAction);
begin
  Action := HandleReconcileError(DataSet, UpdateKind, E)
end;
```

Using the OnReconcileError dialog box is demonstrated in the following steps:

1. If you are using Delphi 2005 or later, select Run | Run without debugging from Delphi's main menu to run the project without the debugger. If you are using Delphi 7 or earlier, after making sure that the project has been compiled, use the Windows Explorer to locate the project's executable and run it.

2. Select ClientDataSet | Load from the applications main menu to load the ClientDataSet.

3. Now run a second instance of the application (this time you can run with the debugger, so you merely need to select Run | Run from Delphi's main menu).

4. From the second copy of the application, select ClientDataSet | Load.

5. In the second application, change the value of the PartNo field of first record to 1313 (or to something else such as 900 if the value is already 1313). Then, from this second application, select File | Apply Updates.

6. Return now to the first copy of the application. Change the PartNo field for the first record to 1946.

7. You now want to enable the OnReconcileError event handler, and instruct it to use the HandleReconcileError dialog box. To do this,

select ClientDataSet | Use OnReconcileError Event Handler and
ClientDataSet | Use HandleReconcileError Dialog Box. Both of these
menu items should now be checked.

8. Now attempt to post your changes with this first application. Select
    File | Apply Updates. The update will fail and you will see the
    HandleReconcileError dialog box shown in Figure 3-5.

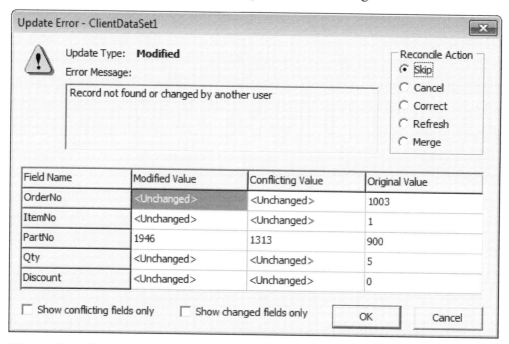

**Figure 3-5: Your users can use the HandleReconcileError dialog box to
work with failed update attempts**

9. Leave the Skip radio button checked, and click OK to accept this
    dialog box. If there were additional failures, they would each be
    displayed in turn, in this dialog box. However, since this was the
    only failure, no more dialog boxes are shown. However, the edit is
    still in the change cache, and it has not been applied.

10. Select File | Apply Updates again. Once again, the
    HandleReconcileError dialog box is displayed. This time, select the
    Refresh radio button and click OK. Notice that now that you have
    returned to the main form, the value of the PartNo field has been
    updated with the current value from the database.

11. Change this value back to 1946 and select File | Apply Updates. This time your change is applied since you have applied a change to a record based on the current value in the database.

Controlling How Updates Are Applied

Up to this point we have concentrated on the default behaviors of the DataSetProvider. While these default behaviors are suitable for many different update situations, there are times when you will need to change these default behaviors. Some of these changes can be accomplished simply by changing default properties of the DataSetProvider or its DataSet, while others involve writing custom code to control precisely how updates are performed.

The following sections begin with a look at the properties that change the default behaviors, and conclude with a look at adding custom code to apply your updates.

Changing the Default Behavior with UpdateMode

As you have learned earlier in this chapter, the DataSetProvider will update the underlying DataSet, one record at a time, using SQL statements generated by a SQLResolver. These SQL statements are based on the metadata information included in the change cache (Delta) that the ClientDataSet provided to the DataSetProvider as part of the ApplyUpdates call, as well as the name of the underlying database table determined from the DataSetProvider's DataSet.

By default, the SQLResolver will generate SQL statements that will only update or delete records where all non-BLOB fields of the original record are intact (unchanged since the record was originally loaded into the ClientDataSet). It does this by creating SQL statements where all non-BLOB fields appear in the WHERE clause. INSERT queries succeed or fail based solely on whether or not a primary key violation occurs, so these statements are not affected.

The DataSetProvider exposes a property that you can use to influence the SQL that the SQLResolver creates. This property is named UpdateMode, and it is of the TUpdateMode type. Following are the TUpdateMode and UpdateMode definitions, which are found in the Provider unit:

```
TUpdateMode = (upWhereAll, upWhereChanged, upWhereKeyOnly);
property UpdateMode: TUpdateMode read FUpdateMode write FUpdateMode
   default upWhereAll;
```

Note: The default keyword in the preceding property declaration doesn't actually make upWhereAll the default. That is done in the constructor of the DataSetProvider class. The default keyword informs the designer that UpdateMode will be set to upWhereAll when the class is created, and that if that property has that value at compile time, it is unnecessary to stream the value of that property to the DFM file.

As mentioned at the outset of this section, when UpdateMode is set to upWhereAll, all non-BLOB fields are included in the WHERE clause of UPDATE and DELETE queries. This results in update failures if any of the non-BLOB fields of the underlying record were modified since the time that the ClientDataSet loaded the record whose updates are being applied.

This approach is known as *optimistic locking*, and when two or more users are trying to apply changes at about the same time, only the first to apply changes will succeed. All others will fail.

When UpdateMode is set to upWhereChanged, only the primary field keys and the fields that have been modified are included in the WHERE clause of UPDATE queries. (Again, INSERTs are not affected. DELETE queries continue to use an exact match criteria since there are no changed fields in a deleted record.) As long as none of the primary key fields of an updated record are affected, and all non-primary key fields that have been modified have also not been posted to the underlying table since the time the data was loaded into the ClientDataSet, these queries should succeed.

Using upWhereChanged permits two or more users to apply their changes to the underlying database so long as none of them have made changes to common fields. For example, if one user changed a field called Address, and another changed a field called PhoneNumber, and neither of these fields are part of the primary key, both users will successfully apply their changes. This sort of update permits merges.

The final UpdateMode value is upWhereKeyOnly. With UpdateMode set to upWhereKeyOnly, the WHERE clause of UPDATE queries only includes the values of the primary key fields. (INSERT and DELETE queries continue to act as they do with upWhereChanged.) Using this mode, so long as the key fields of the underlying record have not been changed, the updates are applied, replacing any updates that other users may have applied.

Assuming that key fields are not touched (this is a pretty safe assumption in most database architectures), the use of upWhereKeyOnly permits everyone to succeed in posting their changes. As a result, the last one to post is the one whose data appears in the underlying database.

Fine Tuning Updates with ProviderFlags

Under normal conditions, the SQL statements generated for the various UpdateMode values are based on the metadata found in the change cache. This metadata includes which fields are key fields and which are not. While this works fine most of the time, there is a bit more tweaking that you can do that has a direct influence on the SQL generated by a SQLResolver.

The metadata included in data that is loaded by a ClientDataSet is influenced in part by the ProviderFlags properties of the DataSet's individual Fields. For example, for most DataSets, a Field that is associated with a column that is part of a result set's primary key will have the pfInKey flag appear in its ProviderFlags property.

It is possible to manually adjust the ProviderFlags property of the Fields of a DataSet, which in turn affects the SQL generated by a SQLResolver.

ProviderFlags is a TProviderFlags property, which is a set of one or more TProviderFlag values. Following are the type declarations for TProviderFlags and TProviderFlag:

```
TProviderFlags = set of TProviderFlag;
TProviderFlag = (pfInUpdate, pfInWhere, pfInKey, pfHidden);
```

Table 3-2 describes the effect of including each TProviderFlag value in the ProviderFlags property of a Field.

pfInUpdate	Include this flag to permit the field to be included in an UPDATE SQL statement. This flag is necessary in order to permit the associated field to be edited, and it is included in ProviderFlags by default.
pfInWhere	Include this field in a WHERE clause of UPDATE and DELETE SQL statements when UpdateMode is set to upWhereAll or in UPDATE statements when UpdateMode is set to upWhereChanged. This flag is in ProviderFlags by default.
pfInKey	Include this field in the WHERE clause of UPDATE SQL statements when UpdateMode is set to upWhereKeyOnly. This is a default flag for key fields, but can be set to include non-key fields in the WHERE clause.
pfHidden	Include this field in the data packet provided to a ClientDataSet, but do not permit it to be modified or

	displayed. You include this flag to include fields that should not be edited in the data packet when those field values are essential for performing record updates or deletions. For example, a key field that is needed for the WHERE clause of an UPDATE or DELETE SQL statement, but which you do not want edited by the ClientDataSet, can have the pfHidden flag set in its ProviderFlags property.

Table 3-2: Flags that Can Be Included in the Field ProviderFlags Property

It is rarely necessary to make changes to the ProviderFlags properties of your DataSet's Fields. Furthermore, if you do make changes to ProviderFlags, the default values that are normally generated will not be generated. This means that if you change ProviderFlags for one Field, you are going to have to manually set the ProviderFlags properties of every Field in the DataSet.

Writing Custom Updates Using BeforeUpdateRecord

At the outset of this chapter, you learned that it is possible to apply the updates in a ClientDataSet's change cache manually, writing each and every change back to the underlying database programmatically. In doing so, you have to take responsibility for handling all of the possible problems that you might encounter. You also learned that the DataSetProvider makes the application of updates relatively easy, in that it handles most of the potential problems.

But what do you do if the DataSetProvider's default behaviors simply cannot handle your data needs? For example, what if your DataSet contains an aggregate query, and you want to be able to project a change made to that result set to a large number of underlying records in one or more tables of your database?

Fortunately, there is an intermediate solution that does not require you to toss out the DataSetProvider altogether. Specifically, there is a solution that allows you to write custom code that takes responsibility for applying the changes found in the change cache, one at a time. You do this by adding your custom code to the BeforeUpdateRecord event handler of the DataSetProvider. This event handler is of the type TBeforeUpdateRecordEvent. The following is the syntax of the TBeforeUpdateRecordEvent type:

```
type
  TBeforeUpdateRecordEvent = procedure(Sender: TObject;
                             SourceDS: TDataSet;
                             DeltaDS: TCustomClientDataSet;
```

```
                                         UpdateKind: TUpdateKind;
                                         var Applied: Boolean) of object;
```

Here's how it works. Recall that when you call ApplyUpdates, the DataSetProvider applies the changes in the change cache one at a time. By default, these changes are applied by executing parameterized SQL statements generated by a SQLResolver. If ResolveToDataSet is set to True, these changes are applied by the DataSetProvider explicitly editing the DataSet to which it points.

When you assign an event handler to the DataSetProvider's BeforeUpdateRecord property, the DataSetProvider applies each change by calling your event handler. From there, you either take complete responsibility for the update, or you defer back to the DataSetProvider, which will then perform its default behavior (which depends on the value of the ResolveToDataSet property).

The parameters of BeforeUpdateRecord provide you with all the information your code needs in order to apply the changes. The first parameter, Sender, is a reference to the DataSetProvider that is executing the event handler.

The second parameter is a reference to the DataSet that the DataSetProvider is referring to in its DataSet property. If there is no DataSet referred to by the DataSetProvider's DataSet property, this value will be nil.

The third parameter is a CustomClientDataSet representing the change cache. Specifically, the current record of this CustomClientDataSet is the record in the change cache that is being applied. You use this CustomClientDataSet to read its Fields, which you will need in order to implement your delete, insert, and update operations.

The forth parameter, UpdateKind, identifies the type of modification that you need to apply. The following is the type declaration of TUpdateKind:

```
type
  TUpdateKind = (ukModify, ukInsert, ukDelete);
```

You use the final parameter, Applied, to control whether the DataSetProvider should perform its default behavior or not. If your code successfully applies its changes (or determines that the changes cannot be applied, in which case your code should raise an exception), you should set this parameter to True, indicating that the DataSetProvider should not execute its default behavior.

When you write BeforeUpdateRecord event handlers, the only responsibility that your code has is to apply the current update associated with the invocation of BeforeUpdateRecord. If there is more than one change in the change cache, BeforeUpdateRecord is invoked for each change.

All other aspects of the update are handled by the DataSetProvider. For example, if your code indicates that one or more updates cannot be applied, the DataSetProvider will automatically stop calling BeforeUpdateRecord once MaxErrors has been exceeded. In addition, the ClientDataSet, if it is employing a OnReconcileError event handler, will be given those records whose data could not be resolved.

This does not mean that writing BeforeUpdateRecord event handlers is a simple matter. Depending on what you need to do with the event handler, they can get complex since you must take responsibility for all aspects of applying each change.

Note: The code project SimpleBeforeUpdateRecord is available from the code download. See Appendix A.

The use of a BeforeUpdateRecord event handler is demonstrated in the SimpleBeforeUpdateRecord project. The main form of this project is shown in Figure 3-6.

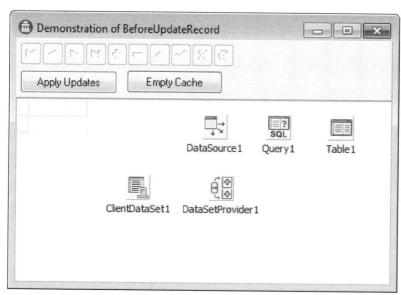

Figure 3-6: The main form of the SimpleBeforeUpdateRecord project

The DataSetProvider that you see in the main form is associated with the Query named Query1. This Query's RequestLive property is set to False, meaning that it returns a readonly result set. It also contains a very simple query, loading all records from the underlying CUSTOMER table. The following is the query associated with the Query's SQL property:

```
SELECT * FROM CUSTOMER
```

ClientDataSet1 is opened from the OnCreate event handler of this main form, so its data will be available for editing as soon as you run the project. If you then make one or more changes to the data and click the Apply Updates button, the DataSetProvider will prepare the change cache that the ClientDataSet provides it, and will then invoke the BeforeUpdateRecord event handler, once for each change in the change cache.

The following is the BeforeUpdateRecord event handler found in this project:

```
procedure TForm1.DataSetProvider1BeforeUpdateRecord(Sender: TObject;
  SourceDS: TDataSet; DeltaDS: TCustomClientDataSet;
  UpdateKind: TUpdateKind; var Applied: Boolean);
var
  i: Integer;
begin
  // Prevent the default behavior
  Applied := True;
  // Post pending cached edits
  // Update the record
  if UpdateKind = ukInsert then
    begin
      Table1.Insert;
      for i := 0 to Table1.Fields.Count - 1 do
        if not DeltaDS.Fields[i].IsNull then
        Table1.Fields[i].Value := DeltaDS.Fields[i].Value;
      try
        Table1.Post;
      except
        Table1.Cancel;
        raise;
      end;
    end
  else
  // Not an insert. Locate the existing record
  if Table1.Locate('CustNo',DeltaDS.Fields[0].OldValue,[]) then
    case UpdateKind of
      ukModify:
        begin
        Table1.Edit;
        for i := 0 to Table1.Fields.Count - 1 do
          if DeltaDS.Fields[i].Value <> Null then
            Table1.Fields[i].Value := DeltaDS.Fields[i].Value;
        try
          Table1.Post;
        except;
          Table1.Cancel;
          raise;
```

```
          end;
          end;
       ukDelete:
          begin
          Table1.Delete;
          end;
      end
    else
      raise ECustomCannotFindRecord.Create(DeltaDS.Fields[0].AsString +
        ' no longer exists');
  end;
```

The code in this event handler is not particularly complicated, but it nicely depicts the degree to which your code is responsible for all aspects of the individual updates. The first step that the code takes is to set Applied to True, indicating that it is going to be responsible for the update. Next, it evaluates the UpdateKind property to determine what kind of update it is being asked to perform.

If the update is an insert, a record is inserted into Table1. Then, for each field in DeltaDS for which data was entered, the data is copied into the newly inserted record. If the change cannot be posted, the newly inserted record of Table1 is cancelled and the exception is re-raised.

If the record was either modified or deleted, the corresponding record is located in Table1 using the Locate method (FindKey could have been used if we were prepared to set an index on Table1). Then, if the record was modified, the located record is updated with the modified fields. If the change cannot be posted, the modifications are cancelled and the exception is re-raised. If the record was deleted, the located record is deleted.

Note that the preceding code assumes that Table1 is already open. In this project, Table1 is opened from the BeforeApplyUpdates event handler of the DataSetProvider and closed in the AfterApplyUpdates event handler. (The ClientDataSet also has these event handlers, and they could have been used just as successfully.)

Use the following steps to get a better feeling about using the BeforeUpdateRecord event handler:

1. Open the BeforeUpdateRecord project.

2. Select the DataSetProvider and double-click the BeforeUpdateRecord event handler on the Events page of the Object Inspector.

3. Move your cursor the line that reads Applied = True; and press F5 to place a breakpoint.

4. Select Run | Run to run the project (make sure to run with the debugger active).

5. Change the name of Kauai Dive Shoppe by changing the spelling of Shoppe to Shop.

6. Click the + button in the DBNavigator to add a new record. Set CustNo to 9999 and Company to Cold Water Diving. Click the post button in the DBNavigator (the one with the checkmark) to post the record.

7. Now, click the button labeled Apply Updates. Delphi now loads the debugger.

8. Press F8 repeatedly to step through the code and watch the first record being updated. When you get to the end of the event handler, press F9 to exit the debugger. Immediately, the debugger loads again as the DataSetProvider invokes BeforeUpdateRecord for the second edit. Press F8 until you complete the execution of the event handler. Press F9 to exit the debugger, and then close the application.

Note: The code project BeforeUpdateRecordProjection is available from the code download. See Appendix A.

The final project of this chapter, BeforeUpdateRecordProjection, demonstrates another aspect of using the BeforeUpdateRecord event handler. Specifically, the data that is loaded into the ClientDataSet is the result of a GROUP BY operation, making the query necessarily readonly. The main form of this project is shown in Figure 3-7.

This project makes use of a table, named DemoTable, which is created when the project's main form is created. If you are interested, you should inspect the OnCreate event handler to see how this table was created.

The DataSet property of DataSetProvider1 is set to Query1, and the SQL property of this Query is shown here:

```
SELECT PartNo FROM DemoTable
  GROUP BY PartNo
  ORDER BY PartNo
```

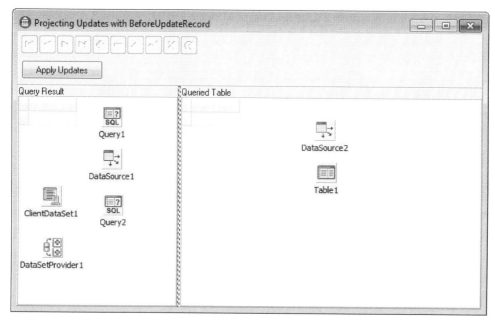

Figure 3-7: The main form of the BeforeUpdateRecordProjection project

As you can see, this query extracts unique PartNo values from the DemoTable. This information is loaded into a ClientDataSet and displayed in the DBGrid on the left side of the main form. Table1, a component that points to DemoTable in the database, is displayed in the DBGrid on the right side.

If you make a change to one or more PartNo values in the left side grid, and then apply those changes, each of those changes is projected to the DemoTable, updating all instances of those part numbers.

To assist with the update, a second Query, named Query2, is employed. This Query holds the parameterized query shown here:

```
UPDATE DemoTable
  SET PartNo = :PartNo
  WHERE PartNo = :OLD_PartNo
```

The actual projection occurs in the BeforeUpdateRecord event handler, which is specifically designed to only handle update operations. The following is the code found in this event handler:

```
procedure TForm1.DataSetProvider1BeforeUpdateRecord(Sender: TObject;
  SourceDS: TDataSet; DeltaDS: TCustomClientDataSet;
  UpdateKind: TUpdateKind; var Applied: Boolean);
begin
  Applied := True;
  if UpdateKind = ukModify then
  begin
    Query2.ParamByName('PartNo').Value :=
```

```
        DeltaDS.FieldByName('PartNo').NewValue;
      Query2.ParamByName('OLD_PartNo').Value :=
        DeltaDS.FieldByName('PartNo').OldValue;
      Query2.ExecSQL;
    end;
end;
```

This BeforeUpdateRecord event handler, which is significantly less complicated than the one from the SimpleBeforeUpdateRecord project, checks for update operations, and ignores all other changes. When an update is detected, it binds the query parameters from the data in the change cache, after which it executes the parameterized query.

Remember that this event handler is executed once for each change in the change cache. If four different part numbers are modified, this event handler will execute four times in response to a single call to ApplyUpdates.

Figure 3-8 depicts how the main form might look after a part number is changed. In this image, the part number 2341 was changed to 2342. After clicking the Apply Updates button, the BeforeUpdateRecord event handler changed all instances of 2341 to 2342 in the DemoTable table. Due to the nature of the Table component, those changes are immediately visible in the records of the grid on the right. If you inspect this figure, you will see that there are at least two records in the grid on the right that contain a part number 2342. I encourage you to play with this project a little to get a feel for what is going on.

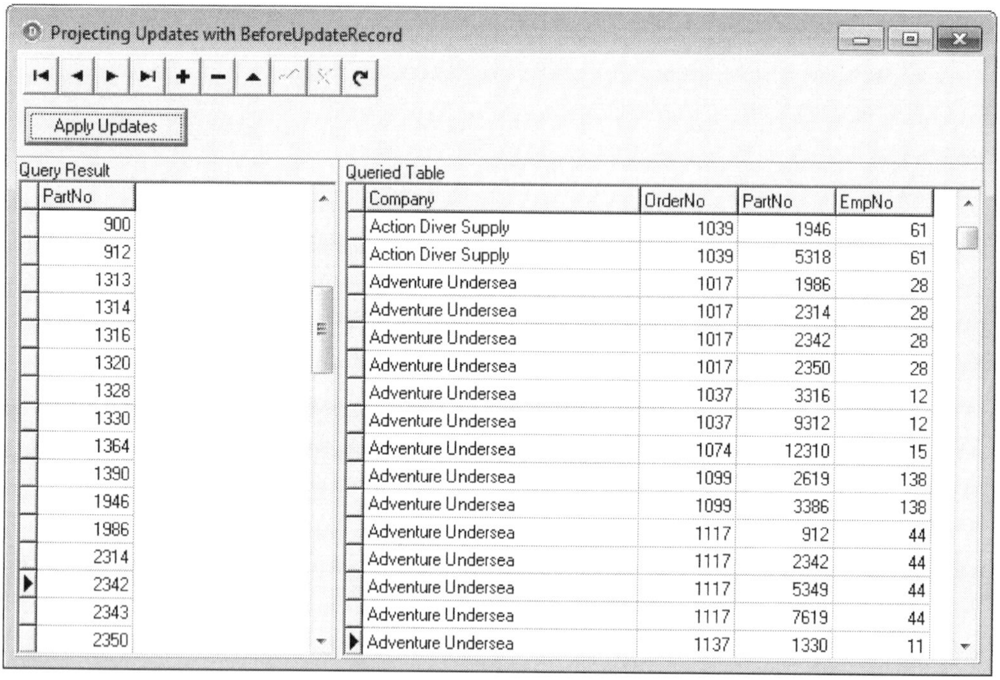

Figure 3-8: The change to one part number has been projected to all instances of that part number

In the next chapter, you will learn how to define the structure of ClientDataSets in those situations where a DataSetProvider is not employed.

Chapter 4
Defining a ClientDataSet's Structure

A ClientDataSet's structure is the definition of its fields and their types. When you load a ClientDataSet from a DataSetProvider, it gets its structure from the DataSetProvider. When you load a ClientDataSet from a previously saved local file (or from a stream), the metadata is obtained from the previously saved file (although sometimes this metadata is supplemented by Fields added to the ClientDataSet itself).

When you need to create an entirely new ClientDataSet, you must define the structure manually. This can be done either at design time or at runtime.

This chapter provides you with a detailed look at the process of defining a ClientDataSet's structure. Here you will learn how to define a ClientDataSet's structure using both FieldDefs as well as Fields. In addition, you will learn how to define these structures at design time and at runtime.

What Is a ClientDataSet's Structure?

A ClientDataSet's structure is the composition of its fields, or columns. The structure of a ClientDataSet defines what kind of data it can hold, and how that data can be used. If the ClientDataSet is not active, its structure can be used to initialize its data store, the in-memory structure that holds a ClientDataSet's data.

Structure has almost nothing to do with how much data a ClientDataSet can hold. A ClientDataSet with structure can be empty. Later on, that same ClientDataSet could contain several megabytes of data. The amount of data a ClientDataSet contains is related to the number of individual records that the ClientDataSet holds. The structure of a ClientDataSet defines what kind of data can be held in each record.

The structure of a ClientDataSet is an essential characteristic. For example, imagine that you have a ClientDataSet that is designed to hold information about your contacts, something similar to a digital phone directory. What kind of structure should that ClientDataSet have?

In the simplest of worlds, the structure of the ClientDataSet could consist of a single memo field called Data. You could store all the information about a given contact in this field, similar to the following:

```
Allen Albright (555) 512-2876 37 1501 Main St. Hancock California …
```

Although this text appears to contain information, it is really rather uninformative. For example, what do the characters 37 mean in this record? Sure, it might be the age, in years, of the contact, but that would be just a guess. And, if it was age, how would that information be used if you wanted to select all contacts who are at least 35 years of age or older from your ClientDataSet?

It's worse, actually. Consider the following text, which could possibly appear as another record in this contact ClientDataSet:

```
Billy Sunday
```

Is this informative? Not really. Is the contact's name Billy Sunday, or is the contact's name Billy, and Sunday is that contact's favorite day of the week? We do not know. That is because the ClientDataSet lacks meaningful structure.

Imagine instead that the contact ClientDataSet has a more organized structure. This might look something like the following:

Field Name	Field Type	Field Size
ContactID	string	6
FirstName	string	14
LastName	string	20
DateOfBirth	date	
PhoneNumber	string	20
…		

This structure is far more useful than a simple memo — it dictates what can be done with the data, and clearly defines the intention of each column's storage. For example, consider the ContactID field. It is of type string. Could it be of type integer instead? Well, yes, and having ContactID as an integer would save 2 bytes of data for each record (assuming that integers are 4 bytes in size).

However, defining a field as an integer implies that the field is a number, and numbers have properties that can be quite handy, such as being sum-able. Would it make sense to add the ContactID value of two contacts together? No. That's why it is best defined as a string.

Consider now DateOfBirth. This field could also have been defined as a string. However, what if we wanted to select all contacts who are 35 years old or older? Storing DateOfBirth as a string would not be that helpful, since a string field places few restrictions on the data it can hold. For example, if DateOfBirth was a string, one record could hold the value 5/3/82 and another could hold 1983 August 8. Yet another record could hold AAAAAAA. As strings, none of these values are really meaningful.

However, as a date field, the ClientDataSet will only accept values that are acceptable date values, and this greatly reduces the universe of values that could appear in that field. Furthermore, you could then do "date things" to those values, such as subtract the value from today's date in order to determine how many years old a given contact is.

Defining Structure

There are two mechanisms for explicitly defining a ClientDataSet's structure (as opposed to the structure that is defined based on data obtained by a DataSetProvider from an underlying DataSet). You can define the structure using the FieldDefs property of the ClientDataSet or you can define it using Fields. Both of these techniques are described in the following sections.

Defining a Table's Structure Using FieldDefs

The FieldDefs property of a ClientDataSet is a collection of TFieldDef instances. Each FieldDef represents a column, or field, that the ClientDataSet contains in its data stored if the ClientDataSet is activated.

You can configure FieldDefs either at design time or at runtime. To define the structure of a ClientDataSet at design time, you use the FieldDefs collection editor to create individual FieldDefs. You then use the Object Inspector to configure each FieldDef, defining the field name, data type, size, or precision, among other options.

At runtime, you define your FieldDef objects by calling the FieldDefs AddFieldDef or Add methods. This section begins by showing you how to create your ClientDataSet's structure at design time. Defining the structure at runtime is shown later in this chapter.

Creating FieldDefs at Design Time

You create FieldDefs at design time using the FieldDefs collection editor. To display this collection editor, select the FieldDefs property of a

ClientDataSet in the Object Inspector and click the displayed ellipsis button. The FieldDefs collection editor is shown in the following figure:

Using the FieldDefs collection editor, click the Add New button (or press Ins) once for each field that you want to include in your ClientDataSet. Each click of the Add New button (or press of Ins) will create a new FieldDef instance, which will be displayed in the collection editor. For example, if you add five new FieldDefs to the FieldDefs collection editor, it will look something like that shown in the following figure:

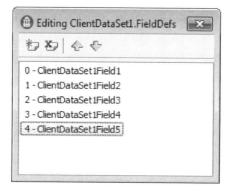

You must configure each FieldDef that is added to the FieldDefs collection editor before you activate the ClientDataSet. To configure a FieldDef, select the FieldDef you want to configure in the collection editor or the Structure Pane (or in older Delphi, the Object TreeView), and then use the Object Inspector to set its properties. Figure 4-1 shows how the Object Inspector looks when a FieldDef is selected. (Notice that the Attributes property has been expanded to display its subproperties.)

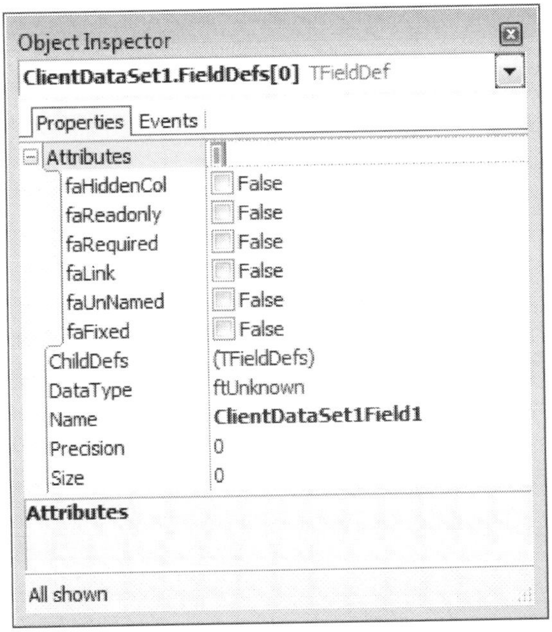

Figure 4-1: A FieldDef selected in the Object Inspector

At a minimum, you must set the DataType property of each FieldDef. You will also want to set the Name property. The Name property defines the name of the corresponding Field that will be created.

Other properties you will often set include the Size property, which you define for String, BCD (binary coded decimal), byte, and VarByte fields, and the precision property for BCD fields. Similarly, if a particular field requires a value before the record to which it is associated can be posted, set the faRequired flag in the Attributes set property.

After setting the necessary properties of each FieldDef, you must create the ClientDataSet's data store before you can use it. You can do this at either design time or runtime.

To create the ClientDataSet's data store at design time, right-click the ClientDataSet and select Create DataSet, as shown in Figure 4-2.

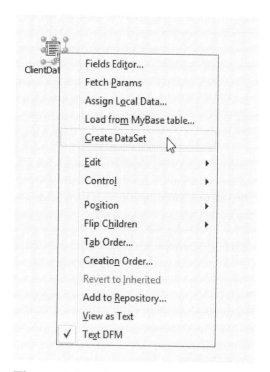

Figure 4-2: After defining its structure, right-click a ClientDataSet and select Create DataSet to make the ClientDataSet active

Creating the ClientDataSet data store at design time makes the ClientDataSet active. This data store is necessarily empty.

There are several advantages to creating the ClientDataSet data store at design time. The first is that the active ClientDataSet has Fields (dynamic fields, to be precise), and these Fields can easily be hooked up to data-aware controls such as DBEdit, DBLabel, and DBImage).

The second advantage is that you can save the ClientDataSet to disk. When you save a ClientDataSet to disk, you are saving its metadata as well as its data. But in this case, there is no data. Nonetheless, the metadata is valuable, in that any ClientDataSet that subsequently loads the saved ClientDataSet from disk will become active and will have the structure that you originally defined.

Saving a ClientDataSet at Design Time

To save your ClientDataSet to disk at design time, right-click the ClientDataSet and select one of the save options, such as Save to MyBase Xml table or Save to binary MyBase file, as shown in Figure 4-3.

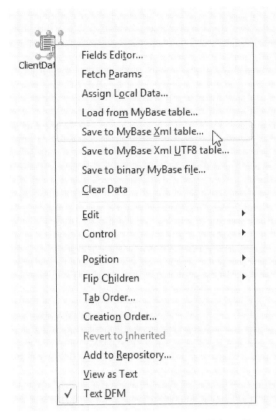

Figure 4-3: Saving a created ClientDataSet to disk

If you save your ClientDataSet to disk at design time, then you will likely need to deploy that file along with any other required files, when you deploy your application (assuming that your application needs this file, which would be the reason you created it in the first place). Alternatively, you can wait to create the ClientDataSet at runtime. You do this by calling the ClientDataSet's CreateDataSet method. For example, consider the following event handler, which might be associated with the OnCreate event handler of the form to which it is associated:

```
procedure TForm1.FormCreate(Sender: TObject);
const
  DataFile = 'mydata.xml';
begin
  ClientDataSet1.FileName :=
    ExtractFilePath(Application.ExeName) + DataFile;
  if FileExists(ClientDataSet1.FileName) then
    ClientDataSet1.Open
  else
    ClientDataSet1.CreateDataSet;
end;
```

This code begins by defining the FileName property of the ClientDataSet, pointing to a file named mydata.xml in the application directory. Next, it tests to see if this file already exists. If it does, it opens the ClientDataSet, loading the specified file's metadata into memory (and possibly any data that had been added to that ClientDataSet during a previous running of the application). If the file does not exist, it is created through a call to CreateDataSet. When CreateDataSet is called, the in-memory structure is created based on the FieldDefs property of the ClientDataSet.

Creating FieldDefs at Runtime

Being able to create FieldDefs at design time is an important capability, in that the Object Inspector provides you with assistance in defining the various properties of each FieldDef you add. However, there may be times when you cannot know the structure of the ClientDataSet that you need until runtime. In these cases, you must define the FieldDefs property at runtime.

As mentioned earlier in this section, there are two methods that you can use to define the FieldDefs property at runtime. The easiest technique is to use the Add method of the TFieldDefs class. The following is the syntax of Add:

```
procedure Add(const Name: String; DataType: TFieldType;
  Size: Integer = 0; Required: Boolean = False);
```

This method has two required parameters and two optional parameters. The first parameter is the name of the FieldDef and the second is its type. If you need to set the Size property, as is the case with fields of type ftString and ftBCD, set the Size property to the size of the field. For required fields, set the fourth property to a Boolean True.

The following code sample creates an in-memory table with five fields:

```
procedure TForm1.FormCreate(Sender: TObject);
const
  DataFile = 'mydata.xml';
begin
  ClientDataSet1.FileName :=
    ExtractFilePath(Application.ExeName) + DataFile;
  if FileExists(ClientDataSet1.FileName) then
    ClientDataSet1.Open
  else
    begin
      with ClientDataSet1.FieldDefs do
      begin
        Clear;
        Add('ID',ftInteger, 0, True);
        Add('First Name',ftString, 20);
        Add('Last Name',ftString, 25);
        Add('Date of Birth',ftDate);
```

```
      Add('Active',ftBoolean);
    end; //with ClientDataSet1.FieldDefs
    ClientDataSet1.CreateDataSet;
  end; //else
end;
```

Like the previous code listing, this code begins by defining the name of the data file, and then tests whether or not it already exists. When it does not exist, the Add method of the FieldDefs property is used to define the structure, after which the in-memory dataset is created using the CreateDataSet method.

If you consider how the Object Inspector looks when an individual FieldDef is selected in the FieldDefs collection editor, you will notice that the Add method is rather limited. Specifically, using the Add method, you cannot create hidden fields, readonly fields, or BCD fields where you define precision. For these more complicated types of FieldDef definitions, you can use the AddFieldDef method of the FieldDefs property. The following is the syntax of AddFieldDef:

```
function AddFieldDef: TFieldDef;
```

As you can see from this syntax, this method returns a TFieldDef instance. Set the properties of this instance to configure the FieldDef. The following code sample shows how to do this:

```
procedure TForm1.FormCreate(Sender: TObject);
const
  DataFile = 'mydata.xml';
begin
  ClientDataSet1.FileName :=
    ExtractFilePath(Application.ExeName) + DataFile;
  if FileExists(ClientDataSet1.FileName) then
    ClientDataSet1.Open
  else
    begin
      with ClientDataSet1.FieldDefs do
      begin
        Clear;
        with AddFieldDef do
        begin
          Name := 'ID';
          DataType := ftInteger;
        end; //with AddFieldDef do
        with AddFieldDef do
        begin
          Name := 'First Name';
          DataType := ftString;
          Size := 20;
        end; //with AddFieldDef do
        with AddFieldDef do
        begin
          Name := 'Last Name';
```

```
        DataType := ftString;
        Size := 25;
      end; //with AddFieldDef do
      with AddFieldDef do
      begin
        Name := 'Date of Birth';
        DataType := ftDate;
      end; //with AddFieldDef do
      with AddFieldDef do
      begin
        Name := 'Active';
        DataType := ftBoolean;
      end; //with AddFieldDef do
    end; //with ClientDataSet1.FieldDefs
    ClientDataSet1.CreateDataSet;
  end; //else
end;
```

Saving a ClientDataSet at Runtime

If you assign a file name to the FileName property of a ClientDataSet whose in-memory table you create using CreateDataSet, and then post at least one new record to the dataset, a physical file will be written to disk when you close or destroy the ClientDataSet. This happens automatically. Alternatively, you can call the SaveToFile method of the ClientDataSet to explicitly save your data to a physical file. The following is the syntax of SaveToFile:

```
procedure SaveToFile(const FileName: string = '';
  Format TDataPacketFormat=dfBinary);
```

Note: The preceding paragraph is accurate with respect to the ClientDataSet in earlier versions of Delphi. Specifically, if you set the FileName property, opening the ClientDataSet loads the data from the specified file, and closing or even freeing the ClientDataSet causes any changes to this data to be saved to disk. This does not work, at least not reliably, in the latest incarnations of the ClientDataSet class. As a result, I highly recommend that you do not rely on this feature. If you want your changes to be saved to disk, specifically invoke the SaveToFile method. I make this recommendation even if you are using an older version of Delphi, in that it makes clear your intent to save the data.

As you can see from the SaveToFile signature, both of the parameters of this method are optional. If you omit the first parameter, the ClientDataSet saves to a file whose name is assigned to the FileName property (or throws an exception if this property is empty).

If you omit the second parameter, the type of file that is written to disk will depend on the file extension of the file to which you are saving the data. If the extension is XML, an XML MyBase file is created. Otherwise, a binary MyBase file is written. You can override this behavior by specifying the type of file you want to write. If you pass dfBinary as the second parameter, a binary MyBase file is created (regardless of the file extension). To create an XML MyBase file when the file extension of the file name is not XML, use dfXML.

An Example of Runtime FieldDefs

Note: The code project FieldDefs is available from the code download. See Appendix A for details.

An example application that demonstrates the use of the FieldDefs AddFieldDef and Add methods can be found in the FieldDefs project. Figure 4-4 shows how the main form of this application looks after File | Create or Load is selected from the main menu.

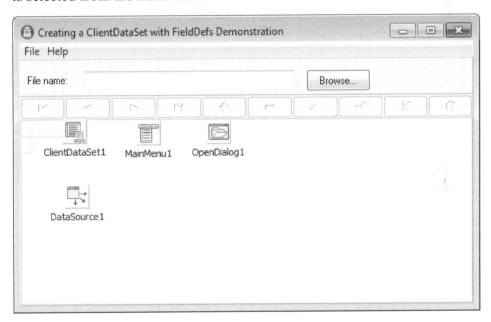

Figure 4-4: The FieldDefs project demonstrates how to create a ClientDataSet at runtime using FieldDefs

Defining a ClientDataSet's Structure Using Fields

While the FieldDefs property provides you with a convenient and valuable mechanism for defining a ClientDataSet's structure, it has several shortcomings.

Specifically, you cannot use FieldDefs to create virtual fields, which include calculated fields, lookup fields, and aggregate fields.

Similar to using FieldDefs to define the structure of a ClientDataSet, you can define a ClientDataSet's structure using Fields either at design time or at runtime. Since the design time technique is the easiest to demonstrate, it is discussed next. Defining a ClientDataSet's structure using Fields at runtime is shown later in this section.

Creating Fields at Design Time

You define the Fields that represent the structure of a ClientDataSet at design time using the Fields Editor. Unfortunately, this process is a bit more work than the process of using FieldDefs. Specifically, using the FieldDefs collection editor, you can quickly add one or more FieldDef definitions, each of which defines the characteristic of a corresponding field in the ClientDataSets' structure. Using the Fields method, you must add one field at a time. All this really means is that it takes a little longer to define a ClientDataSet's structure using Fields than it does using FieldDefs.

To create a Field, right-click a ClientDataSet and select Fields Editor from the displayed context menu:

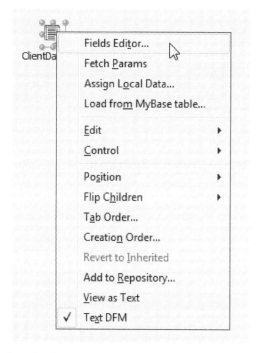

Delphi responds by displaying the Fields Editor.

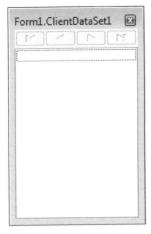

Right-click the Fields Editor and select New Field (or press the Ins key). The New Field dialog box is displayed, as shown in the Figure 4-5.

Figure 4-5: You use the New Field dialog box to define a persistent Field

To define the structure of your ClientDataSet, you typically use Data fields. A Data field is one whose data is stored if the ClientDataSet is saved to disk or a stream. By default, Field Type is set to Data.

Define your field by providing a field name and field type, at a minimum. The value you enter in the Name field defines the name of the column in the ClientDataSet. You set Type to one of the supported Delphi field types, such as String, Integer, DateTime, and so forth.

If your field is one that requires additional information, such as size, provide that information as well. You can also optionally set Component. By default, Component is set to the name of the ClientDataSet concatenated with the Name value. You can set Component manually, but if you do so, ensure that it will be a unique name as this is the name that is used for the Field object that will be created.

When done, select OK to save your new Field.

The Field that is created when you accept the New Field dialog box is one of the descendants of TField, based on the value you set Type to on the New Field dialog box. For example, if you set Type to string, a TStringField descendant is created. By comparison, if you set Type to integer, a TIntegerField descendant is created.

You cannot change a field type once it has been created. If you have mistakenly selected the wrong value for Type, your best bet is to delete that field and create a new replacement.

You also cannot use the New Field dialog box to make changes to a field once it has been created. However, there is really no need to do that, since the created field is a published member of the form, data module, or frame on which your ClientDataSet appears. As a result, you can select the Field in the Object Inspector and make changes there. For example, Figure 4-6 shows the Object Inspector for a string Field that was created by the New Field dialog box. This field can be found in the CDSFields project.

Note: The code project CDSFields is available from the code download. See Appendix A for details.

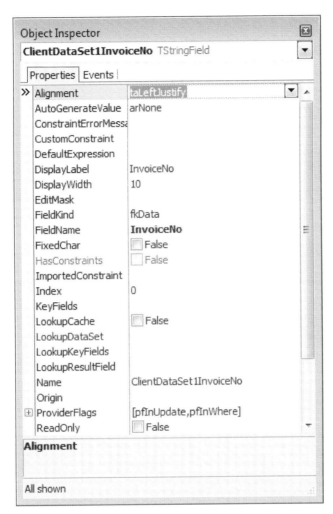

Figure 4-6: Use the Object Inspector to modify a Field that you have created

That Fields are published members of the container on which the ClientDataSet resides results in another interesting feature. They appear in the container's type definition, as shown in the following type definition from the CDSFields project:

```
type
  TForm1 = class(TForm)
    DataSource1: TDataSource;
    DBNavigator1: TDBNavigator;
    DBGrid1: TDBGrid;
    ClientDataSet1: TClientDataSet;
    ClientDataSet1InvoiceNo: TStringField;
    ClientDataSet1PartNo: TStringField;
    ClientDataSet1Price: TCurrencyField;
```

```
   ClientDataSet1Quantity: TIntegerField;
   ClientDataSet1Total: TCurrencyField;
   procedure FormCreate(Sender: TObject);
   procedure FormClose(Sender: TObject; var Action: TCloseAction);
   procedure ClientDataSet1CalcFields(DataSet: TDataSet);
private
   { Private declarations }
public
   { Public declarations }
end;
```

It is interesting to note that these Fields are defined in this fashion even before the ClientDataSet's data store has been created.

Fields that are created prior to a ClientDataSet being made active are known as *persistent fields.* (When you create a ClientDataSet's data store based on FieldDefs, Fields are also created, but those are known as *dynamic fields*, since they are created as part of the activation process.) Persistent fields can be created for any type of DataSet, not just ClientDataSets. However, the role that Fields play in ClientDataSets is different from that for other DataSets, in that a ClientDataSet is the only DataSet whose physical structure can be defined using the Field definitions.

If you want to create the data store of a ClientDataSet whose structure is defined at design time, you use the same steps as you would with a ClientDataSet defined by FieldDefs. Right-click the ClientDataSet and select Create DataSet. Similarly, even though you have defined the Fields at design time, you can still defer the creation of the ClientDataSet's data store until runtime. Again, just as you do with a ClientDataSet whose structure is defined by FieldDefs, you create the ClientDataSet data store at runtime by calling the ClientDataSet's CreateDataSet method.

Note: Saving a ClientDataSet, either to a file or to a stream, saves its structure based on non-virtual fields. Specifically, any dynamic fields created by FieldDefs, or persistent Data fields created through Fields, contribute to the metadata that is persisted. Virtual Fields, by comparison, do not. Virtual fields are features of the ClientDataSet, but not of the internal data store, and therefore, no metadata concerning virtual fields is persisted when you save a ClientDataSet to a file or a stream.

Adding a Calculated Virtual Field

Virtual fields are special fields that, in most cases, do not result in data being stored in a DataSet. Examples of virtual fields are aggregate fields, calculated fields, and lookup fields. Aggregate fields are those that perform a calculation across records, such as summing a column. Calculated fields are fields that display data that results from a calculation. That calculation is performed by adding an OnCalcFields event handler to the ClientDataSet to which the calculated field is associated. Lookup fields can be used to look up data in a separate, related table.

There is a forth virtual field type, called InternalCalc. ClientDataSets are the only type of DataSet that supports InternalCalc fields. This type of virtual field is particularly interesting because it actually stores the value of the calculation in memory, which a regular calculated field does not. Since the value of the calculation is stored, it is possible to create indexes that use those values. Indexes are discussed in Chapter 5, *Understanding ClientDataSet Indexes.*

In almost every other way, InternalCalc and Calculated fields are identical. InternalCalc fields just happen to be more efficient.

Note: Just to be clear, the InternalCalc data is stored entirely in memory. Neither InternalCalc fields nor Calculated fields persist their data to disk when you call SaveToFile.

An example of an InternalCalc field can be found in the CDSFields project. Figure 4-7 shows how the New Field dialog box looked when this field was being defined.

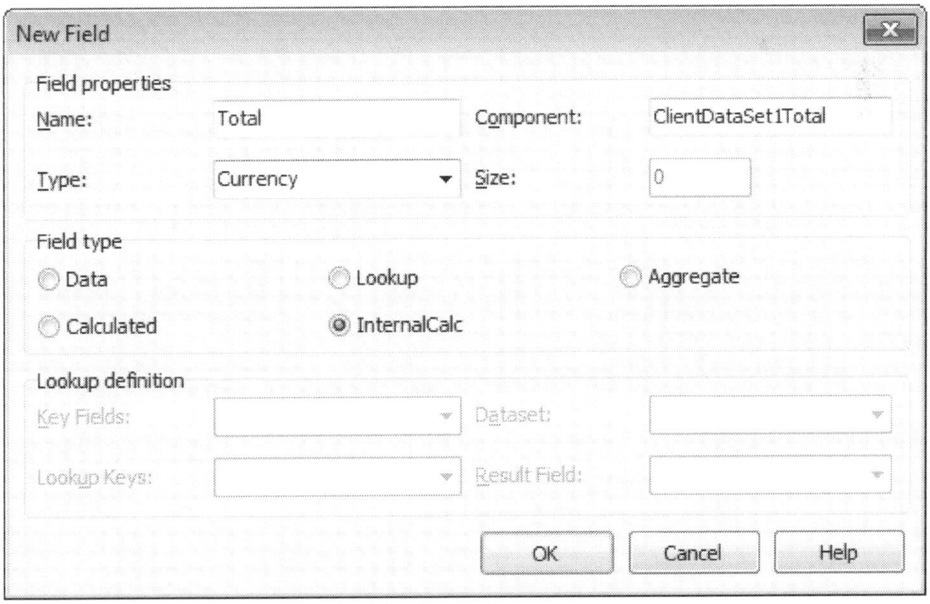

Figure 4-7: Adding the ClientDataSet1Total InternalCalc field

InternalCalc fields, as well as their close relative Calculated fields, are special in that you cannot assign data to them directly, either through data-aware controls or programmatically, with one exception. You can assign data to an InternalCalc or a Calculated field when the DataSet is in the dsCalc state, and if you write an OnCalcField event handler for the ClientDataSet to which at least one of these fields is attached, the ClientDataSet will invoke this event handler when it enters that state. Another way to say this is that you can only assign a value to an InternalCalc or Calculated field from the DataSet's OnCalcFields event handler.

Following is the OnCalcFields event handler found in the CDSFields project. In it, the value of the ClientDataSet1Total field is assigned the product of the ClientDataSet1Price and ClientDataSet1Quantity field values:

```
procedure TForm1.ClientDataSet1CalcFields(DataSet: TDataSet);
begin
  ClientDataSet1Total.AsCurrency :=
    ClientDataSet1Price.AsCurrency *
ClientDataSet1Quantity.AsInteger;
  //If there were additional InternalCalc or Calculated fields in
  //this ClientDataSet, you would perform those calculations here.
end;
```

Figure 4-8 shows the running CDSFields main form. The Total column in the displayed DBGrid contains the results of the calculation performed in the preceding OnCalcFields event handler.

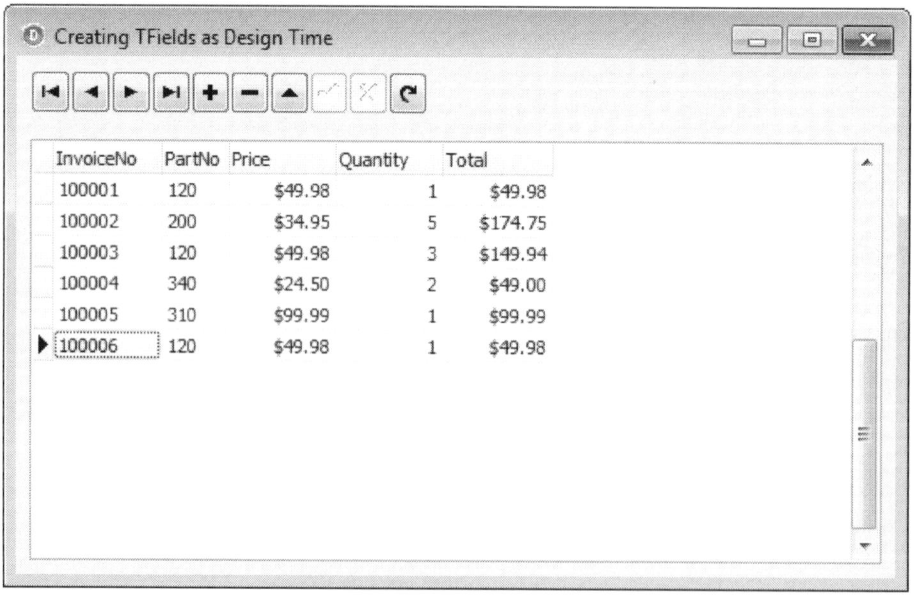

Figure 4-8: An InternalCalc field calculates the total value of an item

Creating a ClientDataSet's Structure at Runtime Using Fields

Earlier in this chapter, where a ClientDataSet's structure was defined using FieldDefs, you learned that you can define the structure of a ClientDataSet both at design time as well as at runtime. As explained in that section, the advantage of using design-time configuration is that you can use the features of the Object Inspector to assist in the definition of the ClientDataSet's structure. It also lets you conveniently hook up data-aware controls. This approach, however, is only useful if you know the structure of your ClientDataSet in advance. If you do not, your only option is to define your structure at runtime.

You define your Fields at runtime using the methods and properties of the appropriate TField descendant class. Specifically, you call the constructor of the appropriate Field, setting the properties of the created object to define its nature. Among the properties of the constructed object, one of the most important is the DataSet property. This property defines to which DataSet you want the object associated (which will be a ClientDataSet in this case, since we are discussing this type of DataSet). After creating all of the Fields, you call the ClientDataSet's CreateDataSet method. Doing so creates the ClientDataSet's structure based on the Fields to which it is associated.

Note: The code project CreatingFieldsAtRuntime is available from the code download. See Appendix A.

The project named CreatingFieldsAtRuntime includes examples of creating a ClientDataSet structures at runtime using both FieldDefs as well as Fields. The following code segment, which demonstrates the creation of a ClientDataSet's data store at runtime using Fields, is taken from that project:

```
with TIntegerField.Create(Self) do
begin
  Name := 'ClientDataSet1ID';
  FieldKind := fkData;
  FieldName := 'ID';
  DataSet := ClientDataSet1;
end; //ID
with TStringField.Create(Self) do
begin
  Name := 'ClientDataSet1FirstName';
  FieldKind := fkData;
  FieldName := 'First Name';
  Size := 20;
  DataSet := ClientDataSet1;
end; //First Name
with TStringField.Create(Self) do
```

```
begin
  Name := 'ClientDataSet1LastName';
  FieldKind := fkData;
  FieldName := 'Last Name';
  Size := 25;
  DataSet := ClientDataSet1;
end; //Last Name
with TDateField.Create(Self) do
begin
  Name := 'ClientDataSet1DateOfBirth';
  FieldKind := fkData;
  FieldName := 'Date of Birth';
  DataSet := ClientDataSet1;
end; //Date of Birth
with TBooleanField.Create(Self) do
begin
  Name := 'ClientDataSet1Active';
  FieldKind := fkData;
  FieldName := 'Active';
  DataSet := ClientDataSet1;
end; //Active Name
ClientDataSet1.CreateDataSet;
```

Figure 4-9 shows a running form from the CreatingFieldsAtRuntime project that uses Fields to create a ClientDataSet structure at runtime.

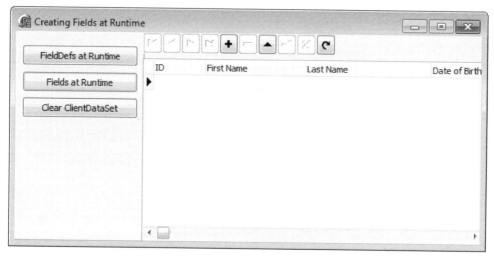

Figure 4-9: A ClientDataSet structure created at runtime using Fields

Fields and FieldDefs Are Different

There are a number of similarities between using FieldDefs and Fields to define your ClientDataSet's structure. Both can be used to define a wide variety of fields in the ClientDataSet's data store. There is another feature that is not obvious, but important. When a ClientDataSet's structure is defined by

FieldDefs, creating the data store results in the creation of Fields. Similarly, if you define a ClientDataSet's structure using Fields, creating the data store results in the creation of FieldDefs.

But there is a significant difference between these two approaches. In short, the structure defined using FieldDefs is transient, while the structure defined using persistent fields, which is what you get when you define the structure using Fields, is fixed.

This issue is complicated, so I am going to walk through it step-by-step. Let's start with a ClientDataSet whose structure is defined using FieldDefs. After defining the structure, whether at design time or runtime, you can create the ClientDataSet's data store by calling CreateDataSet. This call to CreateDataSet causes Fields to be created, one for each of the FieldDefs. These Fields are dynamic fields. If you now explicitly load a previously saved ClientDataSet by calling LoadFromFile, the metadata in that saved file will replace the FieldDefs and create a new set of Fields. In other words, the loaded file's metadata takes precedence, and will completely replace the current structure.

Things are significantly different when you define your structure using Fields. When you explicitly create Fields and associate them with a ClientDataSet at either design time or runtime, those Fields are persistent fields, and that makes all the difference in the world. When persistent fields exist, the process of creating dynamic fields is short-circuited.

As a result, if you define the structure of a ClientDataSet using Fields (whether at design time or runtime), and then attempt to load a previously saved ClientDataSet using LoadFromFile, the structure of the ClientDataSet being loaded does not replace the structure defined by the Fields. If there is a mismatch, an exception is raised and the ClientDataSet cannot become active.

If you define your ClientDataSet's structure using Fields, there are only two situations under which you can load previously saved data into that ClientDataSet. If the structure of the saved data matches the first n persistent fields already defined for the ClientDataSet, all will be fine. The newly loaded data will appear in the data store.

For example, if the previously persisted ClientDataSet has five string fields, all 20 characters in length, and the first five persistent fields of the ClientDataSet being loaded are also 20 character string fields, the data will load. If there are more than five persistent fields, fields 6 and higher will be null (unless they are virtual fields, in which case they may have values, such as those produced by an aggregate or a calculated field).

The second situation under which a previously saved ClientDataSet can be loaded into a ClientDataSet with persistent fields, and the only option when the two structures are incompatible, is to first free the persistent fields, thereby eliminating the previous structure. The previously saved ClientDataSet can now be loaded, and its metadata will dictate the structure.

Don't take this discussion to mean that you should never use Fields to define the structure of a ClientDataSet. In fact, if you read between the lines in the preceding descriptions, you already realize that there are a number of situations where the use of Fields is highly desirable. Specifically, for situations when you need to load data from a file (or stream) and hold that data for display or editing in a ClientDataSet with virtual fields.

For example, consider the CDSFields project discussed earlier in this chapter. The last field in the ClientDataSet is an InternalCalc field. The value in this field will not be saved if you call SaveToFile (nor will metadata about that field be saved), but the data associated with the first four Fields will be saved. If this ClientDataSet is saved to a file and then once again loaded into the ClientDataSet (which is what happens if you run the project, enter some data, close the project, and then run it again), the first four fields of the saved data will match the first four persistent fields in the ClientDataSet's structure, and the fifth persistent field in the ClientDataSet's structure will provide the InternalCalc support.

The issue is similar if you use both FieldDefs and Fields to define the structure of your ClientDataSet (yes, you can use both, if you are careful). The rule is similar to that when loading a previously saved ClientDataSet into a ClientDataSet that has persistent fields. In short, all of the FieldDef definitions must match the corresponding persistent field definitions. There can be more persistent field definitions than FieldDefs, but not less. Typically, those "extra" persistent fields are associated with virtual fields.

A Complex Example Using Fields at Runtime

In this chapter, I have looked at how you define the structure of a ClientDataSet when it is not getting that structure from a DataSetProvider. In particular, I discussed using FieldDefs and Fields, both at design time and at runtime. I also discussed how to create an InternalCalc field at design time.

There are many additional examples that could have been included in this discussion, but some of these rightly belong in other chapters in this book. For example, I am holding off the discussion of how to create an aggregate field at runtime until we examine aggregates in greater detail. That discussion appears in Chapter 10, *Aggregates and Group State.*

Another rich topic, and one that deserves detailed discussion, involve creating nested datasets, both at design time and at runtime. Once again, an entire chapter, Chapter 12, *Using Nested DataSets*, is devoted to this topic.

Note: The code project VideoLibrary is available from the code download. See Appendix A for details.

However, if you are interested in exploring the runtime creation of complex ClientDataSets, I invite you to look more closely at the VideoLibrary project.

The VideoLibrary project includes code that demonstrates how to create data, aggregate, lookup, and nested dataset fields at runtime using Fields. This project, whose running main form is shown in Figure 4-10, includes two primary ClientDataSets. One is used to hold a list of videos and another is used to hold a list of Talent (actors). The ClientDataSet that holds the video information contains two nested datasets: one to hold the list of talent for that particular video and another to hold a list of the video's special features (for instance, a music video found on a DVD).

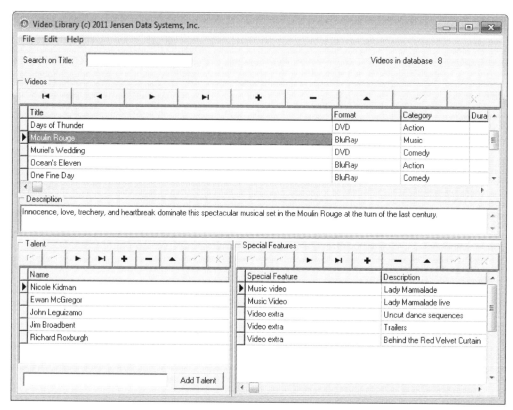

Figure 4-10: A complex ClientDataSet example built using runtime Fields

In the next chapter, we will take a detailed look at ClientDataSet indexes.

Chapter 5
Understanding ClientDataSet Indexes

In many respects, an index on a ClientDataSet is like that on any other DataSet descendant. Specifically, an index controls the order of records in the DataSet, as well as enables or enhances a variety of other operations, such as searches, ranges, and dataset linking.

Unlike a ClientDataSet's structure, which is normally obtained from existing data, a ClientDataSet's indexes are not. Specifically, when a ClientDataSet is loaded with data obtained from a DataSetProvider, or is loaded from a previously saved ClientDataSet file, the ClientDataSet's structure is largely (and usually entirely) defined by the DataSetProvider, or defined by the metadata loaded from the saved file. Indexes, with the exception of two default indexes, are solely the responsibility of the ClientDataSet itself. In other words, even if the underlying table from which a DataSetProvider obtains its data possesses indexes, those indexes are unrelated to indexes on the ClientDataSet loaded from that DataSetProvider.

Consider the CUSTOMER table found in the example DBDEMOS Paradox database that ships with Delphi. There are two customer table-related indexes present in the database: ByOrderNo and PartNo. Regardless of how you load the data from that table into a ClientDataSet, those indexes will be all but ignored by the DataSetProvider, and will be absent in the ClientDataSet. With the exception of the two default indexes that a ClientDataSet creates for its own use, if you want additional indexes in a ClientDataSet, you must define them explicitly.

Index Overview

An index is a data structure that holds subsets of the data in your ClientDataSet, in most cases, about one or more columns. When a ClientDataSet has more than one index, each index is based on either a different column or a different collection of the ClientDataSet's columns. The data in each index is sorted, permitting it to be searched very quickly.

Indexes serve four distinct purposes. These are to:

- Guarantee uniqueness of table data

- Provide quick locates of records

- Provide sorted views of data

- Allow for master-detail joins

First of all, an index can be used to prevent duplicate data from appearing in a table. This type of index is referred to as a *unique index*. A unique index can prevent duplicate values in data that is not loaded through a DataSetProvider. (As mentioned in Chapter 2, *Loading Data with ClientDataSets and DataSetProviders*, a ClientDataSet can obtain constraints that enforce uniqueness from a DataSetProvider.)

For example, in order to ensure that no two customers are assigned the same account number (which would break the association between customers and their invoices), the account number column can have a unique index. If you try to insert a new record that uses an account number that duplicates one that already exists in the ClientDataSet, or try to change the account number of an existing record to one in use by another record, the unique index ensures that the change will be rejected outright (an exception will be raised).

The second purpose of an index is to quickly locate one or more records based on data in the index. These indexes may or may not be unique indexes, depending on the fields used to define the index. Since indexes are already sorted, attempting to located records based on the one or more fields of an index means that the data can be searched very quickly in order to locate the associated records. Searching ClientDataSets is discussed in detail in Chapter 8, *Searching ClientDataSets*.

The third purpose of an index is to provide sorted views of the data in a ClientDataSet. The index does not actually change the order of the records in a ClientDataSet's data store, but instead causes those records to behave as if they were ordered based on the index.

The fourth purpose of an index is closely related to the second and third purposes. An index can be used to create master-detail joins between data in two related ClientDataSets, or between a ClientDataSet and another DataSet. These joins can then be used to create nested datasets. Nested datasets are discussed in detail in Chapter 12, *Using Nested DataSets*.

Indexes and ClientDataSets

In general, the indexes of a ClientDataSet can be divided into three categories: default indexes, temporary indexes, and persistent indexes. Each of these index types is discussed in the following sections.

Default Indexes

At most, an active ClientDataSet has two default index: DEFAULT_ORDER and CHANGEINDEX. These indexes occasionally appear in the IndexDefs collection editor. (We'll talk about the IndexDefs collection editor shortly.) However, they reliably appear in the IndexName dropdown list in the Object Inspector when an active ClientDataSet is selected, as shown in Figure 5-1.

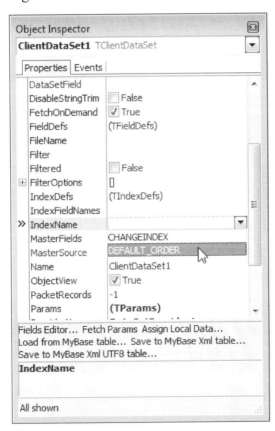

Figure 5-1: When a ClientDataSet is active, its default indexes appear in the IndexName dropdown list of the Object Inspector

DEFAULT_ORDER represents the original order of the records when they were loaded into the ClientDataSet. If the ClientDataSet is loaded through a DataSetProvider, this order matches that of the DataSet from which the DataSetProvider obtained the data.

For example, if the DataSetProvider points to a SQLDataSet that includes a SQL query with an ORDER BY clause, DEFAULT_ORDER will represent the order of the records produced by that ORDER BY clause. If the DataSet to which the DataSetProvider refers does not specify an order, the default order will match the order in which the DataSetProvider scanned the DataSet.

While DEFAULT_ORDER is associated with the original order of the records held in the Data property of the ClientDataSet, CHANGEINDEX is associated with the order of records held in the Delta property, also known as the change cache. CHANGEINDEX is maintained as changes are posted to a ClientDataSet, and it controls the order in which the changed records will be processed by the DataSetProvider when ApplyUpdates is called, as well methods of the ClientDataSet that pertain to change cache order, such as UndoLastChange.

These default indexes have limited utility in most database applications. For example, DEFAULT_ORDER can be used to return data held in a ClientDataSet to the originally loaded order after having switched to some other index. In most cases, however, a ClientDataSet's natural order is of little interest. Most developers want indexes based on specific fields, depending on the needs of the application.

CHANGEINDEX, by comparison, can be used to display only those records that appear in the change cache, and in the order that determines how the updates will be applied if ApplyUpdates is called. Again, this order might be interesting, but most developers are not concerned with the order in which changes are applied.

Even if you are concerned with the order of changes in the change cache, CHANGEINDEX is only marginally useful. For one, it is a readonly index. If you try to make any changes to the records of a ClientDataSet when IndexName is set to CHANGEINDEX, you will get an error.

On the other hand, if you are specifically interested in the contents of the change cache, irrespective of the order of the records, the ClientDataSet provides an alternative option. The ClientDataSet StatusFilter property permits you to display specific changes contained in the change cache. These changes can be displayed using any ClientDataSet index, not just the order in which the changes were applied. StatusFilter is discussed in Chapter 6, *Managing the ClientDataSet Change Cache.*

The bottom line is that these default indexes, while readily exposed through the IndexName property, are designed to be used by the ClientDataSet itself.

Creating Indexes

If you want your ClientDataSet to have one or more indexes, you need to create them yourself, and then instruct your ClientDataSet to use them. This has to be done for each ClientDataSet individually. Recall that indexes are not part of a ClientDataSet's metadata that is persisted when you save a ClientDataSet to a file or a stream. As a result, if you persist a ClientDataSet that has indexes, and you later load that data into another ClientDataSet, the new ClientDataSet must provide for any index definitions that you need. It cannot get them from the data it loads.

Note: Let me clarify this a little bit. If you inspect a saved ClientDataSet, in XML format for example, you might occasionally find an entry in the METADATA section of the XML file that uses the name INDEX. This metadata has nothing to do with custom indexes possessed by the ClientDataSet used to create the file, and cannot be used by a ClientDataSet that loads that data to recreate the custom indexes that existed in the original ClientDataSet.

On the other hand, ClientDataSets have a mechanism that permits you to attach arbitrary data to the file or stream that you persist using SaveToFile or SaveToStream. You can programmatically store information about the indexes that you need when you save a ClientDataSet by calling SetOptionalParam. Similarly, once a ClientDataSet has been loaded with persisted data, GetOptionalParam can be used to read that data, after which your code can create the necessary indexes. SetOptionalParam and GetOptionalParam is discussed in Chapter 6, Managing the ClientDataSet Change Cache.

There are two types of indexes that you explicitly create — temporary indexes and persistent indexes. Each of these index types plays an important role in applications, permitting you to control the order of records that appear in the ClientDataSet, as well as to enable index-based operations, including searches and ranges. These index types are discussed in the following sections.

Temporary Indexes

Temporary indexes are created with the IndexFieldNames property. To create a temporary index, set the IndexFieldNames property to the name of the field or fields you want to base the index on. When you need a multi-field index, separate the field names with semicolons.

For example, imagine that you have a ClientDataSet that contains customer records, including account number, first name, last name, city, state, and so on. If you want to sort this data by last name and first name (and assuming that these fields are named FirstName and LastName, respectively), you can create a temporary index by setting the ClientDataSet's IndexFieldNames property to the following string:

```
LastName;FirstName
```

As with all published properties, this can be done at design time, or it can be done in code at runtime using a statement similar to the following:

```
ClientDataSet1.IndexFieldNames := 'LastName;FirstName';
```

When you assign a value to the ClientDataSet's IndexFieldNames property, the ClientDataSet immediately generates the index. If the contents of the ClientDataSet are being displayed, once the index has been created, those records will appear sorted in ascending order by the fields of the index, with the first field in the index sorted first, followed the second (if present), and so on.

Once the index is active, it is maintained. For example, each time you insert, update, or delete data from the associated ClientDataSet, the index is updated to reflect these changes.

Indexes create this way are temporary in that when you change the value of the IndexFieldNames property, the current index is discarded. If you set IndexFieldNames to a new field or field list, once the current index is discarded, the new index is generated.

For example, imagine that after you create the last name/first name index, you execute the following statement:

```
ClientDataSet1.IndexFieldNames := 'FirstName'
```

This statement will cause the existing temporary index to be discarded and a new index to be generated. If the new index defines a sort order different from the previous index, the record display order is also updated. If you later set the IndexFieldNames property back to 'LastName;FirstName', the first name index will be discarded, and a new last name/first name index will be generated and used.

Note: The project CDSFilter is available from the code download. See Appendix A.

The following code demonstrates one technique that you might be able to adapt that permits the end user to select their own index. This code comes from the CDSFilter project. The main form for the CDSFilter project is shown in Figure 5-2.

The Edit labeled Index On can hold an index definition, but we should not permit the user to define their index without verifying that it is valid. As a result, this Edit is readonly.

In order to enter an index, the user clicks the Select Index button. This button is associated with the OnClick event handler that appears at the top of the following code segment. This event handler calls the GetTemporaryIndexFromUser method, passing in the currently selected index. If GetTemporaryIndexFromUser does not raise an exception, it returns a validated string that can be used to request a temporary index. At this point, the value is assigned to the Edit, which in turn triggers an OnChange event for the Edit. The Edit's OnChange event assigns the value in the Edit to the ClientDataSet's IndexFieldNames property.

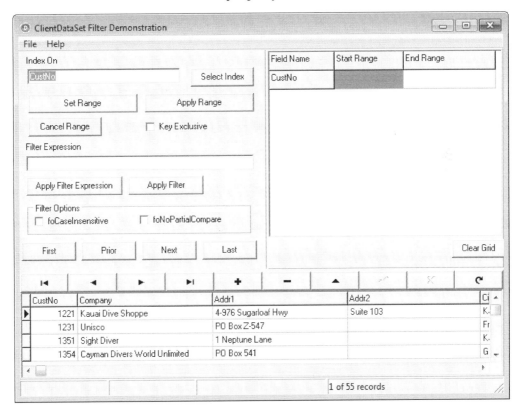

Figure 5-2: The main form of the CDSFilter project. The button labeled Select Index permits a user to choose their own index at runtime

The real work is performed by GetTemporaryIndexFromUser, and this code
is shown below. This method begins by displaying an InputQuery dialog box,
requesting the index text from the user. (A custom dialog box could make this
significantly more convenient in that it could actually contain a list of index-
able fields, and offer drag-and-drop configuration, but it would make the
example much more complicated.) If the user enters a new field or field list, the
code strips off unwanted spaces, verifies that the fields are valid, and then
returns the validated string. If the user does not accept the InputQuery dialog
box, the original index string is returned. If the user enters at least one invalid
field name or invalid character, an exception is raised and the index is
unchanged.

```
procedure TForm1.SelectIndexBtnClick(Sender: TObject);
var
  NewIndexFields: String;
begin
  NewIndexFields :=
GetTemporaryIndexFromUser(IndexFieldNamesEdit.Text);
  if NewIndexFields <> IndexFieldNamesEdit.Text then
  begin
    IndexFieldNamesEdit.ReadOnly := False;
    IndexFieldNamesEdit.Text := NewIndexFields;
    IndexFieldNamesEdit.ReadOnly := True;
    ClearGridBtnClick(Sender);
  end;
end;

procedure TForm1.IndexFieldNamesEditChange(Sender: TObject);
begin
  ClientDataSet1.IndexFieldNames := IndexFieldNamesEdit.Text;
  UpdateGridLabels;
end;

type
  EBadFieldInIndex = class(Exception);

function TForm1.GetTemporaryIndexFromUser(CurrentIndex: String):
String;
  //local function to verify field list
  function FieldsValid(CDS: TClientDataSet; FieldList: String):
Boolean;
  var
    i: Integer;
    SList: TStringList;
  begin
    Result := False;
    SList := TStringlist.Create;
    SList.Delimiter := ';';
    SList.DelimitedText := FieldList;
    try
      if SList.Count = 0 then
      begin
```

```
        Result := True;
        Exit;
      end
      else //if SList.Count = 0
          for i := 0 to Pred(SList.Count) do
            if CDS.FindField(SList[i]) = nil then
              Exit;
          Result := True;
    finally
      SList.Free;
    end;
  end; //function FieldsValid

var
  IndexFields: String;
begin
  Result := IndexFieldNamesEdit.Text;
  if InputQuery('Enter index field(s) [ex: field1;field2]',
    'Index on', Result) then
    begin
    while Pos(' ;',Result) <> 0 do
      Result :=
        StringReplace(Result, ' ;', ';', rfReplaceAll]);
    while Pos('; ',Result) <> 0 do
      Result :=
        StringReplace(Result, '; ', ';', [rfReplaceAll]);
      if not FieldsValid(ClientDataSet1, Result) then
        raise EBadFieldInIndex.Create('IndexFieldNames contains at '+
          'least one invalid field name');
    end; //if InputQuery
end;
```

Temporary indexes are extremely useful in a number of situations, such as in the preceding example where you want to permit your users to sort the data based on any field or field combination. There are, however, some drawbacks to temporary indexes.

All indexes, temporary or otherwise, take some time to build, and temporary indexes usually must be rebuilt more often than persistent indexes. The time it takes a ClientDataSet to build an index is based on the number of records being indexed, the field types being indexed, and the number of fields in the index. Since these indexes are built in memory, even the most complicated temporary index can be built in a fraction of a second so long as there are less than 10,000 records in the ClientDataSet. Even with more than 100,000 records, most indexes can be built in a couple of seconds on a typical workstation.

A more important concern when deciding between temporary and persistent indexes involves index features. Specifically, temporary indexes only produce ascending indexes. In addition, temporary indexes do not support more advanced index options, such as unique indexes and case-sensitive indexes. If you need some of these more sophisticated features, you will need to create persistent indexes.

Persistent Indexes

Persistent indexes, when created, are similar to temporary indexes in many ways. Unlike temporary indexes, though, which persist only so long as IndexFieldNames is set to the index's field or field list, once a persistent index has been built, it remains available to the ClientDataSet so long as the ClientDataSet remains open. Persistent indexes are not discarded until the ClientDataSet against which they were built is closed. For example, if there is a persistent index based on a field named FirstName, setting the ClientDataSet to use this index causes the index to be built. If you then set the ClientDataSet to use another persistent index based on the last name/first name field combination, that index is built, but the first name-based index is not discarded. If you then set the ClientDataSet to use the first name index once again, it immediately switches to that previously created index.

Persistent indexes are defined using the IndexDefs property of the ClientDataSet. You create IndexDefs at design time using the IndexDefs collection editor, shown in the following figure. To display this collection editor, select the IndexDefs property of a ClientDataSet in the Object Inspector and click the ellipsis button that appears:

The IndexDefs property editor may sometimes include the two default indexes.

Click the Add New button on the IndexDefs collection editor toolbar (or press the Ins key) once for each persistent index that you want to define for a ClientDataSet. Each time you click the Add New button (or press Ins), a new IndexDef is created. Complete the index definitions by selecting each IndexDef in the IndexDefs collection editor, one at a time, and configure it using the Object Inspector. The Object Inspector with an IndexDef selected is shown in

Figure 5-3. Note that the Options property has been expanded to show its various flags.

Figure 5-3: An IndexDef selected in the Object Inspector

At a minimum, you must set the Fields property of an IndexDef to the name of the field or fields to be indexed. If you are building a multi-field index, separate the field names with semicolons. You cannot include virtual fields, such as calculated or aggregate fields, in an index, though you can use InternalCalc fields.

By default, indexes created using IndexDefs are ascending indexes. If you want the index to be a descending index, set the ixDescending flag in the Options property. Alternatively, you can set the DescFields property to a semicolon-separated list of the fields that you want sorted in descending order. Using DescFields, you can define an index in which one or more, but not necessarily all, fields are sorted in descending order.

Indexed string fields created with persistent indexes are normally case sensitive. If you want string fields to be indexes without regard to the case of the strings, you can set the ixCaseInsensitive flag in the Options property. Or, you can include a semicolon-separated list of fields whose contents you want sorted case insensitive in the CaseInsFields property. Use the CaseInsFields property when you want to sort some, but not all, string fields without regard to case.

If you want the ClientDataSet to maintain information about groups, set the GroupingLevel property. Groups refer to the unique values on one or more fields of an index. Setting GroupingLevel to 0 maintains no grouping information, treating all records in a ClientDataSet as belonging to a single group. A GroupingLevel of 1 treats all records that contain the same value in the first field of the index as a group. Setting GroupingLevel to 2 treats all records with the combination of values in the first two fields of the index as a group, and so on. GroupingLevel is typically only useful if you are using aggregate fields, or want to call the GetGroupState method. Grouping is discussed in greater detail later in Chapter 10, *Aggregates and GroupState*.

In addition to sorting records, indexes can ensure the uniqueness of records. If you want to ensure that no two records contain the same data in the field or fields of an index, set the ixUnique flag in the IndexDef's Option property.

The remaining properties of the TIndexDef class do not apply to ClientDataSets. For example, ClientDataSets do not support expression, primary, or non-maintained indexes. As a result, do not set the Expression property or add ixNonMaintained or ixPrimary flags to the Options property when defining an IndexDef for a ClientDataSet. Likewise, Source only applies to DataSets that refer to dBase tables. Do not set the Source property when defining an index for a ClientDataSet.

Using Persistent Indexes

A persistent index is created when a ClientDataSet's IndexName property is set to the name of an IndexDef. Doing so will also have the effect of setting IndexFieldNames to an empty string, if necessary.

If IndexName is set at design time, or is set prior to opening a ClientDataSet, that index is built immediately after the ClientDataSet is opened, but before the contents of the ClientDataSet become available.

It is important to note that a ClientDataSet does not build an index (persistent or temporary) until it needs it. Specifically, even if you have fifty different IndexDefs defined for a ClientDataSet, no index is actually built until the ClientDataSet is opened, and then only if the IndexName or IndexFieldNames property has been set.

All persistent indexes that exist for a given ClientDataSet are maintained. Specifically, any time you insert, update, or delete data from the ClientDataSet, all of the current indexes are updated. As you might expect, changes to data have no effect on IndexDef definitions that have not yet been created.

Creating Persistent Indexes at Runtime

To create IndexDefs at runtime, you use either the AddIndex or AddIndexDef methods of the ClientDataSet's IndexDefs property, or you can call the ClientDataSet's AddIndex method. Like the related AddFieldDef, AddIndexDef is more flexible than AddIndex, which makes it the recommended method for adding a persistent index at runtime.

AddIndexDef returns an IndexDef instance, which you use to set the properties of the index. For example, the following statement creates an IndexDef for the data in the ClientDataSet, and then makes this the active index:

```
with ClientDataSet1.IndexDefs.AddIndexDef do
begin
   Name := 'LastFirstIdx';
   Fields := 'LastName;FirstName';
   Options := [ixDescending, ixCaseInsensitive];
end;
ClientDataSet1.IndexName := 'LastFirstIdx';
```

Note: If you use code like the preceding, and the ClientDataSet raises an exception, reporting that the index name is not found, invoke the ClientDataSet's IndexDefs Update method before assigning the IndexName property.

Unlike AddFieldDef, the AddIndex method is a method of the TCustomClientDataSet class. The following is the syntax of AddIndex:

```
procedure AddIndex(const Name, Fields: string;
   Options: TIndexOptions;
   const DescFields: string = ''; const CaseInsFields: string = '';
   const GroupingLevel: Integer = 0);
```

As you can see from this syntax, this method requires at least three parameters. The first parameter is the name of the index you are creating, the second is the semicolon-separated list of the index field names, and the third is the index options. Note, however, that only the ixCaseInsensitive, ixDescending, and ixUnique TIndexOptions are valid when you invoke AddIndex with a ClientDataSet. Using any of the other TIndexOptions flags raises an exception.

The fourth parameter, DescFields, is an optional parameter that you can use to list the fields of the index that you want to sort in descending order. You use this parameter when you want some of the index fields to be sorted in ascending order and others in descending order. When you use DescFields, do not include the ixDescending flag in Options.

Like DescFields, CaseInsFields is an optional String property that you can use to select which fields of the index should be sorted without respect to case. When you use CaseInsFields, do not include the ixCaseInsensitive flag in Options.

The final parameter, GroupingLevel, is an optional parameter that you use to define the grouping level of the index.

An Example: Creating Indexes On-the-fly

A frequently requested feature in a database application is the ability to sort the data displayed in a DBGrid by clicking on the column title. The CDSSortGrid project demonstrates how you can add this feature to any DBGrid that displays data from a ClientDataSet.

Note: The code project CDSSortGrid is available from the code download. See Appendix A.

This project makes use of a generic procedure named SortCustomClientDataSet. This procedure is designed to work with any TCustomClientDataSet descendant, including ClientDataSet, SimpleDataSet, BDEClientDataSet, and IBClientDataSet. However, some of the properties used in this code are not visible in the TCustomClientDataSet class. Specifically, the IndexDefs and IndexName properties are declared protected in TCustomClientDataSet. As a result, this code relies on runtime type information (RTTI) to work with these properties. This means that any unit implementing this procedure must use the TypInfo unit (the unit that implements RTTI).

The following is the SortCustomClientDataSet procedure:

```
uses TypInfo; //TypInfo needed for RTTI GetObjectProp
              //IsPublishedProp, and SetStrProp methods

function SortCustomClientDataSet(DataSet: TCustomClientDataSet;
  const FieldName: String): Boolean;
var
  i: Integer;
  IndexDefs: TIndexDefs;
  IndexName: String;
  IndexOptions: TIndexOptions;
  Field: TField;
```

```
begin
  Result := False;
  Field := DataSet.Fields.FindField(FieldName);
  //If invalid field name, exit.
  if Field = nil then exit;
  //if invalid field type, exit.
  if (Field is TObjectField) or (Field is TBlobField) or
     (Field is TAggregateField) or (Field is TVariantField)
     or (Field is TBinaryField) then exit;
  //Get IndexDefs and IndexName using RTTI
  if IsPublishedProp(DataSet, 'IndexDefs') then
    IndexDefs := GetObjectProp(DataSet, 'IndexDefs') as TIndexDefs
  else
    exit;
  if IsPublishedProp(DataSet, 'IndexName') then
    IndexName := GetStrProp(DataSet, 'IndexName')
  else
    exit;
  //Ensure IndexDefs is up-to-date
  IndexDefs.Update;
  //If an ascending index is already in use,
  //switch to a descending index
  if IndexName = FieldName + '__IdxA'
  then
    begin
      IndexName := FieldName + '__IdxD';
      IndexOptions := [ixDescending];
    end
  else
    begin
      IndexName := FieldName + '__IdxA';
      IndexOptions := [];
    end;
  //Look for existing index
  for i := 0 to Pred(IndexDefs.Count) do
  begin
    if IndexDefs[i].Name = IndexName then
      begin
        Result := True;
        Break
      end;  //if
  end; // for
  //If existing index not found, create one
  if not Result then
      begin
        DataSet.AddIndex(IndexName, FieldName, IndexOptions);
        Result := True;
      end; // if not
  //Set the index
  SetStrProp(DataSet, 'IndexName', IndexName);
end;
```

This code begins by verifying that the field passed in the second parameter exists, and that it is of the correct type. Next, the code verifies that the ClientDataSet passed in the first formal parameter has an IndexDefs property.

If so, it assigns the value of this property to a local variable. It then calculates an index name by appending the characters "__IdxA" or "__IdxD" to the name of the field to index on, with __IdxA being used for an ascending index, and __IdxD for a descending index.

Next, the IndexDefs property is scanned for an existing index with the calculated name. If one is found (because it was already created in response to a previous header click), that index is set to the IndexName property. If the index name is not found, a new index with that name is created, and then the ClientDataSet is instructed to use it.

In the CDSSort project, this code is called from within the DBGrid's OnTitleClick event handler. The following is how this event handler is implemented in the CDSSortGrid project:

```
procedure TForm1.DBGrid1TitleClick(Column: TColumn);
begin
  SortCustomClientDataSet(ClientDataSet1, Column.FieldName);
end;
```

In Figure 5-4, which shows the running main form of the CDSSortGrid project, the header of the LastName column of the DBGrid has been clicked. The contents of the LastName field now appear sorted in ascending order. If the LastName header is clicked once more, this column would appear in descending order.

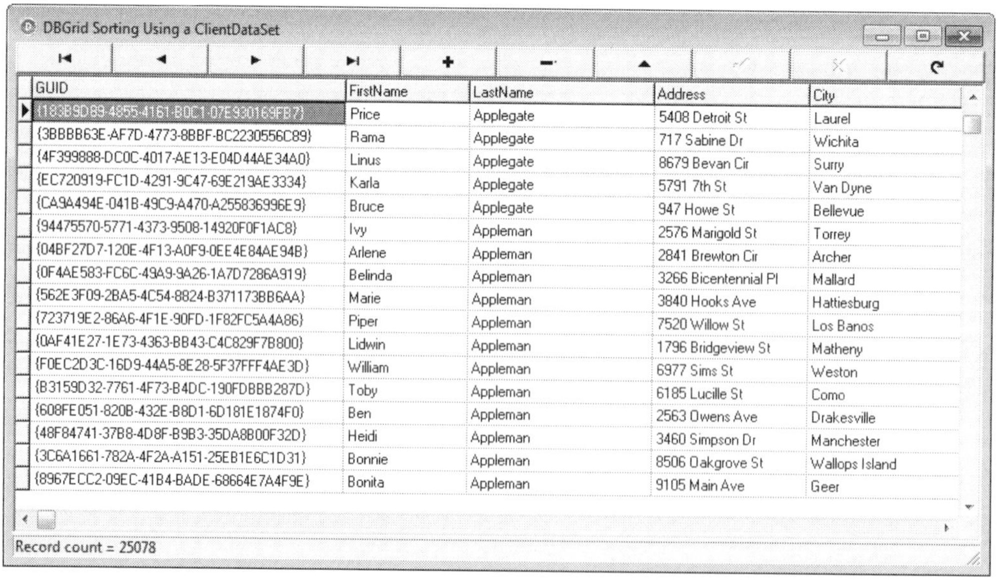

Figure 5-4: The contents of the ClientDataSet have been sorted in response to a click on the PartNo column header

If you look at the StatusBar in the CDSSortGrid project main form, you will notice that it reports that there are more than 25,000 records in the ClientDataSet used by this project. While 25,000 records may sound like a lot, ClientDataSets with several hundred thousand records are not unheard of. For this project, these records are located in a special saved ClientDataSet file provided with the code download.

This file, named BigCDS.cds, is used by a number of different projects used in this book. Specifically, those projects where performance is an issue. Having a large CDS file helps highlight performance differences, since large files exaggerate performance issues. This is why BigCDS.cds was used in this project — generating indexes takes time. Sure, just a few hundred milliseconds, but it is noticeable.

Note: The file BigCDS.cds is available from the code download. See Appendix A.

You will see this if you click on a particular header at least three times. The first two times there will be a slight delay while the ClientDataSet builds the ascending index (first click), and then the descending index (second click). The third time that you click that header, however, the sorting is nearly instantaneous, since the previously created persistent index is reused.

There is one final point I want to make about BigCDS.cds. Since it is used by several projects, and it is several megabytes in size. I wanted to make sure that each of the projects shares this one file, instead of using a separate copy for each project (to keep the code download reasonably small). As a result, each of the projects that use BigCDS.cds expect that file to be in a folder named BigCDS, parallel to the folder in which the project is located. In order for this to work, code like the following appears in the OnCreate event handler for the main form of each of the projects that employ BigCDS.cds:

```
ClientDataSet1.FileName := ExtractFilePath(Application.ExeName) +
  '\..\bigcds\bigcds.cds';
if not FileExists(ClientDataSet1.FileName) then
begin
  ShowMessage('BigCDS.cds not found. This project requires this ' +
    'file, and expects to find it in the folder named BigCDS, ' + '
    which should be located in the folder directly above ' +
    ExtractFilePath(Application.ExeName) + '. Cannot continue.');
  Abort;
end;
```

If you see an error message like the one created by the preceding code, you need to find the BigCDS.cds file, and place it in a folder with the name BigCDS, in the location indicated by the error message.

Returning to the SortCustomClientDataSet procedure, as pointed out earlier, this code has the drawback of requiring RTTI, which is necessary since the IndexDefs and IndexName properties of the TCustomClientDataSet class are protected properties. The CDSSortGrid project also includes a function named SortClientDataSet. This function, shown in the following code segment, is significantly simpler, in that it does not require RTTI. However, it can only be passed an instance of the TClientDataSet class (or one of its descendants), meaning that it cannot be used with other TCustomClientDataSets provided by Delphi, such as BDEClientDataSet and SimpleDataSet.

```
//This version does not require RTTI, but only
//works with ClientDataSets.
function SortClientDataSet(ClientDataSet: TClientDataSet;
  const FieldName: String): Boolean;
var
  i: Integer;
  NewIndexName: String;
  IndexOptions: TIndexOptions;
  Field: TField;
begin
  Result := False;
  Field := ClientDataSet.Fields.FindField(FieldName);
  //If invalid field name, exit.
  if Field = nil then Exit;
  //if invalid field type, exit.
  if (Field is TObjectField) or (Field is TBlobField) or
     (Field is TAggregateField) or (Field is TVariantField)
     or (Field is TBinaryField) then exit;
  //Get IndexDefs and IndexName using RTTI
  //Ensure IndexDefs is up-to-date
  ClientDataSet.IndexDefs.Update;
  //If an ascending index is already in use,
  //switch to a descending index
  if ClientDataSet.IndexName = FieldName + '__IdxA'
  then
    begin
      NewIndexName := FieldName + '__IdxD';
      IndexOptions := [ixDescending];
    end
  else
    begin
      NewIndexName := FieldName + '__IdxA';
      IndexOptions := [];
    end;
  //Look for existing index
  for i := 0 to Pred(ClientDataSet.IndexDefs.Count) do
  begin
    if ClientDataSet.IndexDefs[i].Name = NewIndexName then
      begin
        Result := True;
        Break
      end;  //if
  end; // for
```

```
  //If existing index not found, create one
  if not Result then
      begin
        ClientDataSet.AddIndex(NewIndexName,
          FieldName, IndexOptions);
        Result := True;
      end; // if not
  //Set the index
  ClientDataSet.IndexName := NewIndexName;
end;
```

In the next chapter, you will learn how to manage the change cache.

Chapter 6
Managing the ClientDataSet
Change Cache

The ClientDataSet's change cache is its key to resolving data back to an underlying database. The cache, when enabled, keeps track of the changes made to the data being held by the ClientDataSet. That information is sufficiently detailed to permit a DataSetProvider to resolve those changes to the database from which the data was loaded. Alternatively, you can read the change cache programmatically, using that information to make whatever updates are necessary.

But using the change cache to resolve data is not its only purpose. For example, the change cache permits you examine the whole of a user's edit before saving those changes. This permits you to perform validation across multiple records of the user's edits, verifying that those changes are meaningful and consistent. If not, your application can use the change cache to identify the inconsistencies, permitting the user to make corrections before the data is revalidated. Once the edits are determined to be valid, the data can then be saved.

That the change cache can be persisted is another of its important features. When you save a ClientDataSet to a file or a stream, the change cache is saved along with it. Restoring the ClientDataSet restores the change cache as well. The concept of a briefcase application was introduced in Chapter 3, and that type of application relies extensively on the ability to persist the change cache.

Another type of application that relies on the persistence of the change cache is a DataSnap application. Chapters 13 and 14 describe how the change cache permits a remote application server to resolve changes made by a thin client. The same thing applies to Web service applications that expose Web methods that pass a ClientDataSet back and forth between client applications and the Web service. If a client application makes changes to the ClientDataSet's data before returning it to the Web service, the receiving Web service can use the change cache to determine what changes were made, and to take appropriate action, whatever that may be.

Controlling the Change Cache

Up to this point, I have sung the praises of the change cache, and how useful it is. But this discussion has concentrated primarily on the fact that it exists, and can be used to resolve changes to an underlying database. But what we haven't discussed is in some ways even more amazing. Specifically, you can control almost every aspect of the change cache programmatically.

This programmatic control can be as dramatic as clearing the change cache entirely, thereby erasing all changes in the ClientDataSet, to as subtle as removing the edits from a single record.

Note: The project ChangeCache is available from the code download. See Appendix A for details.

Controlling the change cache is demonstrated in this chapter with a single project named ChangeCache. The main form of this application is shown in Figure 6-1.

In order to make this project rich enough so you can test and verify your change cache operations, this project supports both loading data from a database using a DataSetProvider, as well as saving and loading from a file. In order for this to work correctly, though, the structure of the saved file must be consistent with that of the data being loaded. To ensure this, you should first load the ClientDataSet through the DataSetProvider, and then save it. This project saves the file using a predetermined file name, xmldata.xml, and stores that file in the same directory as the project executable.

There is another detail about the data that you should know before we continue. The data that you will see in the project was originally loaded from the customer.db Paradox table found in the database that ships with Delphi. So that you can edit this file without fear of completely mangling the data, the first time the application runs, it checks to see if there is a custcopy.db table in the Paradox database. If there is not, the application copies the customer.db table, naming that copy custcopy.db. From that point on, all edits are made to custcopy.db.

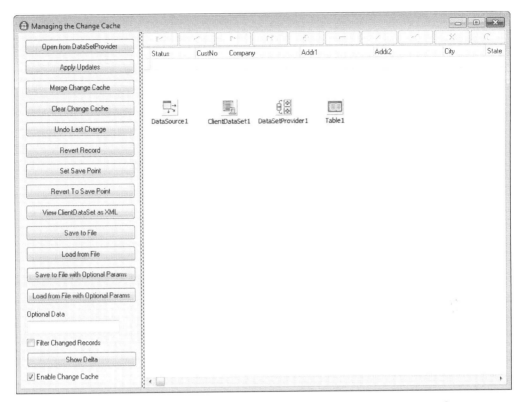

Figure 6-1: The ChangeCache project demonstrates all aspects of managing the change cache

The process of creating the custcopy.db table from customer.db is performed in the OnCreate event handler for the ChangeCache main form, as shown in the following code segment:

```
procedure TForm1.FormCreate(Sender: TObject);
var
  CustomerTable: TTable;
begin
  DataDir := ExtractFilePath(Application.ExeName);
  XMLFileName := DataDir + 'cdsdata.xml';
  if not Table1.Exists then
  begin
    CustomerTable := TTable.Create(Self);
    try
      CustomerTable.DatabaseName := 'DBDEMOS';
      CustomerTable.TableName := 'CUSTOMER.DB';
      Table1.Tablename := 'CustCopy.DB';
      Table1.BatchMove(CustomerTable, batCopy);
      Table1.AddIndex('','CustNo',[ixPrimary, ixUnique]);
      Table1.AddIndex('ByCompany','Company',[ixCaseInsensitive]);
      Table1.Open;
    finally
      CustomerTable.Free;
```

```
      end;
    end;
end;
```

If, during your use of the ChangeCache project, you feel that your data is getting messed up (for example, you have deleted every record and saved those changes to the database), simply delete all files with the custcopy file name from the Paradox database (for example, delete custcopy.*). The next time you run the application, it will re-create custcopy.db from the original customer.db table.

By default, this Paradox database is stored in c:\Program Files\Common Files\Codegear Shared\data. On a 64-bit Windows machine, substitute "program files" with "program files (x86)." If you are using a version of Delphi prior to Delphi 2007, substitute "Codegear Shared" with "Borland Shared."

Another point that you should be aware of while you use the ChangeCache project is that most of the buttons on the main form shown in Figure 6-1 are enabled only under the appropriate conditions. For example, it makes no sense for the Save to File button to be enabled if the ClientDataSet is not active.

This project contains a method, named UpdateButtonStatuses, that toggles the Enabled status of most of the buttons on the main form, based on the status of the ClientDataSet as well as the presence or absence of a previously saved XML file. Buttons that only apply when a change cache is available are disabled when ChangeCount is 0. Buttons that only apply if an XML file exists are disabled if the file is absent. Finally, buttons that only apply when the ClientDataSet is open are disabled when it is not active. UpdateButtonStatuses is shown in the following code segment:

```
procedure TForm1.UpdateButtonStatuses;
var
  Caching: Boolean;
  Loadable: Boolean;
  Active: Boolean;
begin
  //Determine the state of the application
  Caching := ClientDAtaSet1.ChangeCount > 0;
  Loadable := FileExists(XMLFileName);
  Active := ClientDataSet1.Active;
  //Enable or disable the buttons, as appropriate
  ApplyUpdatesButton.Enabled := Caching;
  MergeCacheButton.Enabled := Caching;
  ClearCacheButton.Enabled := Caching;
  UndoLastChangeButton.Enabled := Caching;
  RevertRecordButton.Enabled := Caching;
  SetSavePointButton.Enabled := Caching;
  RevertToSavePointButton.Enabled := Caching;
  ViewXMLButton.Enabled := Caching;
```

```
  SaveToFileButton.Enabled := Active;
  SaveWithParamsButton.Enabled := Active;
  LoadFromFileButton.Enabled := Loadable;
  LoadWithOptionalParams.Enabled := Loadable;
  ShowDeltaButton.Enabled := Caching;
  EnableDisableChangeCache.Enabled := Active;
end;
```

The UpdateButtonStatuses method is called from the DataSource's OnDataChange event handler shown in the following code segment. This event handler ensures that the buttons are updated each time there is a change to the data:

```
procedure TForm1.DataSource1DataChange(Sender: TObject; Field:
TField);
begin
  UpdateButtonStatuses;
end;
```

Change Cache Basics

This section covers change cache basics, including loading and saving the contents of the ClientDataSet. Some of this information was covered in detail in Chapters 2 and 3, but is included here, in a briefer form, for completeness.

Loading the Data

You can use the button labeled Open from DataSetProvider to load the ClientDataSet from DataSetProvider1, which points to Table1. Once the data is loaded, this button's label is changed to 'Close ClientDataSet.' After that, this same button can be used to close the ClientDataSet. The OnClick event handler for this button is shown in the following code segment:

```
procedure TForm1.OpenCloseButtonClick(Sender: TObject);
begin
  if not ClientDataSet1.Active then
  begin
    ClientDataSet1.Open;
    OpenCloseButton.Caption := 'Close ClientDataSet';
  end
  else
  begin
    ClientDataSet1.Close;
    OpenClosebutton.Caption := 'Open from DataSetProvider';
  end;
end;
```

Enabling and Disabling the Change Cache

Once the ClientDataSet has been opened, it begins with a change cache that is empty, but active. If you do not want to maintain the change cache, you disable it by setting the public LogChanges property to False. You enable the change cache once again by setting LogChanges to True.

The most common use for setting LogChanges to False is to permit the ClientDataSet to be loaded programmatically, without those new records being identified as inserts. For example, before reading an external file and parsing its data and inserting that data into a ClientDataSet one record at a time, you usually want to set LogChanges to False. Once the data has been loaded, you set LogChanges to True to enable the change cache. Now you can use the change cache to detect any changes made by a user to the data that was loaded.

The setting of LogChanges is demonstrated in the OnClick event handler for the checkbox that appears in the bottom left corner of the ChangeCache main form. The following is this event handler:

```
procedure TForm1.EnableDisableChangeCacheClick(Sender: TObject);
begin
  ClientDataSet1.LogChanges := EnableDisableChangeCache.Checked;
end;
```

Detecting Changes

If the change cache is empty, the ChangeCount property of the ClientDataSet is equal to 0. If there are any changes in the change cache, ChangeCount represents the number of changes.

An example of using ChangeCount can be found in the UpdateButtonStatuses event handler listed earlier in this chapter. In that example, ChangeCount is used to detect whether a change cache exists or not, and to manage the Enabled property of buttons whose operations require a change cache.

ChangeCount is also used in the OnClose event handler of the form, where the code checks to see if any changes that were made to the data might be lost (which is what would happen if changes have not been saved to a file, or applied to the underlying database, before closing). The following is the OnClose event handler for the form:

```
procedure TForm1.FormClose(Sender: TObject; var Action:
TCloseAction);
begin
  if ClientDataSet1.State in [dsEdit, dsInsert] then
    ClientDataSet1.Post;
```

```
  if ClientDataSet1.ChangeCount > 0 then
  begin
    if MessageDlg('There are changes. Do you want to save them?',
      mtConfirmation, [mbYes, mbNo], 0) = mrYes then
    begin
      //Use 0 so that an exception will be raised if
      //all changes cannot be applied.
      ClientDataSet1.ApplyUpdates(0);
    end;
  end;
end;
```

Note: In the ClientDataSet implementation in early versions of Delphi, ChangeCount is set to 0 when the ClientDataSet is loaded from a file even when that file includes a change cache. This is a bug. Later versions of ClientDataSet work properly, and ChangeCount will accurately reflect the number of changes in the change cache once a file has been loaded. If you need to use ChangeCount to determine the size of the change cache with a just-loaded file, you should test to ensure that it is working correctly with the version of ClientDataSet that you are using.

Saving to File

You can write the contents of a ClientDataSet to a file using SaveToFile. When you save to a file, you are saving metadata, the change cache, and the data. You can also optionally save additional data with the ClientDataSet. Saving optional data with a ClientDataSet is described a bit later in this section.

SaveToFile takes two optional parameters. Use the first parameter to define the file name to which the data will be written. If you omit this parameter, the value of the FileName property is used to define the file to which the data will be written.

You can use the second optional parameter to define which of two file formats to use when writing the data. Use dfBinary to use a proprietary file format, and dfXML to use XML. If you omit this parameter, Delphi will use the file format implied by the extension of the file being written. Delphi will use the XML format if the file extension is XML. Otherwise it will use the binary format.

The binary format is more concise than the XML format, often creating files that are about 50 percent smaller than the XML format. On the other hand, XML is a standard and those XML files can easily be consumed by any client that understands how to read and write XML files.

The use of SaveToFile is shown in the following OnClick event handler, which is associated with the button labeled Save to File:

```
procedure TForm1.SaveToFileButtonClick(Sender: TObject);
begin
  ClientDataSet1.SaveToFile(XMLFileName);
end;
```

Note: The ClientDataSet also supports SaveToStream. You use SaveToStream when you want to persist the ClientDataSet to an in-memory format, which can then be used to transfer the stream across a network or store the ClientDataSet in a BLOB field of a database table.

Loading from File

You load a ClientDataSet from a file by calling its LoadFromFile method. When loading from a file, the ClientDataSet gets its structure from the contents of the file, as well as the change cache and data that was previously saved. Note, however, that as mentioned in Chapter 4, *Defining a ClientDataSet's Structure,* if the ClientDataSet has persistent fields, you can only load an external file if the saved structure is consistent with the structure defined by the persistent fields.

LoadFromFile takes one optional parameter — the name of the file from which to load the data. If you omit this optional parameter, the ClientDataSet loads data from the file specified in the FileName property.

The use of LoadFromFile is shown in the following OnClick event handler, which is associated with the button labeled Load from File:

```
procedure TForm1.LoadFromFileButtonClick(Sender: TObject);
begin
  ClientDataSet1.LoadFromFile(XMLFileName);
  OpenCloseButton.Caption := 'Close ClientDataSet';
  UpdateButtonStatuses;
end;
```

Note: The ClientDataSet also supports the LoadFromStream method. This method loads a previously persistent ClientDataSet from a source that supports streams, such as loading a ClientDataSet from a network stream or a BLOB field in a database.

Saving and Loading with Optional Parameters

ClientDataSets permit you to attach virtually any data to the ClientDataSet's data packet. Once attached, this data is persisted with the data if the ClientDataSet is persisted through a call to SaveToFile or SaveToStream.

Likewise, that data is retrieved when the ClientDataSet is loaded through a call to LoadFromFile or LoadFromStream.

Any time that a ClientDataSet is active, you can attach additional data to the data packet by calling SetOptionalParam. The following is the signature of SetOptionalParam:

```
procedure TCustomClientDataSet.SetOptionalParam(const ParamName: string;
  const Value: OleVariant; IncludeInDelta: Boolean = False); virtual;
```

As you can see, there are two required parameters and a third optional parameter. The first parameter is a name for the optional parameter. You use this name to later retrieve the optional parameter from the data packet.

The second parameter is an OleVariant. As described earlier in this book, an OleVariant is a reference-counted variant that can hold almost any value. (An OleVariant can be a single variant, or a variant array, or an array of variant arrays.) The third parameter is a Boolean parameter that you can use to instruct the ClientDataSet to include the optional parameter in its Delta property. This can be useful if you are writing BeforeUpdateRecord event handlers and want to access the optional parameter from that event handler.

Once an optional parameter has been attached to a data packet, it can be read by calling GetOptionalParam. The following is the signature of GetOptionalParam:

```
function GetOptionalParam(const ParamName: string): OleVariant;
```

When calling GetOptionalParam, you pass a single string parameter with the name of the previously save optional parameter. GetOptionalParam returns an OleVariant, which you read to extract the saved data.

The use of SetOptionalParam and GetOptionalParam is normally done in conjunction with saving and loading a ClientDataSet to and from a file or stream. The optional data often includes information about the saved data, such as a timestamp that holds the date and time when the data was originally loaded into the ClientDataSet from a DataSetProvider, as is often done in briefcase applications. (Briefcase applications were described in some detail in Chapter 3, *Saving Data with ClientDataSets and DataSetProviders.*)

Saving an optional parameter is demonstrated in the OnClick event handler associated with the button labeled Save to File with Optional Params, shown in the following code segment:

```
procedure TForm1.SaveWithParamsButtonClick(Sender: TObject);
begin
  ClientDataSet1.SetOptionalParam('MyData', VarFromDateTime(now));
```

```
    ClientDataSet1.SaveToFile(XMLFileName)
end;
```

Loading previously saved data from an optional parameter can be found in the OnClick event handler associated with the button labeled Load from File with Optional Params, as shown here:

```
procedure TForm1.LoadWithOptionalParamsClick(Sender: TObject);
var
  Data: OleVariant;
begin
  ClientDataSet1.LoadFromFile(XMLFileName);
  OpenCloseButton.Caption := 'Close ClientDataSet';
  UpdateButtonStatuses;
  Data := ClientDataSet1.GetOptionalParam('MyData');
  if not VarIsClear(Data) then
    OptionalDataEdit.Text := DateTimeToStr(Data)
  else
    ShowMessage('No optional data found');
end;
```

A few comments about optional parameters are in order before we leave this topic. First, once you create an optional parameter for a data packet, there is no way to remove it. (Only by reloading the ClientDataSet from a DataSetProvider or a previously saved file or stream that does not contain the optional parameter will it disappear.) Sure, you can set its value to an empty string, but you cannot remove it. This doesn't normally create problems, however, since it is unlikely that you will create an optional parameter and then later want to remove it.

The second comment is that optional parameters are the only way to persist additional data with a ClientDataSet that is saved and loaded using SaveToFile, SaveToStream, LoadFromFile, and LoadFromStream. If, however, you are using DataSnap to communicate between a ClientDataSet and a DataSetProvider in a multi-tier environment, you can pass arbitrary data between the ClientDataSet and the DataSetProvider using one of a number of event handlers, including BeforeGetRecords and AfterGetRecords. These event handlers include an OleVariant parameter that you can use to pass the data. Passing data between a ClientDataSet and a DataSetProvider is described in Chapter 15, *Remote ClientDataSet-DataSetProvider Interaction.*

Viewing the Saved File

If you save the contents of a ClientDataSet to an XML file, you can easily view those saved contents using any XML file viewer, such as the one that is included with recent versions of Microsoft's Internet Explorer.

The ChangeCache application includes a button that makes it simple to view the contents of a persisted XML file. To use this feature, run the application and then click Load from DataSetProvider. Next, click the View ClientDataSet as XML button. You screen may look similar to the one shown in Figure 6-2.

Figure 6-2: The XML representation of the ClientDataSet, including metadata, data, and change cache

The OnClick event handler for the button labeled View ClientDataSet as XML is shown in the following code segment. In this code segment, the value of the XMLData property is saved to a file using a StringList. That file is then opened using the default XML viewer, which in this case was Internet Explorer. Note that the file created using this technique is identical to that created by calling SaveToFile when the file format is dfXML.

```
procedure TForm1.ViewXMLButtonClick(Sender: TObject);
var
  sl: TStringList;
begin
  sl := TStringlist.Create;
  try
    sl.Text := ClientDataSet1.XMLData;
    sl.SaveToFile(Datadir + 'data.xml');
    ShellExecute(Application.Handle, 'open',
```

```
        PChar(DataDir + 'data.xml'), nil, nil, SW_SHOW);
  finally
    sl.Free;
  end;
end;
```

The image shown in Figure 6-2 shows what your screen might look like if you perform these steps. In this case, there are some changes in the change cache, including one edit, one deletion, and one insertion.

If you create one or more optional parameters, those values will appear in the XML file as well. For example, if you click the button labeled Save to File with Optional Params (which creates the optional parameter for the ClientDataSet), and then click the button labeled View ClientDataSet as XML, your screen might look something like that shown in Figure 6-3.

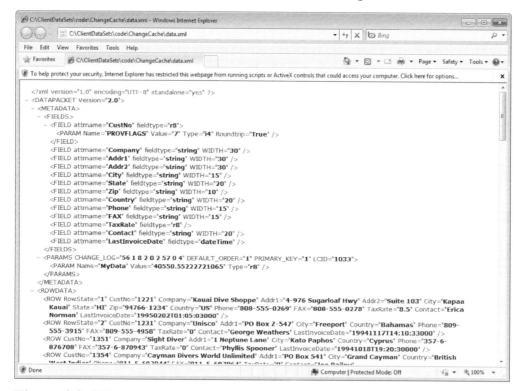

Figure 6-3: When one or more optional parameters have been created, they are also part of the XML that the ClientDataSet creates

Apply Updates with Loaded Data

If there are changes in the change cache, you can apply those changes to an underlying database through a DataSetProvider by calling ApplyUpdates.

ApplyUpdates was described in detail in Chapter 3, *Saving Data with ClientDataSets and DataSetProviders.* The use of ApplyUpdates is demonstrated in the OnClick event handler of the button labeled Apply Updates. This event handler is shown in the following code segment:

```
procedure TForm1.ApplyUpdatesButtonClick(Sender: TObject);
begin
  ClientDataSet1.ApplyUpdates(-1);
end;
```

It is important to note that updates can be applied at any time when a change cache exists, whether that change cache was the result of recent edits to the ClientDataSet or was loaded from a previously persisted ClientDataSet. For example, if you run the ChangeCache application, click Load from DataSetProvider, make some changes and then save those changes by clicking Save to File, you can close the application, run it again, load those changes from the persisted file by clicking Load from File, and then attempt to apply the changes by clicking Apply Updates. (I specifically said "attempt to apply the changes" since in the real world, the attempt to apply the changes may fail depending on what has happened to the original data from which the ClientDataSet was loaded.)

Closing Without Applying Updates

If you open the ClientDataSet through the DataSetProvider, and then make changes to the ClientDataSet, what happens if you close the ClientDataSet without calling ApplyUpdates? The simple answer is that the change cache is lost.

If you had taken the time to click the Save to File button or the Save to File using Optional Params button, you could load that data, which would restored the change cache, after which you could then apply the updates. However, if you close a ClientDataSet that has changes and do not call ApplyUpdates, the data in the change cache is never resolved to the underlying database.

The OnClose event handler of the main form, shown earlier but repeated here for convenience, demonstrates how you might handle a situation where the user has made changes to the ClientDataSet, but has not yet saved that data before closing the ClientDataSet (or by closing the form on which it appears).

In this event handler, we first check to see if the current record was being edited. If so, we post that change. Next, we test ChangeCount. If ChangeCount is greater than 0, there is at least one change that will be lost if the ClientDataSet is closed (unless the user has done something to persist that data, but let's ignore that possibility for now). When changes are detected, the user is

asked whether or not they want to save those changes, and those changes are
saved if they click Yes.

```
procedure TForm1.FormClose(Sender: TObject; var Action:
TCloseAction);
begin
  if ClientDataSet1.State in [dsEdit, dsInsert] then
    ClientDataSet1.Post;
  if ClientDataSet1.ChangeCount > 0 then
  begin
    if MessageDlg('There are changes. Do you want to save them?',
      mtConfirmation, [mbYes, mbNo], 0) = mrYes then
    begin
      //Use 0 so that an exception will be raised if
      //all changes cannot be applied.
      ClientDataSet1.ApplyUpdates(0);
    end;
  end;
end;
```

Controlling the Change Cache

The first sections in this chapter deal with loading and saving data, detecting
changes in the cache, persisting the cache, and applying updates. The remainder
of this chapter is concerned primarily with modifying the change cache, as well
as detecting what types of changes are contained in the change cache.

Merging the Change Cache

You learned earlier in this chapter that if you close a ClientDataSet without
either saving its data (and change cache) to a file or calling ApplyUpdates to
apply all changes in the change cache to an underlying database, the change
cache is lost. There are several additional ways in which the change cache can
be eliminated, and each of these has its purpose.

One way to remove the change cache is to merge it. Merging the change
cache has the effect of making all changes in the change cache permanent with
respect to the data held in the ClientDataSet. Once the changes have been
merged, the change cache is empty (though it will still be active if the
LogChanges property of the ClientDataSet is still set to True).

When you load your data into a ClientDataSet from a DataSetProvider,
merging the change cache is a relatively rare operation that you save for special
purposes. Instead, it is normally reserved for those situations where a
ClientDataSet is being used as a stand-alone database, and only after there is no
longer a need to maintain the change cache.

For example, you might load a ClientDataSet from a file and permit a user to make changes. While the user is working with the data, you will likely keep the change cache active (LogChanges equal to True), in order to permit the user to examine their changes, and even undo individual changes.

However, when the user is ready to save the data back to disk, your code can explicitly call MergeChangeLog to make the changes in the change cache permanent, prior to saving the ClientDataSet to a file. By doing this, you reduce the size of the saved file, and start each new session (re-loading the ClientDataSet with the previously saved file) with an empty change cache. This approach means that a user can examine, and even undo changes during their active session, but cannot examine or undo changes made in any previous sessions.

The use of MergeChangeLog is demonstrated by the OnClick event handler shown in the following code. This event handler is associated with the button labeled Merge Change Cache. If you load the ClientDataSet from a DataSetProvider and make one or more changes, or load the ClientDataSet from a file that contains previously saved changes, this button will be active. Clicking this button removes the change cache (making the data permanent), after which buttons that are active only when there is a change cache become disabled. This includes the ApplyUpdates button, since there are no longer updates to apply.

```
procedure TForm1.MergeCacheButtonClick(Sender: TObject);
begin
  ClientDataSet1.MergeChangeLog;
end;
```

Canceling the Change Cache

While calling MergeChangeLog erases the change cache, it leaves any changes that had been made in the ClientDataSet's data packet (albeit with no way to determine what changes had been made to the data). Another option is the cancel the change cache by calling CancelUpdates.

Canceling the change cache produces two side effects. The first is that following the call to CancelUpdates, like with MergeChangeLog, the change cache is empty (though, again, it will still be active if LogChanges is True). The other side effect is that the ClientDataSet's data is restored to its original state. Specifically, each and every change that appeared in the change cache is removed from the ClientDataSet. This will either result in an empty ClientDataSet (if that's the way the ClientDataSet started out), or will restore the ClientDataSet to the state at which the change cache began collecting information about changes.

For example, if you create a ClientDataSet dynamically, permit the user to enter some data, and then call CancelUpdates, the change cache will be cleared, and the ClientDataSet will return to its empty state. By comparison, if you load a ClientDataSet from a DataSetProvider, permit the user to make changes, and then call CancelUpdates, the ClientDataSet will return to the same state in which it appeared immediately following the completion of the data loading.

The following code segment demonstrates the use of CancelUpdates. This code can be found on the OnClick event handler for the button labeled Clear Change Cache:

```
procedure TForm1.ClearCacheButtonClick(Sender: TObject);
begin
   ClientDataSet1.CancelUpdates;
end;
```

Removing Single Changes from the Cache

It is possible to remove some, but not all, changes from the change cache. You can remove the last change applied to the ClientDataSet, or you can remove an arbitrary change. Let's begin by looking at removing the last change.

You remove the last change from the ClientDataSet by calling UndoLastChange. So long as there is more than one change in the change cache, you can call UndoLastChange repeatedly to systematically undo each change, in reverse order.

Using UndoLastChange is demonstrated in the following code, which appears on the OnClick event handler of the button labeled Undo Last Change:

```
procedure TForm1.UndoLastChangeButtonClick(Sender: TObject);
begin
   ClientDataSet1.UndoLastChange(False);
end;
```

While UndoLastChange performs a LIFO (last in, first out) operation on the change cache, you can use RevertRecord to restore a given record to its previous status, removing that change from the change cache. Unlike UndoLastChange, RevertRecord applies to the current record in the ClientDataSet.

For example, if the current record in the ClientDataSet is one that you inserted (while the change cache was active), you can use RevertRecord to remove that record. This has the effect of removing that inserted record from the ClientDataSet's data, as well as the information in the change cache that could have been used to persist that insertion into an underlying database.

Similarly, you can use RevertRecord to restore a deleted record, which has the effect of placing that record back into the ClientDataSet's data and removing the deletion information from the change cache. "But wait," you might say, "How can a deleted record be the current record?" Good question. In order to use RevertRecord on a deleted record, your ClientDataSet must be displaying deleted records. This is done using StatusFilter, which is discussed a little later in this chapter.

In many cases, you will not want to call RevertRecord on a record that has not been changed, inserted, or deleted. To do this, you must be able to detect the status of the current record in the ClientDataSet. This is done using UpdateStatus.

Determining Single Record Cache Status

You use the UpdateStatus method of the ClientDataSet (which it inherits from DataSet) to determine the status of the ClientDataSet's current record. The following is the definition of the UpdateStatus method:

```
function UpdateStatus: TUpdateStatus; virtual;
```

UpdateStatus returns a TUpdateStatus value, whose declaration is shown here:

```
TUpdateStatus = (usUnmodified, usModified, usInserted, usDeleted);
```

The use of UpdateStatus is demonstrated in two event handlers in the ChangeCache project. The first is from the OnCalcFields event handler for the ClientDataSet. This event handler assigns a value to the virtual calculated field named ClientDataSet1Status, as shown in the following code segment:

```
procedure TForm1.ClientDataSet1CalcFields(DataSet: TDataSet);
begin
  case ClientDataSet1.UpdateStatus of
    usModified: ClientDataSet1Status.Value := 'Modified';
    usDeleted: ClientDataSet1Status.Value := 'Deleted';
    usInserted: ClientDataSet1Status.Value := 'Inserted';
    usUnModified: ClientDataSet1Status.Value := 'Unmodified';
  end;
end;
```

You can see this event handler in action by running the ChangeCache project, and then making a few updates and a few insertions. The Status field for updated records will display the text "Modified," the inserted records will display "Inserted," and the rest will display "Unmodified." This effect can be seen in Figure 6-4. Notice that several of the top-most records in Figure 6-4 contain the words "Modified" or "Inserted" in the Status field. No records in this figure show Deleted in this column, since the normal behavior of a ClientDataSet is to suppress the display of deleted records.

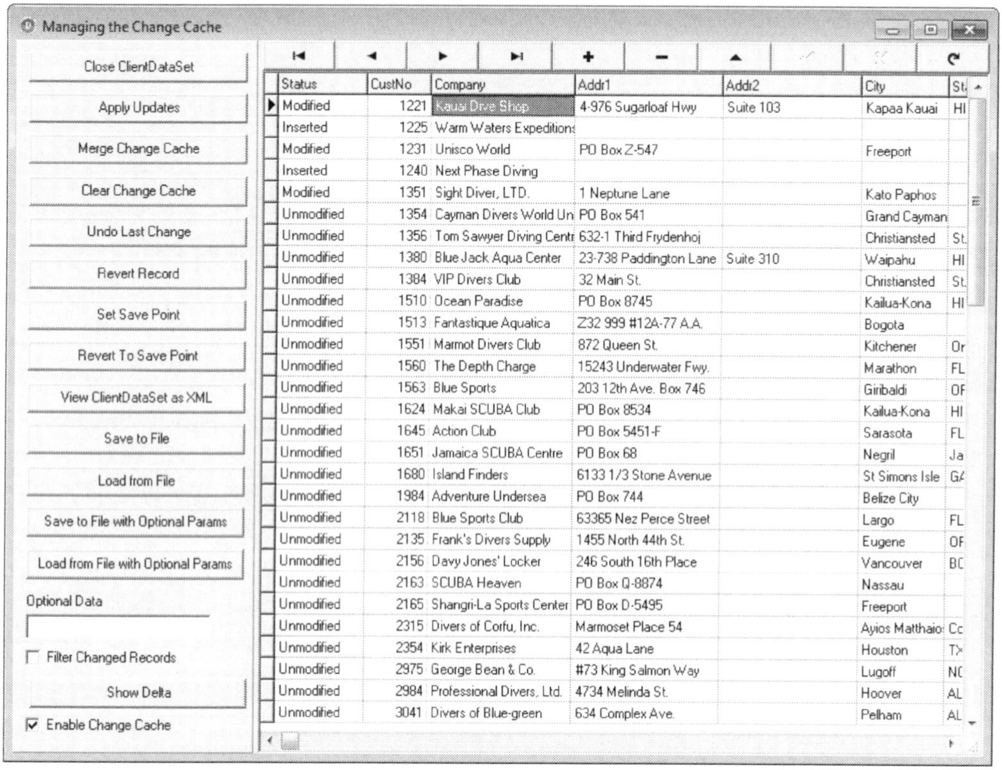

Figure 6-4: Modified and inserted records are identified using the calculated virtual field named Status

The use of UpdateStatus is also demonstrated in the OnClick event handler for the button labeled Revert Record. This event handler, shown here, uses UpdateStatus to determine if the current record is in the change cache. If so, it reverts the record to its original state. Otherwise, it displays a message indicating that the current record has not been changed.

```
procedure TForm1.RevertRecordButtonClick(Sender: TObject);
begin
  if ClientDataSet1.UpdateStatus <> usUnModified then
    ClientDataSet1.RevertRecord
  else
    ShowMessage('The current record is not in the change cache');
end;
```

Using SavePoint

A save point is an integer value that refers to a position in the change cache. You use a save point to record a position in the change cache to which you may want to return by reading the value of the SavePoint property of the ClientDataSet. If later, after making additional changes to the change cache, you set the SavePoint property to the integer that you previously read, those additional changes are removed from the change cache and the associated records are restored to their previous state. For example, inserted records are removed, and deleted records are restored.

Capturing a save point is demonstrated in the following code, which is associated with the button labeled Set Save Point. As you can see from this code, the SavePoint property of the ClientDataSet is assigned to SavedSavePoint, which is a member field of the main form class:

```
procedure TForm1.SetSavePointButtonClick(Sender: TObject);
begin
  SavedSavePoint := ClientDataSet1.SavePoint;
end;
```

Restoring a save point is demonstrated in this code, which is associated with the OnClick event handler for the button labeled Revert to Save Point:

```
procedure TForm1.RevertToSavePointButtonClick(Sender: TObject);
begin
  if SavedSavePoint = -1 then
    ShowMessage('No save point to revert to')
  else
    try
      ClientDataSet1.SavePoint := SavedSavePoint;
    finally
      SavedSavePoint := -1;
    end;
end;
```

The use of a save point may sound like a type of transaction, but it is not. Reverting to a save point usually only works properly when the change cache is in a state in which reverting to the save point makes sense. For example, if you make some changes, capture a save point, make some more changes, and then revert a record that was modified prior to saving the save point, you may not be able to restore to the save point.

Note: It is my experience that you should not try to capture a save point, persist the data to a file, later restoring that file, and attempt to revert to that previous save point. My testing suggests that this simply does not work. If you think you want to use this technique, you should test your code thoroughly before employing it.

Using Status Filters

Earlier in this chapter I noted that you can call RevertRecord to restore the current record to its previous state, including reverting a deleted record. RevertRecord, however, only applies to the current record. How do you make a deleted record the current record? The answer is by using the StatusFilter property of the ClientDataSet.

StatusFilter is a set property, and you can assign to it a set of zero or more of the TUpdateStatus flags. These flags were shown earlier in this chapter, but are repeated here for convenience:

```
TUpdateStatus = (usUnmodified, usModified, usInserted, usDeleted);
```

For example, if you want to view only those records which were inserted, you can use something similar to the following statement:

```
ClientDataSet1.StatusFilter := [usInserted];
```

Following this call, the ClientDataSet will appear to contain only those records that were inserted since the change cache became active. By comparison, if you wanted to view only those records that were deleted, you could use the following statement:

```
ClientDataSet1.StatusFilter := [usDeleted];
```

The use of StatusFilter is demonstrated by the OnClick event handler of the checkbox labeled Filter Changed Records, as shown in the following event handler:

```
procedure TForm1.FilterChangedRecordsClick(Sender: TObject);
begin
if FilterChangedRecords.Checked then
  ClientDataSet1.StatusFilter := [usDeleted, usInserted, usModified]
else
  ClientDataSet1.StatusFilter := [];
end;
```

When the checkbox is checked, the ClientDataSet displays those records that were inserted, modified, and deleted, as shown in Figure 6-5. When StatusFilter includes the usDeleted flag, all deleted records in the change cache are visible in the ClientDataSet. You can then make any of those deleted records the current record, after which calling RevertRecord will restore that record. (Note that calling CancelChanges will restore all changes, including all deleted records.)

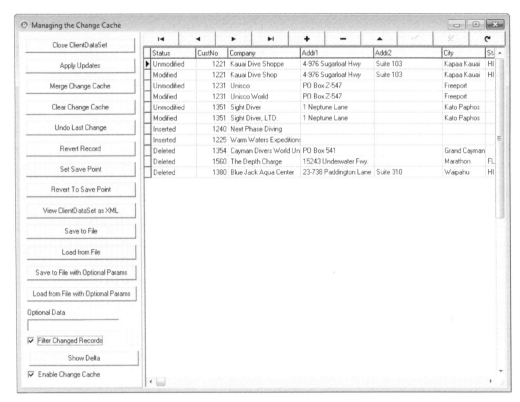

Figure 6-5: Using StatusFilter, you control which records are displayed in the ClientDataSet

It's interesting to note that you restore the original behavior of a ClientDataSet, in which it displays those records that have been updated, inserted, and not changed, by setting StatusFilter to an empty set. When StatusFilter is an empty set, it is as though you set StatusFilter to include the usInserted, usModified, and usUnmodified flags.

StatusFilter Versus Delta

As you learned in Chapter 3, it is possible to assign the Delta property of a ClientDataSet to the Data property of a second ClientDataSet, after which you can display that second ClientDataSet in data-aware controls. What you are seeing as you view the records in that second ClientDataSet is the content of the first ClientDataSet's change cache. If that is the case, do we really need StatusFilter?

The answer is Yes. StatusFilter and the Delta properties are not the same. First, StatusFilter permits you to specifically limit the ClientDataSet to a single type of change, while Delta represents all changes — the change cache, specifically.

Another benefit of StatusFilter over examining Delta directly is that StatusFilter retains all characteristics of the ClientDataSet that owns the change cache. For example, in the Change Cache project the ClientDataSet includes a persistent calculated field. That field would not belong to a ClientDataSet to which you assigned the cache.

Finally, when you load a second ClientDataSet with a ClientDataSet's Delta, the second ClientDataSet does not have a change cache. In other words, the second ClientDataSet has Data but no Delta. As a result, you cannot use the second ClientDataSet to determine which records were inserted and which were deleted. That is something that comes from a ClientDataSet that has a Delta property, which the second ClientDataSet does not.

Granted, these are subtle distinctions, but I wanted to make them here. If you want to compare StatusFilter and Delta, examine what happens when you click the checkbox labeled Filter Changed Records versus what happens when you click the button labeled Show Delta in the ChangeCache project. There's a big difference.

In the next chapter, you will learn how to navigate the contents of a ClientDataSet.

Chapter 7
Navigating ClientDataSets

Delphi's ClientDataSet is a DataSet, in that it implements the DataSet interface. As a result, if you are already familiar with navigating DataSets, such as the BDE Table class, you can skim through this chapter rather quickly. You can probably skip those topics that you are already familiar with. Still, you might pick up a trick or two, such as using the RecNo property to move between records (it's a read/write property).

If, on the other hand, you are coming to ClientDataSets from a SQL, set-based background, or generally have little experience with DataSet navigation, you will want to read this chapter thoroughly. ClientDataSets embrace the navigational model, and you want to be comfortable with moving around a ClientDataSet if you are going to get the most out of this powerful class. And, as an added benefit, many of these techniques are appropriate for any other DataSet that supports navigation, such as SQLDataSets, ADOTables, and IBTables, to name a few.

While this chapter focuses primarily on the use of code to navigate data in a ClientDataSet, a natural place to begin this discussion is with Delphi's data-aware controls and the navigation and editing features they provide.

Navigating with Data-aware Controls

Delphi provides two types of controls that provide data navigation. The first type is a navigation-specific control, and Delphi provides you with one control in this category, the DBNavigator. The second type includes controls that permit navigation as well as data display and editing. We'll begin this section with the first type.

The DBNavigator

The DBNavigator, shown here, provides a video recorder-like interface for navigating data and managing records. Record navigation is provided by the first four buttons, which correspond to First, Prior, Next, and Last. The last six buttons provide record management, and correspond to Insert, Delete, Edit, Post, Cancel, and Refresh.

As you can see in this illustration, some of the buttons are not enabled. This DBNavigator is associated with an active DataSet, and the enabled properties of the buttons are context sensitive. For example, you can tell by this image that the current record is the first record in the DataSet, since the First and Prior buttons are not enabled. Furthermore, the DataSet is in the Browse state, since the Edit button is active, and the Cancel and Post buttons are not.

You can control which buttons are displayed by a DBNavigator through its VisibleButtons property. For example, if you are using the DBNavigator in conjunction with a ClientDataSet that reads and writes its data from a local file, you will want to suppress the display of the Refresh button, since attempting to refresh a ClientDataSet that uses local files raises an exception.

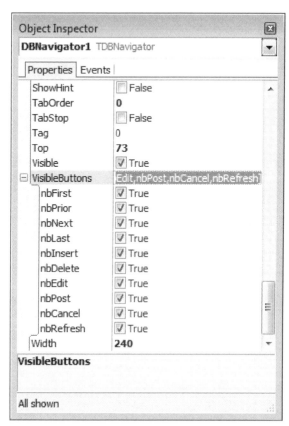

Figure 7-1: Use the Object Inspector at design time to control which buttons are visible in the DBNavigator

You control which buttons of the DBNavigator are visible at design time through the VisibleButtons subproperties editor of the Object Inspector. Figure 7-1 shows this property editor expanded, permitting you to toggle which buttons you want to be available.

Another DBNavigator property whose default value you may want to change is ShowHint. The glyphs used for the various buttons of the DBNavigator are not necessarily obvious to all (take the Edit button, for example). To improve this situation, setting ShowHint to True supplements the glyphs with popup help hints, as shown in the following illustration:

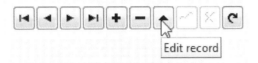

You don't even have to accept the default hints offered by the DBNavigator. Using the Hints property editor, which is a StringList editor, you can supply whatever text you want for each of the buttons in your DBNavigator. To do this, you change the text associated with the corresponding button in the DBNavigator based on the position of the button in the DBNavigator. The StringList editor, with alternative DBNavigator button hints, is shown in Figure 7-2.

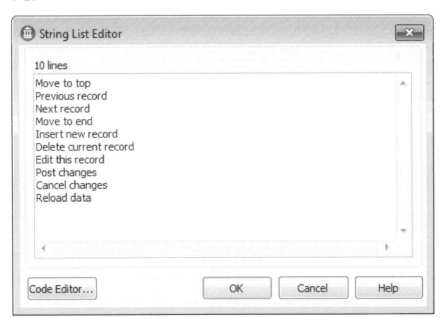

Figure 7-2: Use the Hints property editor, in conjunction with the ShowHint property, to provide custom hints for a DBNavigator

Before leaving this topic, I want to mention an often overlooked gem in Delphi. The Fields Editor, discussed in Chapter 4, includes a small navigator control that you can use to navigate an active DataSet at design time.

This can be seen in Figure 7-3, where a form that includes a DBNavigator and a DBGrid are associated with an active Table. Notice that the small navigator at the top of the Fields Editor and the DBNavigator are both indicating that the DataSet is on the last record, which is confirmed by the small arrow indicator in the DBGrid. Before this figure was captured, the Fields Editor navigator had just been used to move to the last record in the DataSet.

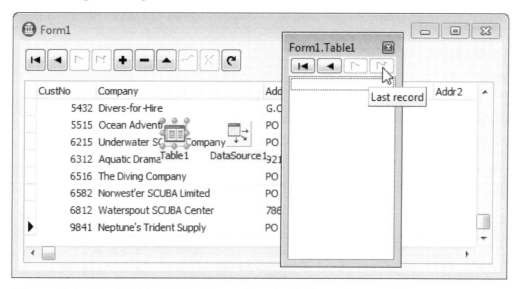

Figure 7-3: The Fields Editor has a handy little navigator that you can use to navigate records of an active DataSet at design time

Displaying Controls that Allow Navigation

The second category of controls that provides navigation is the multi-record controls. Delphi includes two of these controls: DBGrid and DBCtrlGrid. (Other controls are available from third-party vendors, such as Raize Software, TMS Software, and Woll2Woll Software, to name a few.)

Using DBGrids

A DBGrid displays data in a row/column format, as shown in Figure 7-4. By default, all fields of the ClientDataSet are displayed in the DBGrid.

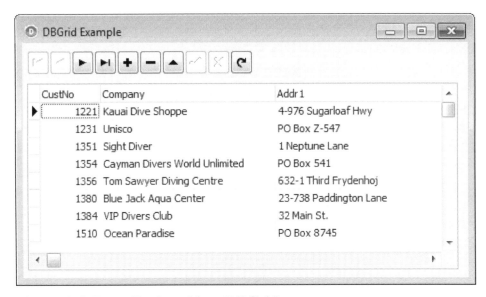

Figure 7-4: Data displayed in a DBGrid

You can control which fields are displayed, as well as specific column characteristics, such as color and typeface, by editing the DBGrid's Columns property using the Columns property editor. To display the Columns property editor, either double-click the DBGrid, right-click the DBGrid and select Columns Editor, or click the ellipsis that appears when the Columns property of a DBGrid is selected in the Object Inspector.

In the following illustration, the Add All Fields button of the Columns property editor has been clicked. These columns can then be selectively deleted, or their properties adjusted by selecting a specific Column in the Columns property editor and then using the Object Inspector to change its properties:

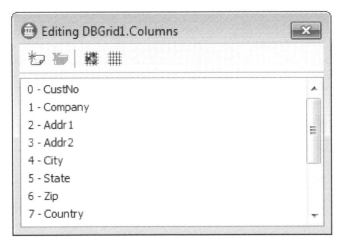

Using DBCtrlGrids

A DBCtrlGrid, by comparison, is a limited, multi-record container. It is limited in that it can only hold certain Delphi components, such as Labels, DBEdits, DBLabels, DBMemos, DBImages, DBComboBoxes, DBCheckBoxes, DBLookupComboBoxes, and DBCharts. The DBCtrlGrid is useful when you want to create a specialized interface, such as the one shown in Figure 7-5. In this example, data from the Paradox country.db table is displayed in a 3 by 3 grid.

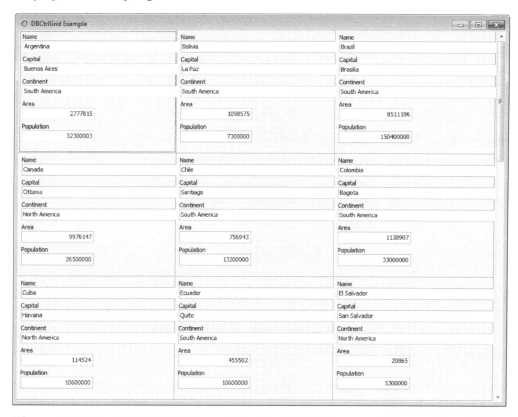

Figure 7-5: The DBCtrlGrid provides flexibility in a multi-record control

Depending on which multi-record control you are using, you can navigate among records using UpArrow, DownArrow, Tab, Ctrl-End, Ctrl-Home, PgDn, PgUp, among others. These keypresses may produce the same effect as clicking the Next, Prior, Last, First, and so on, buttons in a DBNavigator. It is also possible to navigate the records of a ClientDataSet using the vertical scrollbar of these controls.

How you edit a record using these controls also depends on which type of control you are using as well as their properties. Using the default properties of these controls, you can typically press F2 or click twice on a field in one of these controls to begin editing.

Posting a record occurs when you navigate off an edited record. Inserting and deleting records, depending on the control's property settings, can also be achieved using Ins and Ctrl-Del, respectively. Other operations, such as Refresh, are not directly supported. Consequently, in most cases, multi-record controls are combined with a DBNavigator to provide a complete set of record management options.

Detecting Changes to Record State

Changes that occur when a user navigates or manages a record using a data-aware control is something that you may want to control programmatically. For those situations, there are a variety of event handlers that you can use to evaluate what a user is doing, and provide a customized response.

ClientDataSets, as well as all other DataSets, posses the following event handlers: AfterCancel, AfterClose, AfterDelete, AfterEdit, AfterInsert, AfterOpen, AfterPost, AfterRefresh, AfterScroll, BeforeCancel, BeforeClose, BeforeDelete, BeforeEdit, BeforeInsert, BeforeOpen, BeforePost, BeforeRefresh, BeforeScroll, OnCalcFields, OnDeleteError, OnEditError, OnFilterRecord, OnNewRecord, and OnPostError.

There are additional event handlers that are available in most situations where a ClientDataSet is being navigated and edited, and which are always available when data-aware controls are used. These are the event handlers associated with a DataSource. Since all data-aware controls must be connected to at least one DataSource, the event handlers of a DataSource provide you with another source of customization when a user navigates and edits records. These event handlers are: OnDataChange, OnStateChange, and OnUpdateData.

Note: The code project CDSNavigation is available from the code download. See Appendix A.

Several examples of these event handlers are demonstrated in the CDSNavigation project, which is used for the remainder of this chapter. For example, the Open and Close menu items, which appear under the File menu, are enabled and disabled from the ClientDataSet's AfterOpen and AfterClose event handlers, as shown in the following code segments:

```
procedure TForm1.ClientDataSet1AfterClose(DataSet: TDataSet);
begin
```

```
  Open1.Enabled := True;
  Close1.Enabled := False;
end;

procedure TForm1.ClientDataSet1AfterOpen(DataSet: TDataSet);
begin
  Open1.Enabled := False;
  Close1.Enabled := True;
end;
```

Of somewhat greater interest are the event handlers associated with the DataSource in this project. For example, the OnDataChange event handler is used to display which record in the ClientDataSet is the current record in the first panel of the StatusBar, which appears at the bottom of the main form, as shown in Figure 7-6.

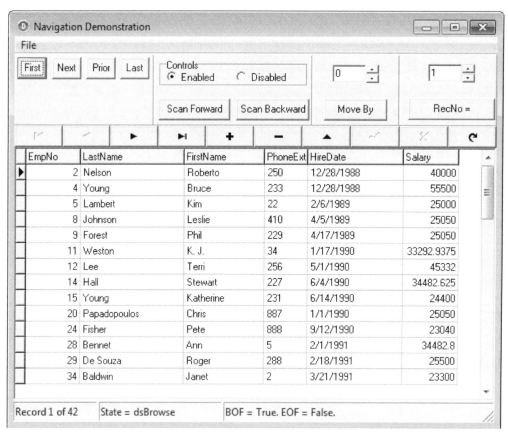

Figure 7-6: The StatusBar on the main form of the CDSNavigation project is updated by OnDataChange and OnStateChange event handlers

This event handler not only displays the current record number, and how many records are in the ClientDataSet, but also indicate in the third panel of the

StatusBar whether an attempt was made to navigate above the first record (Bof) or below the last record (Eof). Bof and Eof are described in a bit more detail a little later in this chapter.

The following is the OnDataChange event handler for the DataSource in this project:

```
procedure TForm1.DataSource1DataChange(Sender: TObject; Field:
TField);
begin
  StatusBar1.Panels[0].Text := 'Record ' +
    IntToStr(ClientDataSet1.RecNo) + ' of ' +
    IntToStr(ClientDataSet1.RecordCount);
  StatusBar1.Panels[2].Text :=
    'BOF = ' + BoolToStr(ClientDataSet1.Bof, True) + '. ' +
    'EOF = ' + BoolToStr(ClientDataSet1.Eof, True) + '. ';
end;
```

The OnStateChange event handler also updates the StatusBar shown in Figure 7-6. In this event handler, RTTI (runtime type information) is used to display the text version of the ClientDataSet's State property, which is of type TDataSetState. Here is the definition of TDataSetState:

```
TDataSetState = (dsInactive, dsBrowse, dsEdit, dsInsert,
  dsSetKey, dsCalcFields, dsFilter, dsNewValue, dsOldValue,
  dsCurValue, dsBlockRead, dsInternalCalc, dsOpening);
```

In Figure 7-6, the ClientDataSet is in the Browse state, as seen in the second panel of the StatusBar. The following is the OnStateChange event handler used by the DataSource:

```
procedure TForm1.DataSource1StateChange(Sender: TObject);
begin
  StatusBar1.Panels[1].Text :=
    'State = ' + GetEnumName(TypeInfo(TDataSetState),
    Ord(ClientDataSet1.State));
end;
```

OnDataChange triggers whenever a ClientDataSet arrives at a new record, when a new value is posted to a field, when an edit is canceled, as well as when a ClientDataSet arrives at the first record when it is initially opened. OnStateChange triggers when a ClientDataSet changes state, such as when it changes from dsBrowse to dsEdit (when a user enters the edit mode), or when it changes from dsEdit to dsBrowse (following the posting or cancellation of a change). Finally, OnUpdateData triggers when the dataset to which the DataSource points is posting its data.

Navigating Programmatically

Whether data-aware controls are involved or not, it is sometimes necessary to use code to navigate a ClientDataSet (for example, to move to a record that you want to change programmatically). For a ClientDataSet, these core navigation methods include First, Next, Prior, Last, MoveBy, and RecNo. Each of these is described in the following sections.

Basic Navigation

The DataSet interface provides for basic navigation through four methods: First, Next, Prior, and Last. These methods are pretty much self-explanatory. Each one produces an effect similar to the corresponding button on a DBNavigator.

There is another type of navigation that is similar to First, Next, and so forth. That navigation, however, is associated with a filter, and is referred to as *filtered navigation.* Filtered navigation is discussed in detail in Chapter 9, *Filtering ClientDataSets.*

Have I Gone Too Far? Bof and Eof

You can determine whether an attempt to navigate has tried to move outside of the range of records in the ClientDataSet by reading the Bof (beginning-of-file)and Eof (end-of-file) properties. Eof will return True if a navigation method attempted to move beyond the end of the table. When Eof returns True, the current record is the last record in the ClientDataSet.

Similarly, Bof will return True if a navigation attempt tried to move before the beginning of the dataset. In that situation, the current record is the first record in the ClientDataSet.

Bof and Eof were used in the OnDataChange event handler shown earlier in this chapter, to indicate in the StatusBar whether the last navigation attempt tried to move before, or beyond the records of the ClientDataSet, respectively. Figure 7-7 shows how the main form of the CDSNavigation project looks when you have used MoveBy to attempt to move beyond the end of the ClientDataSet.

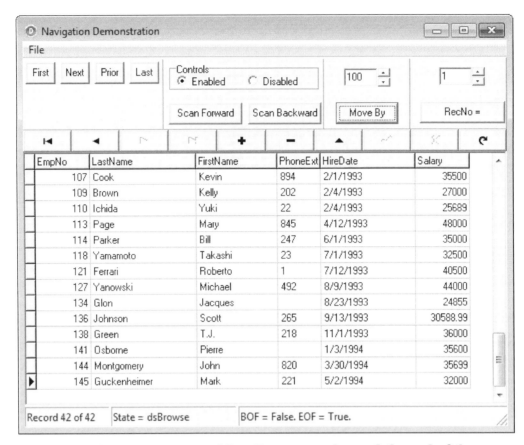

Figure 7-7: An attempt to use MoveBy to move beyond the end of the ClientDataSet has set Eof to True

Using MoveBy

MoveBy permits you to move forward and backward in a ClientDataSet, relative to the current record. For example, the following statement moves the current cursor 5 records forward in the ClientDataSet (if possible):

```
ClientDataSet1.MoveBy(5);
```

To move backwards in a ClientDataSet, pass MoveBy a negative number. For example, the following statement will move the cursor to the record that is 100 records prior to the current records (again, if possible):

```
ClientDataSet1.MoveBy(-100);
```

MoveBy is demonstrated by the OnClick event handler associated with the button labeled MoveBy in the CDSNavigation project. This event handler is shown in the following code segment:

```
procedure TForm1.MoveByBtnClick(Sender: TObject);
begin
  ClientDataSet1.MoveBy(UpDown1.Position);
end;
```

Navigating Using RecNo

The use of RecNo to navigate might come as a surprise. In a ClientDataSet, this property can be used for two purposes. You can read this property to learn the position of the current record in the current record order (based on the index currently in use, or the natural order of the records if no index is selected).

You also can write to this property. Doing so moves the cursor to the record in the position defined by the value you assign to this property. For example, the following statement will move the cursor to the record in the 5th position of the current index order (if possible):

```
ClientDataSet1.RecNo := 5;
```

The description of the preceding example was qualified by the statement that the operation will succeed if possible. This qualification has two aspects to it. First, the cursor movement will not take place if the current record has been edited, but cannot be posted. For example, if a record has been edited but not yet posted, and the data cannot pass at least one of the ClientDataSet's constraints, attempting to navigate off that record will raise an exception, and the navigation will not occur.

The second situation where the record navigation might not be possible is related to the number of records in the dataset. Attempting to set RecNo to a record beyond the end of the table, or prior to the beginning of the table, raises an exception.

The use of RecNo is demonstrated in the following event handler, which is associated with the button labeled RecNo =:

```
procedure TForm1.RecNoBtnClick(Sender: TObject);
begin
  ClientDataSet1.RecNo := UpDown2.Position;
end;
```

Scanning a ClientDataSet

Combining several of the methods and properties described so far provides you with a mechanism for scanning a ClientDataSet. Scanning begins by moving either to the first record or the last record of the ClientDataSet, and then systematically moving to each of the remaining records in the

ClientDataSet, one record at a time. The following pseudo code demonstrates how to scan a ClientDataSet:

```
procedure TForm1.Button1Click(Sender: TObject);
begin
  if not ClientDataSet1.Active then
    ClientDataSet1.Open;
  ClientDataSet1.First;
  while not ClientDataSet1.Eof do
  begin
    //perform some operation based on one or
    //more fields of the ClientDataSet
    ClientDataSet1.Next;
  end;
end;
```

Disabling Controls While Navigating

If the ClientDataSet that you are navigating programmatically is attached to data-aware controls through a DataSource, and you take no other precautions, the data-aware controls will be affected by the navigation. In the simplest case, where you move directly to another record, the update is welcome, causing the controls to repaint with the data of the new record. However, when your navigation involves moving to two or more records in rapid succession, such as is the case when you scan a ClientDataSet, the updates can have severe results.

We talked about this effect in Chapter 2, *Loading Data with ClientDataSets and DataSetProviders,* but let's take a little deeper look into repainting while navigating.

There are two major problems associated with rapid navigation with enabled data-aware controls. First, the flicker caused by the repainting of the data-aware controls as the ClientDataSet arrives at each record is distracting. More importantly, however, is the overhead associated with the repaint itself.

Repainting visual controls is one of the slowest processes in most GUI (graphic user interface) applications. If your navigation involves visiting many records, as is often the case when you are scanning, the repaints of your data-aware controls represent a massive and normally unnecessary amount of overhead.

To prevent your data-aware controls from repainting when you need to programmatically change the current record quickly and repeatedly, you should call the ClientDataSet's DisableControls method. When you call DisableControls, the ClientDataSet stops communicating with any DataSources that point to it. As a result, the data-aware controls that point to those DataSources are never made aware of the navigation.

Once you are done navigating, call the ClientDataSet's EnableControls. This will resume the communication between the ClientDataSet and any DataSources that point to it. It will also result in the data-aware controls being immediately instructed to repaint themselves. However, this repaint occurs only once, in response to the call to EnableControls, and is not due to any of the individual navigations that occurred since DisableControls was called.

It is important to recognize that between the time you call DisableControls and EnableControls, the ClientDataSet is in an abnormal state (the GUI is detached, as least with respect to the ClientDataSet). In fact, if you call DisableControls and never call a corresponding EnableControls, the ClientDataSet will appear to the user to have stopped functioning based on the lack of activity in the data-aware controls.

As a result, it is essential that if you call DisableControls, you structure your code in such a way that a call to EnableControls is guaranteed. One way to do this it to enter a try block immediately after a call to DisableControls, invoking the corresponding EnableControls in the finally block.

This is demonstrated in the OnClick event handler associated with the button labeled Scan Forward on the main form of the CDSNavigation project. In this event handler, if the RadioGroup named ControlsStateBtnGrp is set to 1 (the Disabled radio button is selected), the DisableControls method of the ClientDataSet is called before the scanning takes place. Furthermore, once the scanning is complete, the finally clause ensures that controls are once again enabled (if they were initially disabled).

```
procedure TForm1.ScanForwardBtnClick(Sender: TObject);
begin
if ControlsStateBtnGrp.ItemIndex = 1 then
  ClientDataSet1.DisableControls;
  try
    ClientDataSet1.First;
    while not ClientDataSet1.Eof do
    begin
      //do something with a record
      ClientDataSet1.Next;
    end;
  finally
    if ControlsStateBtnGrp.ItemIndex = 1 then
      ClientDataSet1.EnableControls;
  end;
end;
```

Editing a ClientDataSet

While not technically a navigation issue, one of the primary reasons for navigating a ClientDataSet programmatically is to location a record to change. Since this topic is covered only in passing other chapters of this book, I am going to take this opportunity to once again discuss the programmatic editing of records in a ClientDataSet.

You edit a current record in a ClientDataSet by calling its Edit method, after which you can change the values of one or more of its Fields. Once your changes have been made, you can either move off the record to attempt to post the new values, or you can explicitly call the ClientDataSet's Post method.

In most cases, navigating off an edited record and calling Post produce the same effect. But there are two instances where they do not, and it is due to these situations that an explicit call to Post should be considered essential.

In the first instance, if you are editing the last record in a ClientDataSet and then call Next or Last, the edited record is not posted. The second situation is similar, and involves editing the first record in a ClientDataSet followed by a call to either Prior to First. As long as you always call Post prior to attempting to navigate, you can be assured that your edited record will be posted (or raise an exception due to a failure to post).

If you modify a record, and then decide not to post the change, or discover that you cannot post the change, you can cancel all changes to the record by calling the ClientDataSet's Cancel method. For example, if you change a record, and then find that calling Post raises an exception, you can call Cancel to cancel the changes and return the DataSet to the dsBrowse state.

To insert and post a record, you have several options. You can call Insert or Append, after which your cursor will be on a newly inserted record, assuming that you started from the dsBrowse state. If you were editing a record prior to calling Insert or Append, a new record will not be inserted if the record being edited cannot be posted. Once a record is successfully inserted, assign data to the Fields of that record and call Post to post those changes.

The alternative to calling Insert or Append is to call InsertRecord or AppendRecord. These methods insert a new record, assign data to one or more fields, and attempt to post, all in a single call. The following is the syntax of the InsertRecord method. The syntax of AppendRecord is identical (with the obvious except that the methods have different names).

```
procedure InsertRecord(const Values: array of const);
```

You include in the constant array the data values that you want to assign to each field in the ClientDataSet. If you want to leave a particular field unassigned, include the value null in the constant array. Fields you want to leave unassigned at the end of the record can be omitted from the constant array.

For example, if you are inserting and posting a new record into a four-field ClientDataSet, and you want to assign the first field the value 1000 (a field associated with a unique index), leave the second and fourth fields unassigned, but assign the value 'new' to the third record, your InsertRecord invocation may look something like this:

```
ClientDataSet1.InsertRecord([1001, null, 'new']);
```

The following code segment demonstrates another instance of record scanning, this time with edits that need to be posted to each record. In this example, Edit and Post are performed within try blocks. If the record was placed in the edit mode (which corresponds to the dsEdit state), and cannot be posted, the change is canceled. If the record cannot even be placed into edit state (which for a ClientDataSet should only happen if the ClientDataSet has its ReadOnly property set to True), the attempt to post changes is skipped.

```
procedure TForm1.Button1Click(Sender: TObject);
begin
if not ClientDataSet1.Active then
    ClientDataSet1.Open;
ClientDataSet1.First;
while not ClientDataSet1.EOF do
begin
  try
    ClientDataSet1.Edit;
    try
      ClientDataSet1.Fields[0].Value :=
        UpperCase(ClientDataSet1.Fields[0].Value);
      ClientDataSet1.Post;
    except
      //record cannot be posted. Cancel;
      ClientDataSet1.Cancel;
    end;
  except
    //Record cannot be edited. Skip
  end;
  ClientDataSet1.Next;
end; //while
end;
```

Note: Rather than simply canceling changes that cannot be posted, an alternative except clause would identify why the record could not post, and produce a log that could later be used to apply the change. Also note that if these changes are being cached, the ClientDataSet provides an OnReconcileError event handler that can be used to process failed postings for updates in a subsequent call to ApplyUpdates.

In the next chapter, we take a look at searching a ClientDataSet.

Chapter 8
Searching ClientDataSets

In the context of this chapter, *searching* means attempting to locate a record based on specific data that it contains. For example, attempting to find a record for a particular customer based on their customer id number, is considered searching. Likewise, finding an invoice based on the date of the invoice and the customer id number associated with that invoice is also considered a search operation.

There is a somewhat similar operation that you can perform with ClientDataSets called *filtering*. Filtering, which shares some characteristics with searching, involves selecting subsets of the records in a ClientDataSet based on the data. These operations, while similar, are different in a number of ways. As a result, filtering is covered separately in Chapter 9, *Filtering ClientDataSets*.

ClientDataSets support a number of search operations, and each has its strengths and weaknesses. Some are relatively easy to employ, while others require some setup, such as ensuring that an appropriate index exists and is selected. Depending on your application's needs, one of the most important factors may be the speed of the search.

Let's be clear about this. Most operations on a ClientDataSet, including searches, tend to be pretty fast, since a ClientDataSet's data is stored entirely in memory. Nonetheless, if you have a great deal of data, or you need to perform many searches in rapid succession, speed becomes an important factor. As a result, in this chapter as well as in the one that follows, we will pay particular attention to speed.

Note: The code project CDSSearch is available from the code download. See Appendix A for details.

In order to compare the speed of the various search options, we need to have some means of measuring the speed of searching. This is accomplished in the CDSSearch project through the TimeGetTime function, which is located in Delphi's mmsystem unit. This unit imports functions from the Windows operating system, specifically those associated with multimedia functions, which need precision, as far as time measurement goes.

In order to calculate and display the search times for the various search operations described in this chapter, the CDSSearch project includes two methods — Start and Done. Start is called immediately prior to beginning the search operation, and captures the tick count returned by the TickGetTick Windows API call. The ticks represent milliseconds.

Done is called immediately after the search operation has concluded, and captures the tick count, calculates the difference from that captured in Start, and displays the results in milliseconds in the StatusBar control, which appears at the bottom of the main form shown in Figure 8-1. In this figure, a search operation has been completed, and information about the search speed appears in the StatusBar.

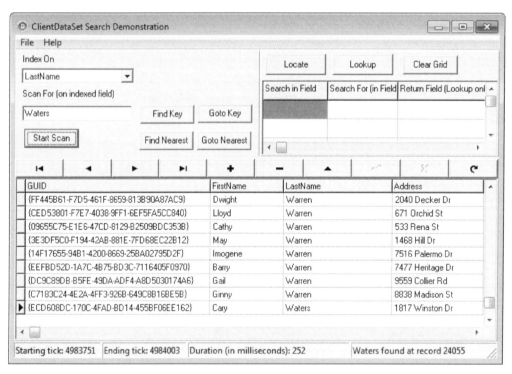

Figure 8-1: The speed of a search operation is displayed in the StatusBar of the CDSSearch project

The following code segments show the Start and Done methods. In these code segments, StartTick and EndTick are private fields of the main form's class. TimeGetTime, as mentioned earlier, is a function imported by Delphi's mmsystem unit, which appears in a uses clause of this project.

```
procedure TForm1.Start;
begin
  StartTick := TimeGetTime;
end;

procedure TForm1.Done;
begin
  EndTick := TimeGetTime;
  StatusBar1.Panels[0].Text := 'Starting tick: ' +
    IntToStr(StartTick);
  StatusBar1.Panels[1].Text := 'Ending tick: ' +
    IntToStr(EndTick);
  StatusBar1.Panels[2].Text := 'Duration (in milliseconds): ' +
    IntToStr(EndTick - StartTick);
end;
```

Before discussing the individual search mechanisms, I also want to mention that we are once again using the BigCDS.cds ClientDataSet file, just as we did in one of the examples in Chapter 5, *Understanding ClientDataSet Indexes.* As you may recall, this saved ClientDataSet file contains more than 25,000 records, making it a good candidate for comparing the speed of the various search mechanisms.

Simple Record-by-Record Searches

The simplest, and typically slowest, mechanism for searching is performed by scanning. As you learned in Chapter 7, *Navigating ClientDataSets,* you can scan a table by moving to either the first or last record in the current index order, and then navigate record by record. When you use scanning for a search operation, you read each record programmatically as you search, comparing the record's data to the search criteria. When you find a record that contains the data you are looking for, you stop scanning.

An example of a scan-based search can be found on the OnClick event handler associated with the button labeled Start Scan in the CDSSearch project. In fact, Figure 8-1 depicts the results of a search operation where a record-by-record scan located the first record in which the name Waters appears in the LastName field.

```
procedure TForm1.ScanBtnClick(Sender: TObject);
var
  Found: Boolean;
begin
  Found := False;
  ClientDataSet1.DisableControls;
  Start;
  try
    ClientDataSet1.First;
```

```
  while not ClientDataSet1.Eof do
  begin
    if ClientDataSet1.Fields[FieldListComboBox.ItemIndex].Value =
      ScanForEdit.Text then
      begin
        Found := True;
        Break;
      end;
    ClientDataSet1.Next;
  end;
  Done;
finally
  ClientDataSet1.EnableControls;
end;
if Found then ShowMessage(ScanForEdit.Text +
  ' found at record ' + IntToStr(ClientDataSet1.RecNo))
else
  ShowMessage(ScanForEdit.Text + ' not found');
end;
```

As you can see from the StatusBar shown in Figure 8-1, the last name Waters was found in record number 24,055, and this search took approximately 252 milliseconds. That's pretty remarkable, if you think about it. Specifically, the code in the preceding event handler evaluated more than 24,000 records in about a quarter of a second before finding a match.

While the scan appears to be very fast, it is nearly always the slowest search you can perform. Many of the remaining search mechanisms discussed in this chapter make use of indexes to perform the search, and this speeds things up significantly.

Searching with Indexes

Indexes, which were introduced in detail in Chapter 5, *Understanding ClientDataSet Indexes,* provide you with a number of features, and speeding up the search process is one of the more significant of these. As you recall, indexes contain information about one or more fields of the ClientDataSet. And since these indexes are ordered by the fields on which they are based, they permit algorithms internal to the ClientDataSet to very quickly locate a record in which a search value appears.

There are two search mechanisms that rely entirely on the presence of indexes. These are FindKey and GotoKey, as well as their close cousins, FindNearest and GotoNearest. FindKey and GotoKey perform their searches based on the fields of the currently selected index. Importantly, it does not matter whether this index is a temporary index created using IndexFieldNames, or a permanent index defined using IndexDefs.

Finding Data

One of the oldest mechanisms for searching a DataSet in Delphi was introduced in Delphi 1. This method, FindKey, permits you to search one or more fields of the current index for a particular value. FindKey, and its close associate, FindNearest, both make use of the current index to perform the search. As a result, the search is always index-based, and always very fast.

Both FindKey and FindNearest take a single constant array parameter (a constant array is a set of one or more comma separated values appearing within square brackets). You include in this array the values for which you want to search on the fields of the index, with the first element in the array being searched for in the first field of the index, the second field in the array (if provided) being searched for in the second field of the index, and so forth. For example, if you have an index based on CustomerNumber, LastName, and FirstName, in that order, you can use FindKey or FindNearest to search on just CustomerNumber, CustomerNumber and LastName, or CustomerNumber and LastName and FirstName.

This pattern cannot be violated. For example, with a CustomerNumber;LastName;FirstName index in place, you cannot use FindKey or FindNearest to search for just LastName, FirstName, or LastName and FirstName. And the search fields must be in the same order as the index, meaning that you cannot search for LastName and CustomerNumber, in that order. Finally, the number of fields being searched cannot exceed the number of fields in the index.

In the CDSSearch project, the only indexes available are temporary indexes associated with a single field in the DataSet. The current temporary index is based on the fields listed in the IndexOnComboBox, which you can use to change which index the ClientDataSet is using. Changing the current index also has the side effect of changing the order in which the records appear in the project's main form. The following code segment is found on the OnClick event handler for this combo box:

```
procedure TForm1.IndexOnComboBoxChange(Sender: TObject);
begin
  ClientDataSet1.IndexFieldNames :=
    IndexOnComboBox.Text;
end;
```

The following single line populates this combo box. This line appears in the OnCreate event handler of the main form, following the code that opens the ClientDataSet (which must be active in order for this code to perform its magic):

```
ClientDataSet1.Fields.GetFieldNames(IndexOnComboBox.Items);
```

The use of FindKey is demonstrated by the code that appears in the OnClick event handler for the button labeled FindKey, shown in the following code segment:

```
procedure TForm1.FindKeyBtnClick(Sender: TObject);
begin
  Start;
  if ClientDataSet1.FindKey([ScanForEdit.Text]) then
  begin
    Done;
    StatusBar1.Panels[3].Text := ScanForEdit.Text +
      ' found at record ' +
      IntToStr(ClientDataSet1.RecNo);
  end
  else
  begin
    Done;
    StatusBar1.Panels[3].Text :=
      ScanForEdit.Text + ' not found';
  end;
end;
```

Figure 8-2 shows how the main form of the CDSSearch project might look following the use of FindKey to locate the first customer whose last name is Waters.

As you can see in this figure, the search took approximately 2 milliseconds, even though the located record was close to the end of the 25,000 record table. If you thought that the scan was fast, consider this the FindKey search is about 100 times faster.

FindKey and FindNearest are identical in syntax. There is, however, a very big difference in what they do. FindKey is a Boolean function method that returns True if a matching record is located. In that case, the cursor is repositioned in the ClientDataSet to the found record, which if there is more than one match, is the first match that is located. If FindKey fails, it returns False and the current record pointer of the ClientDataSet does not change.

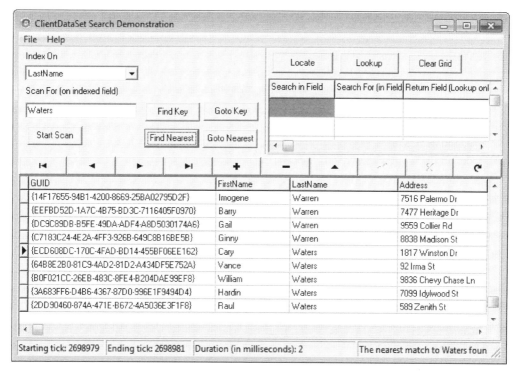

Figure 8-2: FindKey is used to search for the first customer named Waters. This search, which is index-based, is much faster than a scan

Unlike FindKey, which is a function, FindNearest is a procedure method. Technically speaking, FindNearest always succeeds, moving the cursor to the record that most closely matches the search criteria. For example, in Figure 8-3, a search for the city named San Mateo has located a record. This record, however, is not San Mateo. Instead, it is the closest match, San Pablo, which is alphabetically closer to San Mateo than the preceding record, San Marino.

Although FindNearest always succeeds, and always moves to a new current record, the located *nearest* record may actually be the record on which the search started. Specifically, it is possible that the new current record was the old current record, but that would be completely circumstantial.

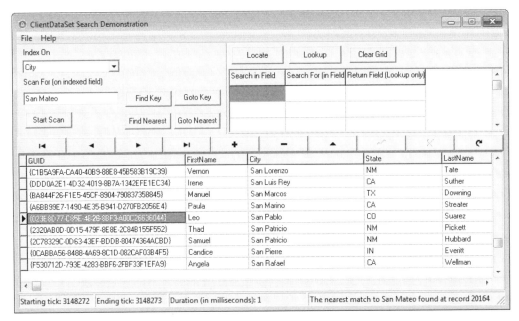

Figure 8-3: FindNearest always succeeds, even if it does not find an exact match

Going to Data

GotoKey and GotoNearest provide the same searching features as FindKey and FindNearest, respectively. The only difference between these two sets of methods is how you define your search criteria. As you have already learned, FindKey and FindNearest are passed a constant array as a parameter, and the search criteria are contained in this array.

Both GotoKey and GotoNearest take no parameters. Instead, their search criteria are defined using the *search key buffer*. The search key buffer contains one field for each field in the current index. For example, if the current index is based on the field LastName, the search key buffer contains one field: LastName. On the other hand, if the current index contains three fields, the search key buffer also contains three fields.

Just as you do not have to define data for each field in the current index when using FindKey and FindNearest, you do not have to define data for each field in the search key buffer. However, those fields that you do define must be associated with the left-most fields in the index definition. For example, if your index is based on LastName and FirstName, you can use the search key buffer to define only the LastName in the search key buffer, or both LastName and

FirstName. Using this same index, you cannot define only the FirstName in the search key buffer.

Once the search key buffer has been populated with the values that you want to search for, you call GotoKey or GotoNearest. At this point, these methods perform the same search, with the same results, as FindKey and FindNearest, respectively.

Fields in the search key buffer can only be modified when the ClientDataSet is in a special state called the dsSetKey state. You call the ClientDataSet's SetKey method to clear the search key buffer and enter the dsSetKey state. If you have previously assigned one or more values to the search key buffer, you can enter the dsSetKey state without clearing the search key buffer's contents by calling the ClientDataSet's EditKey method.

Once the ClientDataSet is in the dsSetKey state, you assign data to Fields in the search key buffer as if you were assigning data to the ClientDataSet's Fields. For example, assuming that the current index is based on the LastName and FirstName fields, the following lines of code assign the value Selman to the LastName field of the search key buffer, and Minnie to the FirstName field of the search key buffer:

```
ClientDataSet1.SetKey;
ClientDataSet1.FieldByName('LastName').Value := 'Selman';
ClientDataSet1.FieldByName('FirstName').Value := 'Minnie';
```

As should be apparent, using GotoKey or GotoNearest requires more lines of code than FindKey and FindNearest. For example, once again assuming that the current index is based on the LastName and FirstName fields, consider the following statement:

```
ClientDataSet1.FindKey(['Selman', 'Minnie']);
```

Achieving the same result using GotoKey requires four lines of code since you must first enter the dsSetKey state and edit the search key buffer. The following lines of code, which use GotoKey, perform precisely the same search as the preceding line of code:

```
ClientDataSet1.SetKey;
ClientDataSet1.FieldByName('FirstName').Value := 'Minnie';
ClientDataSet1.FieldByName('LastName').Value := 'Selman';
ClientDataSet1.GotoKey;
```

Note: In the preceding code segment, I intentionally assigned a value to the FirstName field in the set key buffer before setting a value to the LastName field. Once in the dsSetKey state, it does not matter in which order you assign values to the fields, so long as you respect the other requirements, such as providing values to all of the left-most fields in the index order, without gaps.

The following event handlers are associated with the buttons labeled Goto Key and Goto Nearest in the CDSSearch project:

```
procedure TForm1.GotoKeyBtnClick(Sender: TObject);
begin
  Start;
  ClientDataSet1.SetKey;
  ClientDataSet1.Fields[IndexOnComboBox.ItemIndex].AsString :=
    Trim(ScanForEdit.Text);
  if ClientDataSet1.GotoKey then
  begin
    Done;
    StatusBar1.Panels[3].Text := ScanForEdit.Text +
      ' found at record ' +
      IntToStr(ClientDataSet1.RecNo);
  end
  else
  begin
    Done;
    StatusBar1.Panels[3].Text :=
      ScanForEdit.Text + ' not found';
  end;
end;

procedure TForm1.GotoNearestBtnClick(Sender: TObject);
begin
  Start;
  ClientDataSet1.SetKey;
  ClientDataSet1.Fields[IndexOnComboBox.ItemIndex].AsString :=
    ScanForEdit.Text;
  ClientDataSet1.GotoNearest;
  Done;
  StatusBar1.Panels[3].Text := 'The nearest match to ' +
    ScanForEdit.Text + ' found at record ' +
    IntToStr(ClientDataSet1.RecNo);
end;
```

Since GotoKey and GotoNearest perform essentially the same task as FindKey and FindNearest, though in a more verbose syntax, you might wonder why anyone would use these methods when FindKey and FindNearest are available. There is an answer, and it has to do with EditKey. EditKey places the ClientDataSet in the dsSetKey state, but without clearing the search key buffer. As a result, EditKey permits you to change a single value or a subset of values in the search key buffer without affecting those values you do not want to change. As a result, there are times when GotoKey provides you with a more convenient way to define and change your search criteria. You may never need GotoKey or GotoNearest, but if you do, you'll be glad that these options exist.

Searching with Variants

ClientDataSets provide two additional searching mechanisms, and these involve the use of variants. Unlike FindKey, FindNearest, and their Goto counterparts, these variant-using search mechanisms do not require an index.

This does not mean that these mechanisms do not use indexes. In fact, as you will see, indexes play a role in the performance of these methods. Nonetheless, the point is, they don't require an index, which can be advantageous.

For those search mechanisms that require an index, it means that in order to use them, you must first set the index. While this might not sound like a big deal, setting an index on a ClientDataSet has the effect of changing the sort order of the records as a side effect. While you can sidestep the potential change of record order in the ClientDataSet if you employ a cloned cursor, that too requires additional code. Using cloned cursors is discussed in detail in Chapter 11, *Cloning ClientDataSet Cursors.*

Locating Data

Locate, like FindKey and GotoKey, makes the located record the current record if a match is found. In addition, Locate is a function method and returns a Boolean True if the search produces a match. Lookup is somewhat different in that it returns requested data from a located record, but never moves the current record pointer. Lookup is described separately later in this section.

What makes Locate and Lookup so special is that they do not require you to create or switch indexes, but still provide much faster performance than scanning. In a number of tests that I have conducted, Locate is always faster than scanning, but generally slower than FindKey. Figure 8-4 displays a representative search, in this case, searching for a customer named Waters.

At first glance, Locate looks pretty good as the preceding search results are close to that of the FindKey search shown in Figure 8-2, and significantly faster than scanning. However, upon closer inspection, a wrinkle appears. If you compare Figure 8-4 with Figure 8-1 and Figure 8-2, you will notice that they did not locate the same record. Yes, they located a record with the last name, Waters, but it is not the same record.

Another aspect that is not obvious, unless you spend some time testing various uses of Locate, is that the speed of the search is dependent on the current order of records in the ClientDataSet. For example, in Figure 8-4 the current index is based on FirstName. As a result, the record located is associated with Buddie Waters, which, alphabetically, is the first Waters entry as far as first names go.

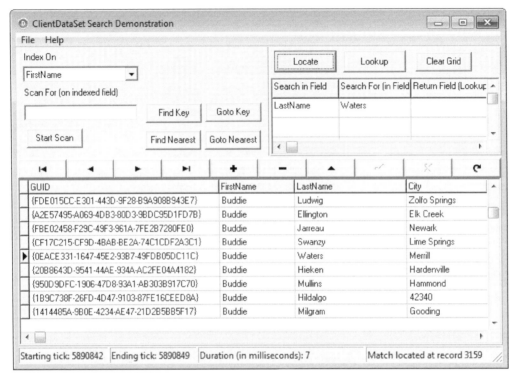

Figure 8-4: A customer with the last name Waters is found using Locate

However, if you were to select the LastName index, where Waters is much later in the order, the Duration would increase from about 7 milliseconds to about 45 milliseconds (on the particular machine on which these tests were executed, and your results may vary). That's a big difference. Yes, it is significantly faster than scanning, but significantly slower than FindKey and GotoKey, even though that index is based on LastName, the field on which the search is being performed.

Should you care? That depends. Locate is fast — FindKey is faster, but Locate and Lookup do not require an index switch. On the other hand, FindKey is fastest, though it requires an index switch (or some cloned cursor mojo). You get it. So let's learn how to use Locate.

Locate has the following syntax:

```
function Locate(const KeyFields: string;
  const KeyValues: Variant; Options: TLocateOptions): Boolean;
```

If you are locating a record based on a single field, the first argument is the name of that field and the second argument is the value you are searching for. To search on more than one field, pass a semicolon-separated string of field names in the first argument, and a variant array containing the search values corresponding to the field list in the second argument.

The third argument of Locate is a TLocateOptions set. This set can contain zero or more of the following flags: loCaseInsensitive and loPartialKey. Include loCaseInsensitive to ignore case in your search and loPartialKey to match any value that begins with the values you pass in the second argument.

If the search is successful, Locate makes the located record the current record and returns a value of True. If the search is not successful, Locate returns False and the cursor does not move.

Imagine that you want to find a customer with the last name Waters. This can be accomplished with the following statement:

```
ClientDataSet1.Locate('LastName', 'Waters',[]);
```

The following is an example of a partial match, searching for a record where the LastName field begins with the letter W or w.

```
ClientDataSet1.Locate('LastName','w',
  [loCaseInsensitive, loPartialKey]);
```

Searching for two or more fields is more complicated in that you must pass the search values using a variant array. The following lines of code demonstrate how you can search for a record where the FirstName field contains Minnie and the LastName field contains Selman:

```
var
  SearchList: Variant;
begin
  SearchList := VarArrayCreate([0, 1], VarVariant);
  SearchList[0] := 'Minnie';
  SearchList[1] := 'Selman';
  ClientDataSet1.Locate('FirstName,LastName',
    SearchList, [loCaseInsensitive]);
```

Instead of using VarArrayCreate, you can use VarArrayOf. VarArrayOf takes a constant array of values from which to create the variant array. This means that you must know at design time how many elements you will need in your variant array. By comparison to VarArrayCreate, the dimensions of the variant array created using VarArrayOf can include variables, which permit you to determine the array size at runtime. The following code performs the same search as the preceding code, but makes use of an array created using VarArrayOf:

```
var
  SearchList: Variant;
begin
  SearchList := VarArrayOf(['Minnie','Selman']);
  ClientDataSet1.Locate('FirstName;LastName',SearchList,
    [loCaseInsensitive]);
```

If you refer back to the CDSSearch project main form shown in the earlier figures in this section, you will notice a StringGrid in the upper-right corner. Data entered into the first two columns of this grid are used to create the KeyFields and KeyValues arguments of Locate, respectively. The following methods, found in the CDSSearch project, generate these parameters:

```
function TForm1.GetKeyFields(var FieldStr: String): Integer;
const
  FieldsColumn = 0;
var
  i : Integer;
  Count: Integer;
begin
  Count := 0;
  for i := 1 to 20 do
  begin
    if StringGrid1.Cells[FieldsColumn,i] <> '' then
    begin
      if FieldStr = '' then FieldStr :=
        StringGrid1.Cells[FieldsColumn,i]
      else
        FieldStr := FieldStr + ';' +
          StringGrid1.Cells[FieldsColumn,i];
      inc(Count);
    end
    else
      Break;
  end;
  Result := Count;
end;

function TForm1.GetKeyValues(Size: Integer): Variant;
const
  SearchColumn = 1;
var
  i: Integer;
begin
  Result := VarArrayCreate([0,Pred(Size)], VarVariant);
  for i := 0 to Pred(Size) do
    Result[i] := StringGrid1.Cells[SearchColumn, Succ(i)];
end;
```

The following code is associated with the OnClick event handler of the button labeled Locate in the CDSSearch project. As you can see in this code, the Locate method is invoked based on the values returned by calling GetKeyFields and GetKeyValues:

```
procedure TForm1.LocateBtnClick(Sender: TObject);
var
  FieldList: String;
  Count: Integer;
  SearchArray: Variant;
begin
  FieldList := '';
  Count := GetKeyFields(FieldList);
  SearchArray := GetKeyValues(Count);
  Start;
  if ClientDataSet1.Locate(FieldList, SearchArray, []) then
  begin
    Done;
    StatusBar1.Panels[3].Text :=
      'Match located at record ' +
      IntToStr(ClientDataSet1.RecNo);
  end
  else
  begin
    Done;
    StatusBar1.Panels[3].Text := 'No match located';
  end;
end;
```

Using Lookup

Lookup is similar in many respects to Locate, with one very important difference. Instead of moving the current record pointer to the located record, Lookup returns a variant containing data from the located record without moving the current record pointer. The following is the syntax of Lookup:

```
function Lookup(const KeyFields: string;
  const KeyValues: Variant; const ResultFields: string): Variant;
```

The KeyFields and KeyValues parameters of Lookup are identical in purpose to those in the Locate method. The ResultFields parameter is a semicolon-separated string of field names whose values you want returned.

If Lookup fails to find the record being search for, it returns a null variant. Otherwise, it returns a variant containing the field values requested in the ResultFields parameter.

The event handler associated with the Lookup button in the CDSSearch project makes use of the GetKeyFields and GetKeyValues methods for defining the KeyFields and KeyValues parameters of the call to Lookup, based again on the first two columns of the StringGrid in the CDSSearch project. In addition, this event handler makes use of the GetResultFields method to construct the ResultFields parameter from the third column of the grid. The following is the code associated with the GetResultFields method:

```
function TForm1.GetResultFields: String;
const
  ReturnColumn = 2;
var
  i: Integer;
begin
  for i := 1 to Succ(StringGrid1.RowCount) do
    if StringGrid1.Cells[ReturnColumn, i] <> '' then
      if Result = '' then
        Result := StringGrid1.Cells[ReturnColumn, i]
      else
        Result := Result + ';' +
          StringGrid1.Cells[ReturnColumn, i]
    else
      Break;
end;
```

The following is the code associated with the OnClick event handler of the button labeled Lookup:

```
procedure TForm1.LookupBtnClick(Sender: TObject);
var
  ResultFields: Variant;
  KeyFields: String;
  KeyValues: Variant;
  ReturnFields: String;
  Count, i: Integer;
  DisplayString: String;
begin
  Count := GetKeyFields(KeyFields);
  DisplayString := '';
  KeyValues := GetKeyValues(Count);
  ReturnFields := GetResultFields;
  Start;
  ResultFields := ClientDataSet1.Lookup(KeyFields,
    KeyValues, ReturnFields);
  Done;
  if VarIsNull(ResultFields) then
    DisplayString := 'Lookup record not found'
  else
    if VarIsArray(ResultFields) then
      for i := 0 to VarArrayHighBound(ResultFields,1) do
        if i = 0 then
          DisplayString := 'Lookup result: ' +
            VarToStr(ResultFields[i])
        else
          DisplayString := DisplayString +
            ';' + VarToStr(ResultFields[i])
    else
```

```
        DisplayString := VarToStr(ResultFields);
    StatusBar1.Panels[3].Text := DisplayString
end;
```

Figure 8-5 shows the main form of the CDSSearch project following a call to Locate. Notice that the current record is still the first record in the ClientDataSet (as indicated by the DBNavigator buttons), even though the data returned from the call to Locate was found much later in the current index order.

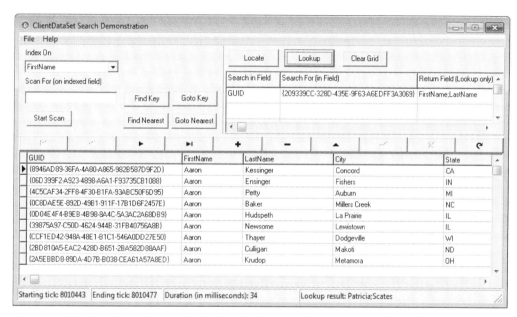

Figure 8-5: Lookup is a relatively high-speed way to get data from a record without changing the current record of a ClientDataSet

In the next chapter, you will learn how to filter ClientDataSets.

Chapter 9
Filtering ClientDataSets

When you filter a ClientDataSet, you restrict access to a subset of records contained in the ClientDataSet's in-memory store. For example, imagine that you have a ClientDataSet that includes one record for each of your company's customers, worldwide. Without filtering, all customer records are accessible in the ClientDataSet. That is, it is possible to navigate, view, and edit any customer in the ClientDataSet.

Through filtering, you can make the ClientDataSet appear to include only those customers who live in the United States or in London, England, or who live on a street named 6th Avenue. This example, of course, assumes that there is a field in the ClientDataSet that contains country names, or fields containing City and Country names, or a field holding street names. In other words, a filter limits which records in a ClientDataSet are accessible based on data that is stored in the ClientDataSet.

While a filter is similar to a search, it is also different in a number of significant ways. For example, when you apply a filter, it is possible that the current record in the ClientDataSet will change. This will happen if the record that was current before the filter was applied no longer exists in the filtered ClientDataSet. When performing a search, the current record may change as well, specifically if the record you are searching for is not the current record. However, the record that was the current record prior to the search operation is still accessible in the ClientDataSet.

Another difference is that a search operation never changes the number of records in the ClientDataSet, as reflected by the ClientDataSet's RecordCount property. By comparison, if at least one record in the ClientDataSet does not match the filter criteria, RecordCount will be lower following the application of the filter, and will change again when the filter is dropped.

ClientDataSet Filters

A ClientDataSet supports two fundamentally different mechanisms for creating filters. The first of these involves a *range,* which is an index-based filtering mechanism. The second, called a *filter,* is more flexible than a range, but is slower to apply and cancel. Both of these approaches to filtering are covered in the following sections.

But before addressing filtering directly, there are a couple of additional points that I need to make. The first is that filtering is a client-side operation. Specifically, the filters discussed here are applied to the data that is loaded into the ClientDataSet. For example, you may load 10,000 records into a ClientDataSet (every customer record, for instance), and then apply a filter that limits access to only those customers located in Philadelphia.

Once applied, the filter may make the ClientDataSet appear to contain only 300 records (assuming that 300 of your customers are located in Philadelphia). Although the filtered ClientDataSet provides access only to these 300 records, all 10,000 records remain in memory. In other words, a filter does not reduce the overhead of your ClientDataSet — it simply restricts your access to a subset of the ClientDataSet's records, those that match the filter criteria.

The second point is that instead of using a filter on the data loaded into your ClientDataSet, you may be better off limiting how many records you load into the ClientDataSet in the first place. Consider the preceding example where 10,000 customer records are loaded into the ClientDataSet. Instead of loading all 10,000 records, it might be better to load only those customer records associated with customers who live in Philadelphia. While partial loading is not an option when you load a ClientDataSet through a call to LoadFromFile or LoadFromStream, it is an option when you load a ClientDataSet through a DataSetProvider.

For example, imagine that your DataSetProvider points to a SQLDataSet whose CommandText contains the following SQL query:

```
SELECT * FROM CUSTOMER WHERE CITY = 'Philadelphia'
```

When the ClientDataSet's Open method is called, this SQL SELECT statement is executed, and only those 300 or so records from your Philadelphia-based customers are loaded into the ClientDataSet. This approach greatly reduces the memory overhead of the ClientDataSet, since fewer records need to be stored in memory.

While the preceding query seems rather limiting, in that it only allows the selection of customers from Philadelphia, the ClientDataSet allows you to be much more flexible. For example, imagine that your DataSetProvider points to a SQLDataSet whose query is parameterized, like that shown in the following SQL statement:

```
SELECT * FROM CUSTOMER WHERE CITY = :City
```

With this query in play, and with a single Param named City defined in the ClientDataSet's Params property, you could use code similar to the following to allow the end user to select into the ClientDataSet customer records from any city:

```
var
  CityName: String;
begin
  if InputQuery('Select Customers from Which City',
    'City', CityName) then
  begin
    ClientDataSet1.Params[0].AsString := CityName;
    ClientDataSet1.Open;
  end;
```

Nonetheless, from the perspective of this discussion, these techniques are not technically ClientDataSet filtering, since they do not limit access within the ClientDataSet to a subset of its loaded records.

So when do you use filtering as opposed to loading only selected records into a ClientDataSet? The answer boils down to four issues: bandwidth, source of data, the amount of data, and client-side features.

When loading a ClientDataSet from a DataSetProvider, and the DataSetProvider exists on another computer on your network, bandwidth is a concern. In distributed applications like these (we are talking DataSnap here), it is usually best to load only selected records when bandwidth is low. In this situation, loading records that are not going to be displayed consumes bandwidth unnecessarily, affecting the performance of your application as well as that of others that share the bandwidth. On the other hand, if bandwidth is plentiful and the entire result set is relatively small, it is often easier to load all data and filter on those records that you want displayed.

The second consideration is data location. If you are loading data from a previously saved ClientDataSet (using LoadFromFile or LoadFromStream), you have no choice. Filtering is the only option for showing just a subset of records. Only when you are loading data through a DataSetProvider do you have a choice between using a filter and selectively loading the data.

The third consideration is the amount of data. If your DataSetProvider points to a data source that has a very large amount of data, it may not even be possible to load all of that data into a ClientDataSet. For example, if the DataSetProvider points to a query that returns millions of records, or that contains a very large number of really big BLOB fields, it may not be possible to load all of that data into memory at the same time. In these cases, you must use some technique, such as using a well considered WHERE clause to load only that data you need or can handle.

The final consideration is related to client-side features, the most common of which is speed. Once data is loaded into a ClientDataSet, most filters are applied very quickly, even when a large amount of data needs to be filtered. As a result, filtering permits you to rapidly alter which subset of records is displayed. A simple click of a button or a menu selection can almost instantly switch your ClientDataSet from displaying customers from Philadelphia to displaying customers from Dallas, without a network roundtrip.

The use of filters is demonstrated in the CDSFilter project. The main form for this project is shown in Figure 9-1.

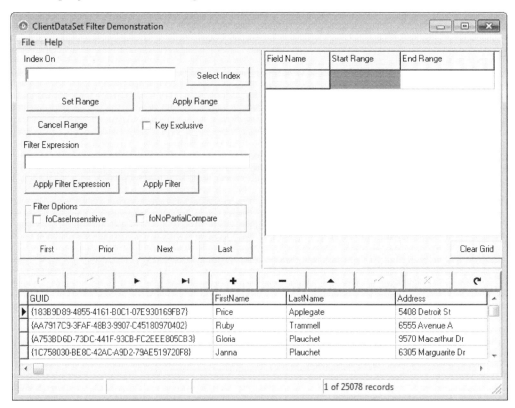

Figure 9-1: The main form of the CDSFilter project

Note: The code project CDSFilter is available from the code download. See Appendix A for details.

Several types of filters are demonstrated in the CDSFilter project, which is used for the remainder of this chapter. This project also makes use of BigCDS.cds, a saved ClientDataSet file that contains more than 25,000 records. This file, which is assumed to be located in a directory named BigCDS in a folder parallel to the one in which the CDSFilter project is located, is loaded from the OnCreate event handler of the main form. This event handler will also display an error message if BigCDS.cds cannot be located.

As mentioned earlier, there are two basic approaches to filtering: ranges and filters. Let's start by looking at ranges.

Setting a Range

Ranges, although less flexible than filters, provide the fastest option for displaying a subset of records from a ClientDataSet. In short, a range is an index-based mechanism for defining the low and high values of records to be displayed in the ClientDataSet. For example, if the current index is based on the customer's last name, a range can be used to display all customers whose last name is Jones. Or, a range can be used to display only customers whose last name begins with the letter J. Similarly, if a ClientDataSet is indexed on an integer field called Credit Limit, a range can be used to display only those customers whose credit limit is greater than (US) $1,000, or between $0 and $1000.

Setting ranges with a ClientDataSet bears a strong resemblance to the index-based search mechanisms covered in Chapter 8, *Searching ClientDataSets*. First, both of these mechanisms require that you set an index, be that a temporary index or a permanent index. The range, like the index, is then based on one or more fields on the current index. A second similarity between ranges and index-based searches is that there are two ways to set a range. One technique involves a single method call, similar to FindKey, while the other employs the set key buffer, like GotoKey.

Let's start by looking at the easiest mechanism for setting a range — the SetRange method. SetRange defines a range using a single method invocation. In Delphi, SetRange has the following syntax:

```
procedure SetRange(const StartValues, EndValues: array of const);
```

As you can see from this syntax, you pass two constant arrays when you call SetRange. The first array contains the low values of the range for the fields of the index, with the first element in the array being the low value of the range for the first field in the index, the second element being the low value of the range for the second field in the index, and so on. The second array contains the high end values for the index fields, with the first element in the second array being the high end value of the range on the first field of the index, the second element being the high value of the range on the second field of the index, and so forth. These arrays can contain fewer elements than the number of fields in the current index, but cannot contain more.

Consider again our example of a ClientDataSet that holds all customer records. Given that there is a field in this ClientDataSet named City, and you want to display only records for customers who live in Pleasantville, you can use the following statements:

```
ClientDataSet1.IndexFieldNames := 'City';
ClientDataSet1.SetRange(['Pleasantville'], ['Pleasantville']);
```

The first statement creates a temporary index on the City field, while the second sets the range. Of course, if the ClientDataSet is already using an index where the first field of the index was the City field, you omit the first line in the preceding code segment.

The preceding example sets the range on a single field, but it is often possible to set a range on two or more fields of the current index. For example, imagine that you want to display only those customers whose last name is Waters and who live in Pleasantville, New York. The following statements show you how:

```
ClientDataSet1.IndexFieldNames := 'LastName;City;State';
ClientDataSet1.SetRange(['Waters', 'Pleasantville', 'NY'],
                        ['Waters', 'Pleasantville', 'NY']);
```

Each of these examples sets the range to a single value in all fields. It is sometimes possible to set a range that includes a range of values. For example, imagine that you want to find all customers who live in California and in a city whose name begins with A. You could achieve this with the following statements:

```
ClientDataSet1.IndexFieldNames := 'State;City';
ClientDataSet1.SetRange(['CA', 'Aa'],
                        ['CA', 'Az']);
```

The use of SetRange is demonstrated in the OnClick event handler associated with the button labeled Set Range. Unfortunately, due to the syntax of the SetRange method, in order to make the CDSFilter project flexible, allowing you to create ranges on one or more fields, this event handler is somewhat clumsy.

You define an index by clicking the Select Index button. The event handler on this button was described in some detail in Chapter 5, *Understanding*

ClientDataSet Indexes, so I won't go into a lot of detail here. But suffice it to say that this event handler ensures that the user can enter in a valid set of fields for the current ClientDataSet (which it assigns to the ClientDataSet's IndexFieldNames property). Once the index is set, it also initializes the StringGrid that appears in the upper-right side of the main form, displaying the name of each index field, and providing fields for you to enter the low and high values for one or more fields of the index.

The clumsy part is due to the use of constant arrays in the SetRange method. In short, you have to know the size of a constant array at design time. As a result, the OnClick event handler for the button labeled Set Range must provide one call to SetRange for each possible constant array size. For example, there is one call for situations where you want to set a range on a single field, and a second call for calls involving two fields. In fact, the Set Range button actually includes five different calls to SetRange. This can be seen in the following code:

```
procedure TForm1.SetRangeBtnClick(Sender: TObject);
var
  MaxItems: Integer;
begin
if ClientDataSet1.IndexFieldNames = '' then
  begin
    ShowMessage('Set index field names before trying to set a
range');
    Exit;
  end;
  MaxItems := GetMaxRangeItems;
  case MaxItems of
  0: ShowMessage('Enter a range');
  1: begin
    Start;
    ClientDataSet1.SetRange(
      [StringGrid1.Cells[1,1]],
      [StringGrid1.Cells[2,1]]);
    Done;
    end;
  2: begin
    Start;
    ClientDataSet1.SetRange(
      [StringGrid1.Cells[1,1],
      StringGrid1.Cells[1,2]],
      [StringGrid1.Cells[2,1],
      StringGrid1.Cells[2,2]]);
    Done;
    end;
  3:  begin
     Start;
     ClientDataSet1.SetRange(
       [StringGrid1.Cells[1,1],
       StringGrid1.Cells[1,2],
```

```
            StringGrid1.Cells[1,3]],
          [StringGrid1.Cells[2,1],
          StringGrid1.Cells[2,2],
          StringGrid1.Cells[2,3]]);
        Done;
        end;
   4:   begin
        Start;
        ClientDataSet1.SetRange(
          [StringGrid1.Cells[1,1],
          StringGrid1.Cells[1,2],
          StringGrid1.Cells[1,3],
          StringGrid1.Cells[1,4]],
          [StringGrid1.Cells[2,1],
          StringGrid1.Cells[2,2],
          StringGrid1.Cells[2,3],
          StringGrid1.Cells[2,4]]);
        Done;
        end;
   5:   begin
        Start;
        ClientDataSet1.SetRange(
          [StringGrid1.Cells[1,1],
          StringGrid1.Cells[1,2],
          StringGrid1.Cells[1,3],
          StringGrid1.Cells[1,4],
          StringGrid1.Cells[1,5]],
          [StringGrid1.Cells[2,1],
          StringGrid1.Cells[2,2],
          StringGrid1.Cells[2,3],
          StringGrid1.Cells[2,4],
          StringGrid1.Cells[2,5]]);
        Done;
        end;
   6..MaxInt: ShowMessage('This example project limited to '+
     'a maximum of 5 fields in a range');
   end;
   if MaxItems < 6 then
     CancelRangeBtn.Enabled := True;
end;
```

Figure 9-2 shows a how the CDSFilter project looks after a range has been set on two fields. This range displays all records associated with people from Des Moines whose last name begins with the letter S.

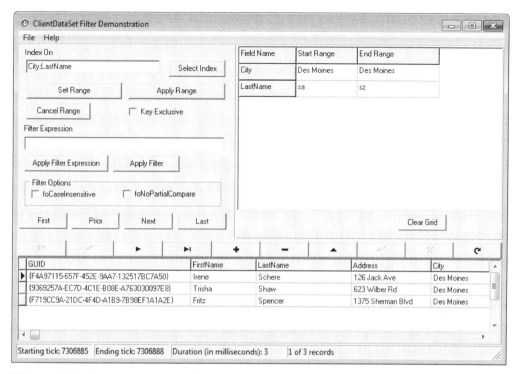

Figure 9-2: A range on two fields has been applied to the ClientDataSet

Using ApplyRange

ApplyRange is the range equivalent to the GotoKey search. To use ApplyRange, you begin by calling SetRangeStart (or EditRangeStart). Doing so places the ClientDataSet in the dsSetKey state. While in this state, you assign values to one or more of the Fields involved in the current index to define the low values of the range. As is the case with SetRange, if you define a single low value it will be used to define the low end of the range on the first field of the current index. If you define the low values of the range for two fields, they must necessarily be the first two fields of the index.

After setting the low range values, you call SetRangeEnd (or EditRangeEnd). You now assign values to one or more fields of the current index to define the high values for the range. Once both the low values and high values of the range have been set, you call ApplyRange to filter the ClientDataSet on the defined range.

For example, the following statements use ApplyRange to display only customers who live in Philadelphia:

```
ClientDataSet1.IndexFieldNames := 'City';
ClientDataSet1.SetRangeStart;
```

```
ClientDataSet1.FieldByName('City').Value := 'Philadelphia';
ClientDataSet1.SetRangeEnd;
ClientDataSet1.FieldByName('City').Value := ' Philadelphia ';
ClientDataSet1.ApplyRange;
```

Just like SetRange, ApplyRange can be used to set a range on more than one field of the index, as shown in the following example:

```
ClientDataSet1.IndexFieldNames := 'LastName;City;State';
ClientDataSet1.SetRangeStart;
ClientDataSet1.FieldByName('LastName').Value := 'Waters';
ClientDataSet1.FieldByName('City').Value := 'Pleasantville';
ClientDataSet1.FieldByName('State').Value := 'NY';
ClientDataSet1.SetRangeEnd;
ClientDataSet1.FieldByName('LastName').Value := 'Waters';
ClientDataSet1.FieldByName('City').Value := 'Pleasantville';
ClientDataSet1.FieldByName('State').Value := 'NY';
ClientDataSet1.ApplyRange;
```

Both of the preceding examples made use of SetRangeStart and SetRangeEnd. In some cases, you can use EditRangeStart and/or EditRangeEnd instead. In short, if you have already set low and high values for a range, and want to modify some, but not all, values, you can use EditRangeStart and EditRangeEnd. Calling SetRangeStart clears any previous values in the range. By comparison, if you call EditRangeStart, the previously defined low values remain in the range fields. If you want to change some, but not all, of the low range values, call EditRangeStart and modify only those fields whose low values you want to change. Likewise, if you want to change some, but not all, of the high range values, do so by calling EditRangeEnd.

For example, the following code segment will display all records in which the customer's credit limit is between (US) $1,000 and (US) $5,000:

```
ClientDataSet1.IndexFieldNames := 'CreditLimit';
ClientDataSet1.SetRange([1000],[5000]);
```

If you then want to set a range between $1,000 and $10,000, you can do so using the following statements:

```
ClientDataSet1.EditRangeEnd;
ClientDataSet1.FieldByName('CreditLimit').Value := 10000;
ClientDataSet1.ApplyRange;
```

At first glance, ApplyRange sounds like it is more verbose than SetRange, and this is true when you know in advance how many fields on which your range is based. Ironically, when you do not know how many fields you need to set a range on in advance, ApplyRange can actually be more concise.

Consider the OnClick event handler associated with the button labeled Apply Range. This event handler, shown in the following code segment, performs the same task as the hideous Set Range event handler shown earlier. As you can see, this event handler is much shorter. It can also handle any number of fields in the index without requiring more code.

```
procedure TForm1.ApplyRangeBtnClick(Sender: TObject);
var
  MaxItems: Integer;
  i: Integer;
begin
if ClientDataSet1.IndexFieldNames = '' then
  begin
    ShowMessage('Set index field names before trying to set a range');
    Exit;
  end;
  MaxItems := GetMaxRangeItems;
  if MaxItems = 0 then
  begin
    ShowMessage('Enter a range');
    Exit;
  end;
  Start;
  ClientDataSet1.SetRangeStart;
  for i := 1 to MaxItems do
    ClientDataSet1.FieldByName(StringGrid1.Cells[0,i]).Value :=
      Trim(StringGrid1.Cells[1,i]);
  ClientDataSet1.SetRangeEnd;
  for i := 1 to MaxItems do
    ClientDataSet1.FieldByName(StringGrid1.Cells[0,i]).Value :=
      Trim(StringGrid1.Cells[2,i]);
  ClientDataSet1.ApplyRange;
  Done;
  if MaxItems < 6 then
    CancelRangeBtn.Enabled := True;
end;
```

Canceling a Range

Whether you have created a range using SetRange or ApplyRange, you cancel that range by calling the ClientDataSet's CancelRange method. Canceling a range is demonstrated by the OnClick event handler associated with the button labeled Cancel Range, as shown in the following code:

```
procedure TForm1.CancelRangeBtnClick(Sender: TObject);
begin
  ClientDataSet1.CancelRange;
  CancelRangeBtn.Enabled := False;
end;
```

A Comment About Ranges

Earlier I mentioned that it is *sometimes* possible to set a range on two or more fields where a range of values is included in the result (all customers with a credit limit above 1000) compared to setting a range where all records in the range have the same value (all customers from Pleasantville). The implication of this statement is that sometimes it is not possible to set a range where the records have a range of values, and that is intentional since it is a correct conclusion.

When setting a range on two or more fields, only the last field of the range can specify a range of values; all other fields must have the same value for both the low and high ends of the range. For example, the following range will display all records in which the credit limit is between $1,000 and $5,000 for customers living in Des Moines:

```
ClientDataSet1.IndexFieldNames := 'City;CreditLimit';
ClientDataSet1.SetRange(['Des Moines', 1000], [' Des Moines', 5000]);
```

By comparison, the following statement will display all records for customers whose credit limit is between $1,000 and $5,000, regardless of which city they live in:

```
ClientDataSet1.IndexFieldNames := 'CreditLimit;City';
ClientDataSet1.SetRange([1000, 'Des Moines'], [5000, 'Des Moines']);
```

The difference between these two range examples is that in the first example, the low and high value in the first field of the range is a constant value, Des Moines. In the second, a range appears (1000-5000). Because a range of values, instead of a constant value, appears in the first field of the range the second field of the range is ignored.

There is another aspect of ranges that is rather odd when working with ClientDataSets. This is related to the KeyExclusive property inherited by the ClientDataSet from TDataSet. With BDE components, such as Table and Query, this property can be used to define how ranges are applied. When KeyExclusive is False (its default value), the range includes both the low and high values of the range. For example, if you set a range on CreditLimit to a low of 1000 and a high of 5000, records where the credit limit is 1000 or 5000 will also appear in the range. If KeyExclusive is set to True, only customer records where the credit limit is greater than 1000 but less than 5000 will appear in the range. Customers with credit limits of exactly 1000 or 5000 will not.

When you attempt to set the value of KeyExclusive to True on a ClientDataSet, an exception is raised. The error message, however, warns that the ClientDataSet is not in the dsEdit or dsInsert mode. This really doesn't make a lot of sense. As a result, I have concluded that KeyExclusive does not apply to ClientDataSets.

Using Filters

Because ranges rely on indexes, they are applied very quickly. For example, using the BigCDS.cds table with an index on the FirstName field, setting a range to show only records for customers where the first name is Scarlett was applied in about 2 milliseconds on my computer.

Filters, by comparison, do not use indexes. Instead, they operate by evaluating the records of the ClientDataSet, displaying only those records that pass the filter. Since filters do not use indexes, they are not as fast (filtering on the first name Scarlett took just under 40 milliseconds in my tests, which is 20 times slower). On the other hand, filters are much more flexible.

A ClientDataSet has four properties that apply to filters. These are: Filter, Filtered, FilterOptions, and OnFilterRecord (an event property). In its simplest case, a filter requires that you use two of these properties: Filter and Filtered. Filtered is a Boolean property that you use to turn filtering on and off. If you want to filter records, set Filtered to True: Otherwise, set Filtered to False (the default value).

When Filtered is set to True, the ClientDataSet uses the value of the Filter property to identify which records will be displayed. You assign to this property a Boolean expression containing at least one comparison operation involving at least one field in the ClientDataSet. You can use any comparison operators, including =, >, <, >=, <=, and <>. As long as the field name does not include any spaces, you include the field name directly in the filter expression without delimiters. For example, if your ClientDataSet includes a field named City, you can set the Filter property to the following expression to display only customers living in Dayton (when Filtered is True):

```
City = 'Dayton'
```

Note that the single quotes are required here, since Dayton is a string. If you want to assign a value to the Filter property at runtime, you must include the single quotes in the string that you assign to the property. The following is one example of how to do this:

```
ClientDataSet1.Filter := 'City = ' + QuotedStr('Philadelphia');
```

The preceding code segment used the QuotedStr function, which is located in the SysUtils unit. The alternative is to use something like the following. Personally, I prefer using QuotedStr, as it is much easier to debug and maintain.

```
ClientDataSet1.Filter := 'City = ''Philadelphia''';
```

In the preceding examples, the field name of the field in the filter does not include spaces. If one or more fields that you want to use in a filter include spaces in their field names, or characters that would otherwise be interpreted to mean something else, such as the > (greater than) symbol, enclose those field names in square brackets. (Square brackets can also be used around field names that do not include spaces.) For example, if your ClientDataSet contains a field named 'Last Name,' you can use a statement similar to the following to create a filter:

```
ClientDataSet1.Filter := '[Last Name] = ' + QuotedStr('Williams');
```

These examples have demonstrated only simple expressions. However, complex expressions can be used. Specifically, you can combine two or more comparisons using the AND, OR, and NOT logical operators. Furthermore, more than one field can be involved in the comparison. For example, you can use the following Filter to limit records to those where the City field is San Francisco and the Last Name is Martinez:

```
ClientDataSet1.Filter := '[City] = '+ QuotedStr('San Francisco') +
   'and [Last Name] = ' + QuotedStr('Martinez');
```

Assigning a value to the Filter property does not automatically mean that records will be filtered. Only when the Filtered property is set to True does the Filter property actually produce a filtered ClientDataSet. Furthermore, if the Filter property contains an empty string, setting Filtered to True has no effect.

By default, filters are case sensitive and perform a partial match to the filter criteria. You can influence this behavior using the FilterOptions property. This property is a set property that can contain zero or more of the following two flags: foCaseInsensitive and foNoPartialCompare. When foCaseInsensitive is included in the set, the filter is not case sensitive.

When foNoPartialCompare is included in the set, partial matches are excluded from the filtered DataSet. When foNoPartialCompare is absent from the FilterOptions property, partial matches are identified by an asterisk ('*') in the last character of your filter criteria. All fields whose contents match the characters to the left of the asterisk are included in the filter. For example, consider the following filter:

```
ClientDataSet1.Filter := 'City = '+ QuotedStr('San *');
```

As long as foNoPartialCompare is absent from the FilterOptions property, this filter will include any city whose name begins 'San ,' such as San Francisco or San Antonio.

Partial matches can also be used with compound Boolean expressions. For example, the following filter will display all customers whose names begin with the letter R, and who live in a city whose name begins with 'New,' such as Newcastle or New York City:

```
ClientDataSet1.Filter := 'City = '+ QuotedStr('New*') +
  'and [Last Name] = ' + QuotedStr('R*');
```

Filtering is demonstrated from two event handlers in the CDSFilter project. The first is associated with the OnClick event of the button labeled Apply Filter Expression. This code assigns the value entered into the provided Edit to the ClientDataSet's Filter property:

```
procedure TForm1.ApplyFilterExpressionBtnClick(Sender: TObject);
begin
  Start;
  ClientDataSet1.Filter := FilterExpressionEdit.Text;
  Done;
end;
```

As pointed out earlier, assigning a value to Filter does not actually cause the ClientDataSet to filter the records it displays. That only happens when you set the Filtered property to True, which is performed by the OnClick event handler of the button labeled Apply Filter. This event handler is shown here:

```
procedure TForm1.ApplyDropFilterBtnClick(Sender: TObject);
begin
  Start;
  ClientDataSet1.Filtered := not ClientDataSet1.Filtered;
  Done;
  if ClientDataSet1.Filtered then
    ApplyDropFilterBtn.Caption := 'Drop Filter'
  else
    ApplyDropFilterBtn.Caption := 'Apply Filter';
end;
```

Figure 9-3 shows the CDSFilter project after a filter has been applied. In this filter, the filter expression selects all records for which the City name is Philadelphia and the last name begins with the letter S. This filter is case insensitive, and partial compares are allowed.

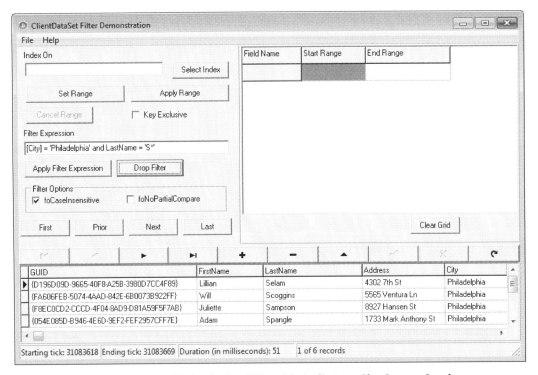

Figure 9-3: A filter has limited the ClientDataSet to display only six records

Using the OnFilterRecord Event Handler

There is a second, somewhat more flexible way to define a filter. Instead of using the Filter property, you can attach code to the OnFilterRecord event handler of a ClientDataSet. When Filtered is set to True, this event handler triggers for every record in the ClientDataSet. When called, this event handler is passed a Boolean parameter by reference, named Accept, that you use to indicate whether or not the current record should be included in the filtered view.

From within this event handler you can perform almost any test you can imagine. For example, you can verify that the current record is associated with a record in another table. If, based on this test, you wish to exclude the current record from the view, you set the value of the Accept formal parameter to False. This parameter is True by default.

The Filter property normally consists of one or more comparisons involving values in fields of the ClientDataSet. OnFilterRecord event handlers, however, can include any comparison you want. And there lies the danger. Specifically, if the comparison that you perform in the OnFilterRecord event handler is time consuming, the filter will be slow. In other words, you should try to optimize any code that you place in an OnFilterRecord event handler, especially if you need to filter a lot of records.

The following is a simple example of an OnFilterRecord event handler:

```
procedure TForm1.ClientDataSet1FilterRecord(DataSet: TDataSet;
  var Accept: Boolean);
begin
  Accept := ClientDataSet1.Fields[1].AsString = 'Scarlett';
end;
```

Navigating Using a Filter

Whether you have set Filtered to True or not, you can still use a Filter for the purpose of navigating selected records. For example, although you may want to view all records in a database, you may want to quickly move among records that meet specific criteria. For example, you may want to be able to quickly navigate among those records where the customer has a credit limit in excess of (USD) $5,000.

ClientDataSets exposes four methods for navigating using a filter. These methods are FindFirst, FindLast, FindNext, and FindPrior. When you execute one of these methods, the ClientDataSet will locate the requested record based on the current Filter property or OnFilterRecord event handler. This navigation, however, does not require that the Filtered property be set to True. In other words, while all records of the ClientDataSet may be visible, the filter can be used to quickly navigate among those records that match the filter.

When you execute the methods FindNext or FindPrior, the ClientDataSet sets a property named Found. If Found is True, a next record or a prior record was located, and is now the current record. If Found returns False, the attempt to navigate failed. However, all of the filtered navigation methods are function methods that return Boolean True if the operation was successful. For example, after setting the filter expression, a call to FindFirst or FindLast returns False if no records match the filter expression.

The use of filtered navigation is demonstrated in the event handlers associated with the buttons labeled First, Prior, Next, and Last. These event handlers are shown here:

```
procedure TForm1.ApplyFilterExpressionBtnClick(Sender: TObject);
begin
  Start;
  ClientDataSet1.Filter := FilterExpressionEdit.Text;
  Done;
end;
```

```
procedure TForm1.FirstBtnClick(Sender: TObject);
begin
  Start;
  if not ClientDataSet1.FindFirst then
  begin
    Done;
    ShowMessage('There are no matching records');
  end
  else
    Done;
end;

procedure TForm1.PriorBtnClick(Sender: TObject);
begin
  Start;
  if not ClientDataSet1.FindPrior then
  begin
    Done;
    ShowMessage('No prior record found');
  end
  else
    Done;
end;

procedure TForm1.NextBtnClick(Sender: TObject);
begin
  Start;
  ClientDataSet1.FindNext;
  Done;
  if not ClientDataSet1.Found then
    ShowMessage('No next record found');
end;
```

Notice that the NextBtnClick method uses the Found property of the ClientDataSet to determine if the navigation was successful. By comparison, the PriorBtnClick simply uses the return value of FindPrior to measure success. The values returned by the calls to FindFirst and FindLast are also used in this code to evaluate whether or not any records matched the expression entered into the provided Edit.

Figure 9-4 shows how the CDSFilter project looks after a filtered navigation. After entering the filter expression FirstName = 'Scarlett' into the Edit, and clicking the Apply Filter Expression button, the button labeled First was clicked. This moved the cursor to record number 510. The Next button was then clicked, and the record at position 878 became the current record. The navigation is being performed on records where the first name field contains the value Scarlett, even though all records from the ClientDataSet are visible in the DBGrid.

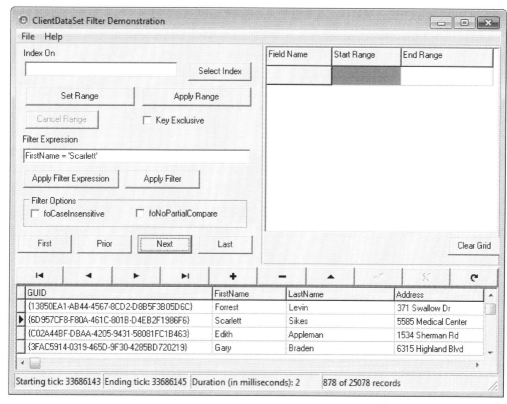

Figure 9-4: Filtered navigation uses the filter expression to navigate, even when Filtered is set to False

Using Ranges and Filters Together

Ranges make use of indexes and are very fast. Filters are slower, but are more flexible. Fortunately, both ranges and filters can be used together. Using ranges with filters is especially helpful when you cannot use a range alone, and your filter is a complicated one that would otherwise take a long time to apply. In those situations, it is best to first set a range, limiting the number of records that need to be filtered to the smallest possible set that includes all records of the filter. The filter can be applied on the resulting range. Since fewer records need to be evaluated for the filter, the combined operations will be faster than using a Filter alone.

In the next chapter, you will learn how to create aggregate virtual fields and use GroupState.

Chapter 10
Aggregates and GroupState

One of the advantages to using a ClientDataSet in your applications is the large number of features it enables. Two of the more interesting features that fall into this category are aggregates and group state. Aggregates are objects that can perform the automatic calculation of basic descriptive statistics based on the data stored in a ClientDataSet. Group state, by comparison, is information that identifies the relative position of the current record within a group of records, based on an index. Together, these two features permit you to add easy-to-maintain capabilities to your applications.

If you are unfamiliar with either aggregates or group state, you might be wondering why they are being covered together in this chapter. The answer is simple. Both are associated with grouping level, which is an index-related feature. Because the discussion of aggregates necessarily involves grouping level, the coverage of group state is a natural addition. This section begins with a look at aggregates. Group state is covered later in this section.

Using Aggregates

An aggregate is an object that can automatically perform a simple descriptive statistical calculation across one or more records in a ClientDataSet. For example, imagine that you have a ClientDataSet that contains a list of all purchases made by your customers. If each record contains fields that identify the customer, the number of items purchased, and the total value of the purchase, an aggregate can calculate the sum of all purchases across all records in the table. Another aggregate can calculate the average number of items purchased by each customer, and a third aggregate can calculate the average cost of a given customer's items.

ClientDataSet aggregates support a total of five statistics. These are: Count, minimum, maximum, sum, and average.

There are two types of objects that you can use to create aggregates: Aggregates and AggregateFields. An Aggregate is a CollectionItem descendant, and an AggregateField is a descendant of the TField class.

While these two aggregate types are similar in how you configure them, they differ in their use. Specifically, an AggregateField, because it is a TField descendant, can be associated with data-aware controls, permitting the aggregated value to be displayed automatically. By comparison, an Aggregate is an object whose value must be explicitly read at runtime.

One characteristic shared by both types of aggregates is that they require quite a few specific steps to configure them. If you have never used aggregation in the past, be patient. If your aggregates do not appear to work at first, you probably missed one or more steps. However, after you get comfortable configuring aggregates, you will find that they are relatively easy to use.

Because AggregateField instances are somewhat easier to use, we will consider them first. Using Aggregates is discussed later in this chapter.

Creating Aggregate Fields

AggregateFields are virtual, persistent fields. While they are similar to other virtual, persistent fields, such as calculated and lookup fields, there is one very important difference. Specifically, introducing one or more aggregate fields does not preclude the automatic, runtime creation of dynamic fields.

By comparison, creating at least one other type of persistent field, such as a data field, lookup field, or calculated field, prevents the ClientDataSet from creating any other Fields for that ClientDataSet at runtime. These runtime-created fields are referred to as *dynamic fields*. As a result, you can always create AggregateFields at design time, whether or not you intend to instantiate any other Field instances at design time.

> Note: The code project AggregatesAndGroupState is available from the code download. See Appendix A.

As mentioned earlier, adding an aggregate requires a number of specific steps in order to configure it correctly. These are:

- Add an AggregateField or an Aggregate collection item to a ClientDataSet. AggregateFields can be added at design time using the Fields Editor, or at runtime using the AggregateField's constructor. Aggregate collection items are added using the Aggregates property editor at design time, or by calling the Aggregate's constructor at runtime.

- Set the aggregate's Expression property to define the calculation that the aggregate will perform.

- Set the aggregate's IndexName property to identify the index on which to base grouping level.

- Set the aggregate's GroupingLevel property to identify which records to perform the aggregation across.

- Set the aggregate's Active property to True to activate it.

- Set the aggregate's Visible property to True.

- Set the AggregatesActive property of the ClientDataSet to which the aggregate is associated to True.

Because there are so many steps here, and some of them must be performed before others, it is best to learn how to create an AggregateField by doing it. Use the following steps in Delphi to create a simple project to which you will add an AggregateField:

1. Create a new VCL Forms Application project.

2. Add to your main form a DBNavigator, a DBGrid, a ClientDataSet, a DataSetProvider, a Table, and a DataSource.

3. Set the Align property of the DBNavigator to alTop, and the Align property of the DBGrid to alClient.

4. Next, set the DataSource property of both the DBNavigator and the DBGrid to DataSource1.

5. Now set the DataSet property of DataSource1 to ClientDataSet1.

6. Select Table1 and set its DatabaseName property to DBDEMOS and the TableName property to orders.db.

7. Set the DataSet property of the DataSetProvider to Table1.

8. Set the ProviderName property of the ClientDataSet to DataSetProvider1.

9. Finally, set the Active property of the ClientDataSet to True. Your main form should look something like that shown in Figure 10-1.

OrderNo	CustNo	SaleDate	ShipDate	EmpNo	ShipToContact	ShipToAddr1
▶ 1269	1221	12/16/1994	12/16/1994	28		
1271	1560	12/20/1994	12/20/1994	145		
1275	1351	12/22/1994	12/22/1994	20		
1278	1231	12/23/1994	12/23/1994	71		
1280	1356	12/26/1994	12/26/1994	118		
1283	1563	12/30/1994	12/30/1994	113		
1292	1354	1/1/1995	1/1/1995	136		
1294	1984	1/4/1995	1/4/1995	85		
1295	2156	1/6/1995	1/6/1995	45		
1296	5412	1/8/1995	1/8/1995	34		
1298	2315	1/9/1995	1/9/1995	11		
1300	1384	1/10/1995	1/10/1995	28		
1302	1231	1/16/1995	1/16/1995	52		
1305	1356	1/20/1995	1/20/1995	65		
1309	3615	1/22/1995	1/22/1995	94		
1315	1651	1/26/1995	1/26/1995	121		
1317	1984	2/1/1995	2/1/1995	138		

(DataSource1, ClientDataSet1, DataSetProvider1, Table1 components shown on form)

Figure 10-1: A newly created form

Adding the Aggregate Field

At design time, you add an AggregateField using the ClientDataSet's Fields Editor. Use the following steps to add an aggregate field.

1. Right-click the ClientDataSet and select Fields Editor.

2. Right-click the Fields Editor and select New Field (or press Ctrl-N). Delphi displays the New Field dialog box.

3. At Name, enter CustomerTotal and select the Aggregate radio button in the Field type area. Your New Field dialog box should now look something like that shown in Figure 10-2.

4. Click OK to close the New Field dialog box. You will see the newly added aggregate field in the Fields Editor, as shown here:

Notice that the newly added CustomerTotal field appears in its own little window at the bottom of the Fields Editor. All AggregateFields appear in this window, which serves to separate AggregateFields from any other dynamic fields. This separation serves to emphasize the distinction between AggregateFields and other virtual fields. As mentioned earlier in this chapter, this distinction is that the presence of persistent AggregateFields does not preclude the automatic creation of dynamic data fields.

Figure 10-2: A new virtual AggregateField being defined in the New Field Editor

Defining the Aggregate Expression

The Expression property of an aggregate defines the calculation the aggregate will perform. This expression can consist of constants, field values, and aggregate functions. The aggregate functions are AVG, MIN, MAX, SUM, and COUNT. For example, to define a calculation that will total the AmountPaid field in the ClientDataSet, you use the following expression:

```
SUM(AmountPaid)
```

The argument of the aggregate function can include two or more fields in an expression, if you like. For example, if you have two fields in your table, one named Quantity and the other named Price, you can use the following expression:

```
SUM(Quantity * Price)
```

The expression can also include constants. For example, if the tax rate is 8.25%, you can create an aggregate that calculates total plus tax, using something similar to this:

```
SUM(Total * 1.0825)
```

You can also set the Expression property to perform an operation on two aggregate functions, as shown here:

```
MIN(SaleDate) - MIN(ShipDate)
```

In addition, you can perform an operation between an expression function and a constant, as in the following:

```
MAX(ShipDate) + 30
```

You cannot, however, include an aggregate function as the expression of another aggregate function. For example, the following is illegal:

```
SUM(AVG(AmountPaid)) //illegal
```

Nor can you use an expression that contains a calculation between an aggregate function and a field. For example, if Quantity is the name of a field, the following expression is illegal:

```
SUM(Price) * Quantity //illegal
```

In the case of the CustomerTotal AggregateField, we want to calculate the total of the AmountPaid field. To do this, use the following steps:

1. Select the AggregateField in the Fields Editor. By default, this field should have the name ClientDataSet1CustomerTotal.

2. Using the Object Inspector, set the Expression property to SUM(AmountPaid) and its Currency property to True. Your Object Inspector should now look something like that shown in Figure 10-3.

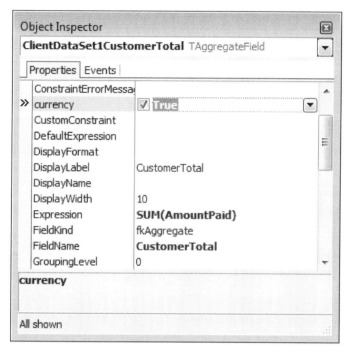

Figure 10-3: An AggregateField is being configured to calculate the total of the AmountPaid field

Setting Aggregate Index and Grouping Level

An aggregate needs to know across which records it will perform the calculation. This is done using the IndexName and GroupingLevel properties of the aggregate. Actually, if you want to perform a calculation across all records in a ClientDataSet, you can leave IndexName blank and GroupingLevel set to 0.

If you want the aggregate to perform its calculation across groups of records, you must have a persistent index whose initial fields define the group. For example, if you want to calculate the sum of the AmountPaid field separately for each customer, and a customer is identified by a field name CustNo, you must set IndexName to the name of a persistent index whose first field is CustNo. If you want to perform the calculation for each customer for each purchase date, and you have fields named CustNo and SaleDate, you must set IndexName to the name of a persistent index that has CustNo and SaleDate as its first two fields (the order of these fields in the index is irrelevant).

The persistent index whose name you assign to the IndexName property can have more fields than the number of fields you want to group on. This is where GroupingLevel comes in. You set GroupingLevel to the number of fields of the index that you want to treat as a group.

For example, imagine that you set IndexName to an index based on the CustNo, SaleDate, and PaymentMethod fields. If you set GroupingLevel to 0, the aggregate calculation will be performed across all records in the ClientDataSet. Setting GroupingLevel to 1 performs the calculation for each customer (since CustNo is the first field in the index). Setting GroupingLevel to 2 will perform the calculation for each customer for each sale date (since these are the first two fields in the index).

It is interesting to note that the TIndexDef class type, the class type used to define a persistent index, also has a GroupingLevel property. If you set this property for the index, the index will contain additional information about record grouping. So long as you are setting an aggregate's GroupingLevel to a value greater than 0, you can improve the performance of the aggregate by setting the persistent index's GroupingLevel to a value at least as high as the aggregate's GroupingLevel. Note, however, that a persistent index whose GroupingLevel property is set to a value greater than 0 takes a little longer to generate and update, since it must also produce the grouping information. This overhead is minimal, but should be considered if the speed of index generation and maintenance are concerns.

The following steps walk you through the process of creating a persistent index on the CustNo field, and then setting the AggregateField to use this index with a grouping level of 1:

1. Select the ClientDataSet in the Object Inspector and select its IndexDefs property. Click the ellipsis button of the IndexDefs property to display the IndexDefs collection editor.

2. Click the Add New button in the IndexDefs collection editor toolbar to add a new persistent index.

3. Select the newly added index in the IndexDefs collection editor. Using the Object Inspector, set the Name property of this IndexDef to CustIdx, its Fields property to CustNo, and its GroupingLevel property to 1. Close the IndexDefs collection editor.

4. With the ClientDataSet still selected, set its IndexName property to CustIdx.

5. Next, using the Fields Editor, once again select the AggregateField. Set its IndexName property to CustIdx, and its GroupingLevel property to **1**. The Object Inspector should look something like that shown in Figure 10-4.

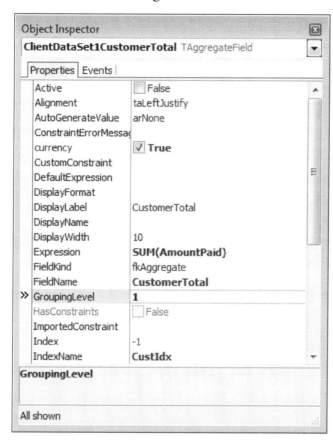

Figure 10-4: The AggregateField is configured to calculate the sum of AmountPaid for each customer

Making the Aggregate Field Available

The AggregateField is almost ready. In order for it to work, however, you must set both the AggregateField's Active and Visible properties to True. In addition, you must set the ClientDataSet's AggregatesActive property to True. After doing this, the aggregate will automatically be calculated when the ClientDataSet is made active.

With AggregateFields, there is one more step than with Aggregates, which is to associate the AggregateField with a data-aware control (if this is what you want to do).

The following steps demonstrate how to activate the AggregateField, as well as make it visible in the DBGrid:

1. With the AggregateField selected in the Object Inspector, set its Active property to True and its Visible property to True.

2. Next, select the ClientDataSet and set its AggregatesActive property to True and its Active property to True. At this point, the aggregate value is being calculated for each customer in the ClientDataSet. However, it is not yet visible in the DBGrid. The following steps will make the new AggregateField visible.

3. Right-click the DBGrid and select Columns to display the Columns collection editor.

4. Click the Add All button on the Columns collection editor toolbar to add persistent columns for each dynamic field in the ClientDataSet. If you were to scroll to the bottom of the Columns collection editor, you will notice that the AggregateField was not added. That is something that you will have to do manually.

5. Click the Add New button on the Columns collection editor toolbar to add one more Column to the collection:

6. With this new Column selected, use the Object Inspector to set its FieldName property to CustomerTotal. Setting this property also has

the side effect of changing the name of the new Column in the Columns Editor. Next, change the position of this Column in the Columns Editor by dragging it the sixth position, immediately below the EmpNo Column, as shown here:

If you have followed all of these steps correctly, your newly added AggregateField should be visible in the sixth column of your DBGrid, as shown in the Figure 10-5.

OrderNo	CustNo	SaleDate	ShipDate	EmpNo	CustomerTotal	ShipToContact	ShipToAddr1
1269	1221	12/16/1994	12/16/1994	28	$51,450.80		
1023	1221	7/1/1988	7/2/1988	5	$51,450.80		
1176	1221	7/26/1994	7/26/1994	52	$51,450.80		
1076	1221	12/16/1994	4/26/1989	9	$51,450.80		
1123	1221	8/24/1993	8/24/1993	121	$51,450.80		
1169	1221	7/6/1994	7/6/1994	12	$51,450.80		
1173	1231	7/16/1994	7/16/1994	127	$85,643.60		
1178	1231	8/2/1994	8/2/1994	24	$85,643.60		
1160	1231	6/1/1994	6/1/1994	110	$85,643.60		
1202	1231	10/6/1994	10/6/1994	145	$85,643.60		
1102	1231	6/6/1992	6/6/1992	105	$85,643.60		
1302	1231	1/16/1995	1/16/1995	52	$85,643.60		
1278	1231	12/23/1994	12/23/1994	71	$85,643.60		
1060	1231	2/28/1989	3/1/1989	94	$85,643.60		
1073	1231	4/15/1989	4/16/1989	2	$85,643.60		
1163	1351	6/14/1994	6/14/1994	83	$260,325.80		
1055	1351	2/4/1989	2/5/1989	29	$260,325.80		

Figure 10-5: The configured AggregateField appears next to the EmpNo field in the DBGrid

Turning Aggregates On and Off

A couple of additional comments about active aggregates are in order. First, the ClientDataSet's AggregatesActive property is one that you might find yourself turning on and off at runtime. Setting AggregatesActive to False is extremely useful when you must add, remove, or change a lot of records at runtime. If you make changes to a ClientDataSet's data, and these changes affect the aggregate calculation, these changes will be much slower if AggregatesActive is True since the aggregate calculations will be updated with each and every change. As a result, you may want to set AggregatesActive to False before changing many records. When you later set AggregatesActive to True, any aggregates associated with that ClientDataSet will then be recalculated, one time.

Rather than turning all aggregates off or on, the Active property of individual aggregates can be manipulated at runtime. This can be useful if you have many aggregates, but only need one or two to be updated during changes to the ClientDataSet. Subsequently turning other aggregates back on will immediately trigger their recalculation. At runtime, you can read the ClientDataSet's ActiveAggs TList property to see which aggregates are currently active for a given grouping level.

Creating Aggregate Collection Items

Aggregate collection items, like aggregate fields, perform the automatic calculation of simple descriptive statistics. However, unlike AggregateFields, Aggregates must be read at runtime in order to use their values.

Aggregate collection items cannot be hooked up to data-aware controls. But with that exception in mind, nearly all other aspects of the configuration of aggregate collection items are the same as for AggregateFields.

The following steps demonstrate how to add and use an Aggregate collection item in a project. These steps assume that you have been following along with the steps provided earlier to define the AggregateField:

1. Select the ClientDataSet in the Object Inspector and select its Aggregates property. Click the ellipsis button to display the Aggregates collection editor:

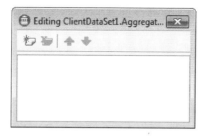

2. Click the Add New button twice on the Aggregates collection editor's toolbar to add two aggregates to your ClientDataSet.

3. Select the first Aggregate in the Aggregates collection editor. Using the Object Inspector, set the aggregate's Expression property to AVG(AmountPaid), its AggregateName property to CustAvg, its IndexName property to CustIdx, its GroupingLevel property to 1, its Active property to True, and its Visible property to True.

4. Select the second Aggregate in the Aggregates collection editor. Using the Object Inspector, set its Expression property to MIN(SaleDate), its AggregateName property to FirstSale, its IndexName property to CustIdx, its GroupingLevel property to 1, its Active property to True, and its Visible property to True.

5. Add a PopupMenu from the Standard page of the Tool Palette to your project. Using the Menu Designer (double-click the PopupMenu to display this editor), add a single MenuItem, setting its caption to "About this customer."

6. Set the PopupMenu property of the DBGrid to PopUpMenu1.

7. Finally, add the following event handler to the Add this customer MenuItem:

```
procedure TForm1.Aboutthiscustomer1Click(Sender: TObject);
begin
  ShowMessage('The average sale to this customer is ' +
  Format('%.2m',
    [StrToFloat(ClientDataSet1.Aggregates[0].Value)]) +
    '. The first sale to this customer was on '+
    DateToStr(ClientDataSet1.Aggregates[1].Value));
end;
```

If you now run this project, your main form should look something like that shown in the Figure 10-6.

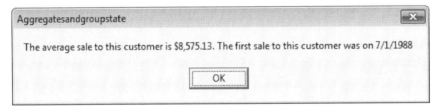

Figure 10-6: A project with one AggregateField and two Aggregates

To see the values calculated by the Aggregate collection items, right-click a record and select About this customer. The displayed dialog box should look something like this:

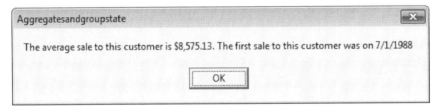

Understanding Group State

Group state refers to the relative position of a given record within its group. Using group state, you can discover whether the current record is the first record in its group (given the current index), the last record in its group, neither the last nor the first record in the group, or the only record in the group. You determine group state for the current record by calling the ClientDataSet's GetGroupState method. This method has the following syntax:

```
function GetGroupState(Level: Integer): TGroupPosInds;
```

When you call GetGroupState, you pass an integer indicating grouping level. Passing a value of 0 (zero) to GetGroupState will return information about the current record's relative position within the entire ClientDataSet. Passing a value of 1 will return the current record's group state with respect to the first field of the current index, passing a value of 2 will return the current record's group state with respect to the first two fields of the current index, and so on.

GetGroupState returns a set of TGroupPosInd flags. TGroupPosInd is declared as follows:

```
TGroupPosInd = (gbFirst, gbMiddle, gbLast);
```

As should be obvious, if the current record is the first record in the group, GetGroupState will return a set containing the gbFirst flag. If the record is the last record in the group, this set will contain gbLast. When GetGroupState is called for a record somewhere in the middle of a group, the gbMiddle flag is returned. Finally, if the current record is the only record in the group, GetGroupState returns a set containing both the gbFirst and gbLast flags.

GetGroupState can be particularly useful for suppressing redundant information when displaying a ClientDataSet's data in a multi-record view, like that provided by the DBGrid component. For example, consider the preceding figure of the main form. Notice that the CustomerTotal AggregateField value is displayed for each and every record, even though it is being calculated on a customer-by-customer basis. Not only is the redundant aggregate data unnecessary, it makes reading the data more difficult (this is a signal-to-noise ratio type problem).

Using GetGroupState, you can test whether or not a particular record is the last record for the group, and if so, display the value for the CustomerTotal field. For records that are not the last record in their group (based on the CustIdx index), you can suppress the display of the data. Displaying total amounts for a customer in the last record for that customer serves to emphasize the fact that the calculation is based on all of the customer's records.

Determining group state and suppressing or displaying the data can be achieved by adding an OnGetText event handler to the CustomerTotal AggregateField. The following is the OnGetText event handler for the ClientDataSet1CustomerTotal AggregateField in the AggregatesAndGroupState project:

```
procedure TForm1.ClientDataSet1CustomerTotalGetText(Sender: TField;
  var Text: String; DisplayText: Boolean);
begin
  if gbLast in ClientDataSet1.GetGroupState(1) then
    Text := Format('%.2m',[StrToFloat(Sender.Value)])
  else
    Text := '';
end;
```

If you think about it, you might also want to suppress the CustNo field for all but the first records in the group. This event handler can be associated the CustNo field at design time, but only if you have added persistent data fields for all of the fields that you want displayed in the DBGrid. If you want to use dynamic fields with your DBGrid, you will need to hook the OnGetText event handler to the dynamic CustNo field at runtime.

The following is the OnGetText event handler associated with the persistent ClientDataSet1CustNo data field in the AggregatesAndGroupState project:

```
procedure TForm1.ClientDataSet1CustNoGetText(Sender: TField;
  var Text: String; DisplayText: Boolean);
begin
  if gbFirst in ClientDataSet1.GetGroupState(1) then
    Text := Sender.Value
  else
    Text := '';
end;
```

If you want to hook this event handler to a dynamic CustNo field at runtime, you can do this using something similar to the following from the OnCreate event handler of your form:

```
ClientDataSet1.FieldByName('CustNo').OnGetText :=
  ClientDataSet1CustNoGetText;
```

Figure 10-7 shows the main form of the running AggregatesAndGroupState project, which demonstrates the techniques described in this chapter. Notice that the CustNo and CustomerTotal fields are displayed only for the first and last records in each group, respectively.

Creating AggregateFields at Runtime

You learned how to create data fields and calculated fields at both design time and runtime in Chapter 4, *Defining a ClientDataSet's Structure*. As described in that chapter, one reason that you might defer the creation of Fields until runtime is that you might not know until runtime which types of fields you will need. For example, the structure of a given table may be based on the needs of the individual users, in which case you provide them with some sort of interface where they select the types of data they need to store, and you then create the table structure programmatically based on that input.

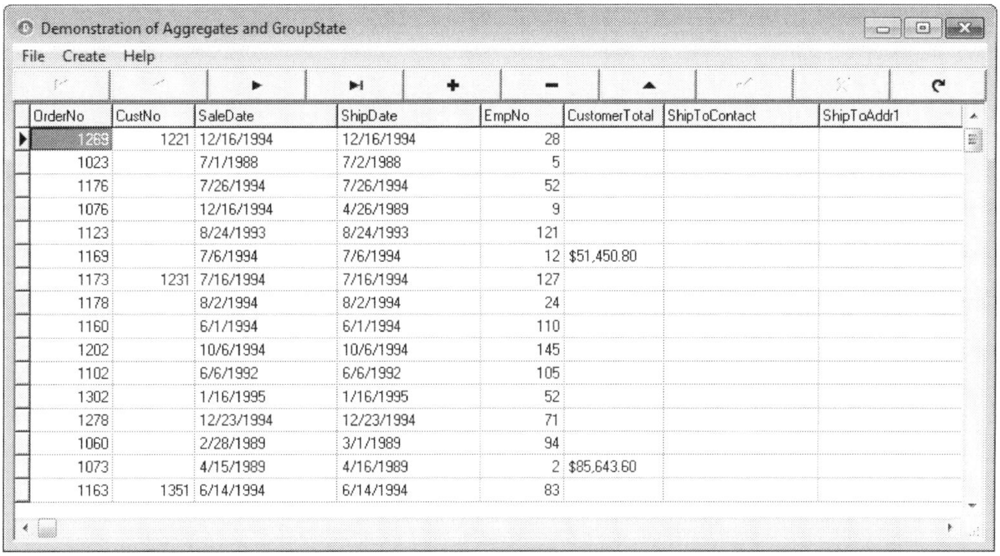

OrderNo	CustNo	SaleDate	ShipDate	EmpNo	CustomerTotal	ShipToContact	ShipToAddr1
1269	1221	12/16/1994	12/16/1994	28			
1023		7/1/1988	7/2/1988	5			
1176		7/26/1994	7/26/1994	52			
1076		12/16/1994	4/26/1989	9			
1123		8/24/1993	8/24/1993	121			
1169		7/6/1994	7/6/1994	12	$51,450.80		
1173	1231	7/16/1994	7/16/1994	127			
1178		8/2/1994	8/2/1994	24			
1160		6/1/1994	6/1/1994	110			
1202		10/6/1994	10/6/1994	145			
1102		6/6/1992	6/6/1992	105			
1302		1/16/1995	1/16/1995	52			
1278		12/23/1994	12/23/1994	71			
1060		2/28/1989	3/1/1989	94			
1073		4/15/1989	4/16/1989	2	$85,643.60		
1163	1351	6/14/1994	6/14/1994	83			

Figure 10-7: GroupState is used to display CustNo and CustomerTotal values for selected records within a group

AggregateFields, because of their potential uses in analytics, are more likely than many other field types to be unknown in advance, and therefore need to be created at runtime. For example, you may provide users with an interface where they can specify the types of statistics that they want to see for groups of their data. You can then create those AggregateFields on-the-fly.

In short, creating AggregateFields, as well as Aggregate collection items, at runtime requires the same type of configuration as does creating those objects at design time. The obvious difference is that you cannot use the design tools, such as the Fields Editor or the Object Inspector, to set the various properties at runtime.

The creation of a new AggregateField at runtime is demonstrated in the code associated with the AggregatesAndGroupState project. This code can be found on the OnClick event handler for the menu item labeled Create Aggregate. This event handler is shown in the following code segment:

```
procedure TForm1.NewAggregateField1Click(Sender: TObject);
begin
  ClientDataSet1.DisableControls;
  ClientDataSet1.Close;
  try
    with TAggregateField.Create(Self) do
    begin
      FieldName := 'NumberOfSales';
      Expression := 'COUNT(OrderNo)';
      IndexName := 'CustIdx';
```

```
      GroupingLevel := 1;
      Active := True;
      Visible := True;
      Name := 'ClientDataSet1NumberOfSales';
      DataSet := ClientDataSet1;
    end;
    with DBGrid1.Columns.Add do
    begin
      FieldName := 'NumberOfSales';
      Title.Caption := 'Number of Sales';
      Index := 6;
    end;
    //Hook up the OnGetText event handler
    ClientDataSet1.FieldByName('NumberOfSales').OnGetText :=
      ClientDataSet1GetNumberSales;
    //Disable the menu to that creates the new AggregateField
    Create1.Enabled := False;
  finally
    //Enable controls and re-open the ClientDataSet
    ClientDataSet1.EnableControls;
    ClientDataSet1.Open;
  end;
end;
```

As you can see from this code, the event handler begins by disabling the ClientDataSet, which will prevent its subsequent closing from causing a flicker on the DBGrid. Next, the AggregateField is created and configured. Then, a new Column is added to the DBGrid for the display of this new virtual field. The new Column is put in position 7 of the DBGrid, which will cause it to be display to the right of the CustomerTotal field.

Next, the OnGetText event handler is set to the ClientDataSet1GetNumberSales method. Like the ClientDataSet1CustomerTotalGetText method used by the CustomerTotal field, this event handler displays the count of orders in the last record of the group. Unlike the ClientDataSet1CustomerTotalGetText event handler, however, it does not format the number as a currency value.

The following is the code associated with the ClientDataSet1GetNumberSales method:

```
procedure TForm1.ClientDataSet1GetNumberSales(Sender: TField;
  var Text: String; DisplayText: Boolean);
begin
  if gbLast in ClientDataSet1.GetGroupState(1) then
    Text := Sender.Value
  else
    Text := '';
end;
```

The menu item used to create this AggregateField is then disabled (since trying to create another persistent field using the same name would raise an exception). Finally, the ClientDataSet is hooked back to its DataSource by calling EnableControls, and the ClientDataSet is re-opened.

If you run this project, and select Create | New AggregateField, the main form will look something like that shown in Figure 10-8.

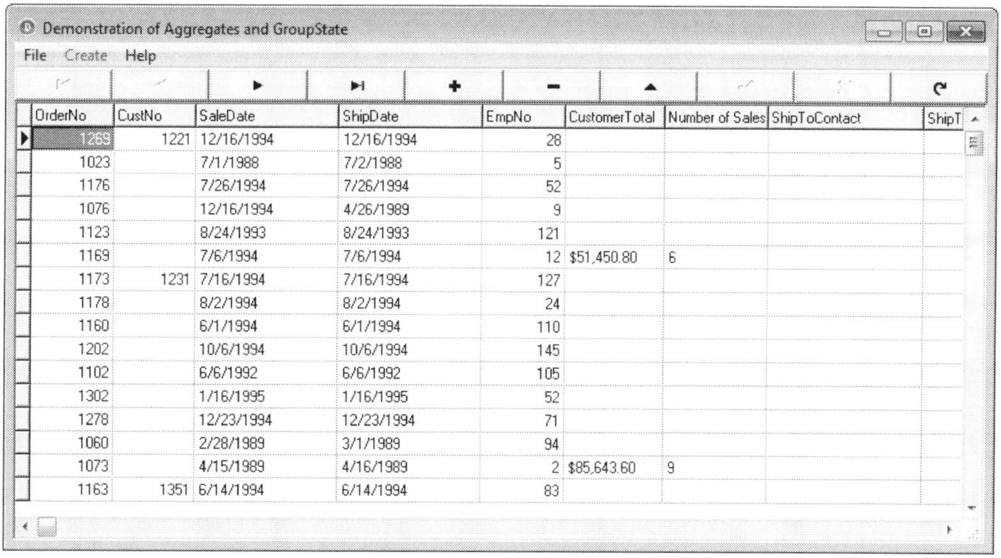

Figure 10-8: An AggregateField has been added to the ClientDataSet and the DBGrid at runtime

In the next chapter you will learn how to clone a ClientDataSet's cursor.

Chapter 11
Cloning ClientDataSet Cursors

Normally, the data that you load into a ClientDataSet is retrieved from another DataSet or from a file. But what do you do when you need two different views of the same data at the same time?

One alternative is to load a second copy of the data into a second ClientDataSet. This approach, however, results in an unnecessary increase in network traffic (or disk access) and places redundant data in memory. In some cases, a better option is to clone the cursor of an already populated ClientDataSet. When you clone a cursor, you create a second, independent pointer to an existing ClientDataSet's memory store, including Delta (the change cache). Importantly, the cloned ClientDataSet has an independent current record, filter, index, provider, and range.

It is difficult to appreciate the power of cloned cursors without actually using them, but some examples can help. I have mentioned several times already in earlier chapters in this book that the data held by a ClientDataSet is stored entirely in memory. Imagine that you have loaded 25,000 records into a ClientDataSet, and you want to compare two separate records in that ClientDataSet programmatically.

One approach is to locate the first record and save some of its data into local variables. You can then locate the second record and compare the saved data to that in the second record. Yet another approach is to load a second copy of the data in memory. You can then locate the first record in one ClientDataSet, the second record in the other ClientDataSet, and then directly compare the two records.

A third approach, and one that has advantages over the first two, is to utilize the one copy of data in memory, and clone a second cursor onto this memory store. The cloned ClientDataSet cursor appears as if it were a second copy of the data in memory, in that you now have two cursors (the original and the clone), and each can point to a different record and utilize a different index. Importantly, only one copy of the data is stored in memory, and the cloned cursor provides a second, independent pointer into it. You can then point the original cursor to one record, the cloned cursor to the other, and directly compare the two records.

Here's another example. Imagine that you have a list of customer invoices stored in memory using a ClientDataSet. Suppose further that you need to display this data to the end user using two different sort orders, simultaneously. For example, imagine that you want to use one DBGrid to display this data sorted by customer account number, and another DBGrid to display this data by invoice date.

While your first inclination might be to load the data twice using two ClientDataSets, a cloned cursor performs the task much more efficiently. After loading the data into a single ClientDataSet, you can use a second ClientDataSet to clone the cursor of the first. The first ClientDataSet can be sorted by customer account number and the second can be sorted by invoice date. Even though the data appears in memory only once, each of the ClientDataSets contains a different view.

Cloning a cursor is easy. The hard part involves changing how you think about a ClientDataSet's data. The ClientDataSet is the only DataSet that ships with Delphi that supports cloned cursors. As a result, even if you have extensive experience with other DataSets, unless you've used ClientDataSet cloned cursors, this technique is likely to be unfamiliar to you.

This chapter begins with a look at the fundamentals of cloning a ClientDataSet's cursor. Later sections of this chapter show you several different, yet valuable, techniques that would be almost impossible to do without the ability to clone a ClientDataSet's cursor.

Cloning a ClientDataSet's Cursor

You clone a ClientDataSet's cursor by invoking a ClientDataSet's CloneCursor method. This method has the following syntax:

```
procedure CloneCursor(Source :TCustomClientDataSet;
  Reset: Boolean; KeepSettings: Boolean = False);
```

When you invoke CloneCursor, the first argument that you pass is a reference to an active ClientDataSet whose cursor you want to clone. The second parameter, Reset, is used to either keep or discard the original ClientDataSet's view. If you pass a value of False, the values of the IndexName (or IndexFieldNames), Filter, Filtered, MasterSource, MasterFields, OnFilterRecord, and ProviderName properties are set to match that of the source ClientDataSet. Passing True in the second parameter resets these properties to their default values. (A special case with respect to filters is discussed later in this section.)

For example, if you invoke CloneCursor, passing a value of True in the second parameter, the cloned ClientDataSet's IndexFieldNames property will contain an empty string, regardless of the value of the IndexFieldNames property of the original ClientDataSet. To put this another way, the cloned cursor may or may not start out with similar properties to the ClientDataSet from which it was cloned, depending on the second parameter.

You include the third, optional parameter, passing a value of True, typically in conjunction with a Reset value of False. In this situation, the properties of the cloned cursor match that of the original dataset, but may not actually be valid, depending on the situation. In most cases, a call to CloneCursor only includes the first two parameters.

Although the cloned cursor may not share many view-related properties with the ClientDataSet it was cloned from, it may present a view that nearly matches the original. For example, the current record of a cloned cursor is typically the same record that was current in the original. Similarly, if a ClientDataSet uses an index to display records in a particular order, the clone's natural order will match the indexed view of the original, even though the IndexName or IndexFieldNames properties of the clone may be empty.

This view duplication also applies to ranges. Specifically, if you clone a ClientDataSet that has a range set, the clone will employ that range, regardless of the values you pass in the second and third parameters. However, you can easily change that range, by either setting a new range or dropping the range by calling the ClientDataSet's CancelRange method. These ranges are independent, however, in that each ClientDataSet pointing to a common memory store can have a different range, or one can have a range and the other can employ no range.

Note: In general, I think it is a good idea to make few assumptions about the view of a cloned cursor. In other words, your safest bet is to clone a cursor, passing a value of True in the Reset formal parameter. If you pass a value of False in the Reset parameter, I suggest that you insert a comment or Todo List item into your code, and document how you expect the view of the clone to appear. Doing so may help you fix problems that could potentially be introduced if future implementations of the CloneCursor method change the view of the clone.

A single ClientDataSet can be cloned any number of times, creating many different views and many different current records for the same data store.

Furthermore, you can clone a clone to create yet another pointer to the original data store. You can even clone the clone of a clone. It really does not matter. There is a single data store, and at least one ClientDataSet points to it, whether or not it was created by cloning.

Here is another way to think of this. Once a ClientDataSet is cloned, the clone and the original have equal status, as far as the memory store is concerned. For example, you can load one ClientDataSet with data, and then clone a second ClientDataSet from it. You can then close the original ClientDataSet, either by calling its Close method or by setting its Active property to False (or even by calling Free). Importantly, the clone will remain open. To put this another way, so long as one of the ClientDataSets remains open, whether it was the original ClientDataSet used to load the data or a clone, the data and change cache remain in memory.

Why this works this way is easier to understand when you recall that a ClientDataSet's memory store is an OleVariant. OleVariants are reference counted. As long as one ClientDataSet is referring to the memory store, it stays in memory. When the last ClientDataSet referring to a particular memory stored closes or gets freed, the OleVariant holding the data is released from memory.

Note: The code project CloneAndFilter is available from the code download. See Appendix A.

Cloning a is demonstrated in the ViewData form of the CloneAndFilter project, which is based closely on the CDSFilter project discussed in Chapter 9, *Filtering ClientDataSets*. The ViewData form of this project is shown in Figure 11-1.

What is different about this project, when compared to the CDSFilter project, is that it includes two additional buttons at the top of the main form. These buttons are labeled Clone Cursor with Reset and Clone Cursor without Reset. As the labels imply, the first button clones a ClientDataSet with True passed in the second parameter of the CloneCursor method, and the second button clones a cursor with False passed in the second parameter.

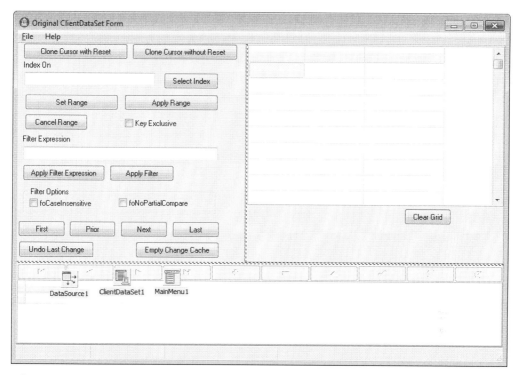

Figure 11-1: The main form of the CloneAndFilter project

The OnClick event handlers for these two buttons are shown in the following code segment:

```
procedure TViewData.CloneResetBtnClick(Sender: TObject);
var
  ViewData: TViewData;
begin
  ViewData := TViewData.Create(Application, True);
  ViewData.ClientDataSet1.CloneCursor(Self.ClientDataSet1, True);
  ViewData.CancelRangeBtn.Enabled := Self.CancelRangeBtn.Enabled;
  ViewData.Caption := 'Cloned ClientDataSet with Reset';
  ViewData.Show;
end;

procedure TViewData.CloneNoResetBtnClick(Sender: TObject);
begin
  ViewData := TViewData.Create(Application, True);
  ViewData.ClientDataSet1.CloneCursor(Self.ClientDataSet1, False);
  ViewData.CancelRangeBtn.Enabled := Self.CancelRangeBtn.Enabled;
  ViewData.Caption := 'Cloned ClientDataSet without Reset';
  ViewData.Show;
end;
```

The overloaded constructor called from these event handlers takes a Boolean second parameter. As seen in the following code segment, this overloaded constructor assigns a value to a private member field of the form named

FCloning. This variable is used by the OnCreate event handler to detect whether or not it is being called by the form's inherited constructor. If it is, it loads the ClientDataSet from the BigCDS.cds file. If it is not, the ClientDataSet gets its data from a cloned cursor. This extra code is necessary since many different copies of the ViewData form may be created at runtime.

```
constructor TViewData.Create(AOwner: TComponent; Cloning: Boolean);
begin
  FCloning := Cloning;
  inherited Create(AOwner);
end;

procedure TViewData.FormCreate(Sender: TObject);
begin
  if not FCloning then
  begin
    ClientDataSet1.FileName := ExtractFilePath(Application.ExeName) +
      '\..\bigcds\bigcds.cds';
    if not FileExists(ClientDataSet1.FileName) then
    begin
      ShowMessage('BigCDS.cds not found. This project requires this ' +
        'file, and expects to find it in the folder named BigCDS, ' +
        'which should be located in the folder directly above ' +
        ExtractFilePath(Application.ExeName) + '. Cannot continue.');
      Abort;
    end;
    ClientDataSet1.Open;
  end;
  StringGrid1.RowCount := 2;
  StringGrid1.ColCount := 3;
  StringGrid1.Cells[0,0] := 'Field Name';
  StringGrid1.Cells[1,0] := 'Start Range';
  StringGrid1.Cells[2,0] := 'End Range';
  StringGrid1.FixedRows := 1;
  StringGrid1.FixedCols := 1;
end;
```

Here is the code that is associated with the OnCreate event handler of the main form. This form creates the first copy of the ViewData form:

```
procedure TForm1.FormCreate(Sender: TObject);
begin
  Self.SetBounds(1, 1, Self.Width, Self.Height);
  with TViewData.Create(Self) do
    Show;
end;
```

As you can see from this event handler, the main form repositions itself to the upper-left corner of the screen, after which it creates and displays the first instance of the ViewData form. The simple main form is shown here:

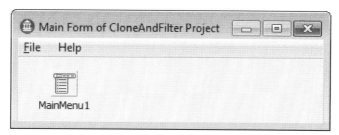

There are two additional buttons located just above the DBGrid on the ViewData form. These buttons permit you to call the ClientDataSet's UndoLastChange and ClearChanges methods, respectively, so you can see how changes to the change cache affect all ClientDataSets sharing a common data stored. These event handlers are shown in the following code segment:

```
procedure TViewData.UndoLastBtnClick(Sender: TObject);
begin
  ClientDataSet1.UndoLastChange(True);
end;

procedure TViewData.CancelChangesBtnClick(Sender: TObject);
begin
  ClientDataSet1.CancelUpdates;
end;
```

You will gain a better understanding of cloned cursors if you run this project and then observe what happens when you clone one or more cursors. For example, there are two instances of the ViewData form shown in Figure 11-2. One of these instances employs an index, and the second, a clone, does not. Although there is only one copy of BigCDS.cds in memory, the ClientDataSets on the two forms are sharing the single memory store.

If you run this project, and then create one or more clones, you will observe that navigation on one form has no affect on the other forms. Nor does changing an index, setting a range, or applying a filter.

On the other hand, if you post a change to data on one form, that change is immediately visible to all of the other forms. How and why is described in the next section.

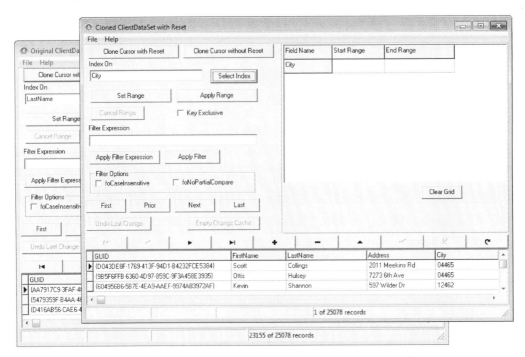

Figure 11-2: Both of these forms display data from a single in-memory data store

The Shared Data Store

The fact that all clones share a common data store has some important implications. Specifically, any changes made to the common data store directly affect all ClientDataSets that use it. For example, if you delete a record using a cloned cursor, the record instantly appears to be deleted from all ClientDataSets pointing to that same store and an associated record appears in the change cache (assuming that the ClientDataSet's LogChanges property is set to True, its default value). Similarly, calling ApplyUpdates from any of the ClientDataSets attempts to apply the changes in the change cache.

Likewise, if you have at least one change in the change cache, calling RevertRecord, or even CancelChanges, affects the shared change cache. For example, if you delete a record from a cloned ClientDataSet, it will appear to be instantly deleted from the views of all the ClientDataSets associated with the single data store. If you then call UndoLastChange on one of the ClientDataSets, that deleted record will be removed from the change cache, and will instantly reappear in all of the associated ClientDataSets.

There is another point, one that has been alluded to earlier in this chapter. When you are using cloned cursors, the memory store belongs to all of the

ClientDataSets equally. To say this a bit differently, the memory store does not belong to the original ClientDataSet that loaded the data. In fact, you can free the ClientDataSet that originally loaded the data, and any existing ClientDataSets created by cloning the freed ClientDataSet will continue to function perfectly. It is even possible to load a ClientDataSet, make some changes to data, clone the ClientDataSet, free the original, and then call ApplyUpdates on the clone. Assuming that the properties of the clone associate it with a properly configured DataSetProvider (something that you may have to do programmatically), the changes will be correctly applied to the underlying database.

You can actually test this using the CloneAndFilter project. This project makes this possible because it contains a main form separate from the instances of ViewData. This main form simply displays the first instance ViewData, causing it to load the ClientDataSet from the BigCDS.cds file.

If you run the CloneAndFilter project, and then create a clone, you can then close the form with the caption Original ClientDataSet Form. Any remaining cloned cursors will continue to display the data from the shared memory store, and can also be used to create new clones.

Cloning a Filtered ClientDataSet: A Special Case

Similar to cloning a ClientDataSet that uses a range, there is an issue with cloning ClientDataSets that are filtered. Specifically, if you clone a ClientDataSet that is currently being filtered (its Filter property is set to a filter expression and Filtered is True), and you pass a value of False (no reset) in the second parameter of the CloneCursor invocation, the cloned ClientDataSet will also employ the filter. However, unlike when a cloned cursor has a range, which can be canceled, the cloned cursor will necessarily be filtered. In other words, in this situation, the clone can never cancel the filter it gets from the ClientDataSet it was cloned from. (Actually, you can apply a new filter to the filtered view, but that does not cancel the original filter. It merely adds an additional filter on top of the original filter.)

This effect does not occur when Filter is set to a filter expression and Filtered is set to False. Specifically, if Filter is set to a filter expression and Filtered is False, cloning the cursor with a Reset value of False will cause the cloned view to have a filter expression, but it will not be filtered. Furthermore, you can set an alternative Filter expression, and set or drop the filter, in which case, the clone may include more records than the filtered ClientDataSet from which it was cloned.

The discrepancy in the way a non-reset clone works with respect to the Filtered property is something that can potentially cause major problems in your application. Consequently, I suggest that you pass a value of True in the Reset formal parameter of CloneCursor if you are cloning an actively filtered ClientDataSet. You can then set the filter on the clone, in which case the filters will be completely independent.

Cloning Examples

Cloning a cursor is easy, but until you see it in action, it is hard to really appreciate the power that cloned cursors provide. The CloneAndFilter project does a nice job of demonstrating the basics of cloned cursors, but it does little to incite the imagination about how cloned cursors can be applied in a real world environment.

This section discusses two examples where cloned cursors perform tasks that would otherwise be difficult or impossible to duplicate. In the first example, a single table is used to produce a self-referencing master-detail view of its data. The second example demonstrates how to delete a range of values from a ClientDataSet without needing to first set an index on a ClientDataSet that is displaying the data from which the range will be deleted.

Self-Referencing Master-Details

Most database developers have some experience creating master-detail views of data. This type of view, sometimes also called a one-to-many view or a parent-child view, involves displaying the zero or more records from a detail table that are associated with the currently selected record in a master table. You can easily create this kind of view using the MasterSource and MasterFields properties of a ClientDataSet, given that you have two tables with the appropriate relationship (such as the sample customer.db and orders.db Paradox tables that ship with Delphi).

Note: Creating dynamic master-detail relationships between tables using MasterSource and MasterFields is discussed in some detail in Chapter 12, Using Nested DataSets.

While most master-detail views involve two tables, what do you do if you want to create a similar effect using a single table? In other words, what if you want to select a record from a table and display other related records from that same table in a separate view?

Sounds weird? Well, not really. Consider the items.db Paradox table that ships with Delphi. Each record in this file contains an order number, a part number, the quantity ordered, and so forth. Imagine that when you select a particular part associated with a given order, you also want to see, in a separate view, all orders from this same table in which this same part was ordered. In this example, all of the data resides in a single table (items.db).

Note: The code project MasterDetailClone is available from the code download. See Appendix A.

Fortunately, cloned cursors give you a powerful way of displaying master-detail relationships within a single table. This technique is demonstrated in the MasterDetailClone project.

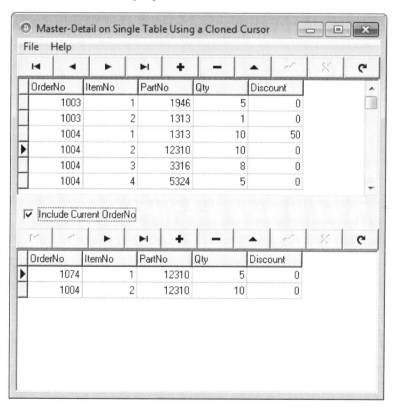

Figure 11-3: Selecting a record in the top DBGrid displays all orders containing this same part number in the bottom DBGrid. Both DBGrids display data from a single memory store

The main form of this running project can be seen in the Figure 11-3. Notice that when a record associated with part number 12310 is selected (in this case, for order number 1004), the detail view, which appears in the lower grid on this form, displays all orders that include part number 12310 (including order number 1004).

This form also contains a checkbox that permits you to either include or exclude the current order number from the detail list. When this checkbox is not checked, the current order in the master table does not appear in the detail view, as shown in Figure 11-4.

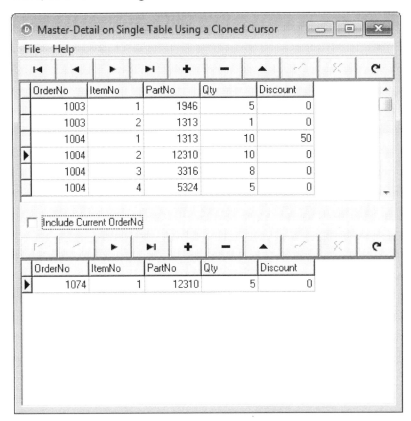

Figure 11-4: When Include Current OrderNo is not checked, the bottom DBGrid displays all other orders in which this same part was ordered.

The detail view is created in the MasterDetailClone project using a cloned cursor of the master table (ClientDataSet1) from the OnCreate event handler of the main form. The following is the code associated with this event handler:

```
procedure TForm1.FormCreate(Sender: TObject);
begin
  ClientDataSet1.Open;
  //Assign the OnDataChange event handler after
  //opening the ClientDataSet
  DataSource1.OnDataChange := DataSource1DataChange;
```

```
  //Clone the detail cursor.
  ClientDataSet2.CloneCursor(ClientDataSet1, True);
  //Create and assign an index to the cloned cursor
  ClientDataSet2.AddIndex('PartIndex','PartNo',[]);
  ClientDataSet2.IndexName := 'PartIndex';
  ClientDataSet2.Filtered := True;
  //Invoke the OnDataChange event handler to
  //create the detail view
  DataSource1DataChange(Self, PartFld);
end;
```

Once this ClientDataSet1 is opened, there are three additional steps that must occur in order for this technique to work.

The first step is that an OnDataChange event handler, which creates the detail view, is assigned to DataSource1. This is the DataSource that points to ClientDataSet1. Once this assignment is made, the detail table view is updated each time OnDataChange is invoked (which occurs each time a change is made to ClientDataSet1, as well as each time ClientDataSet1 arrives at a new current record). The runtime assignment of this event handler is necessary to prevent this event handler from triggering upon the opening of the ClientDataSet, which would fail since the cloned cursor has not been created yet.

The second operation performed by this event handler is the cloning of the detail table cursor, assigning an appropriate index, and setting the cloned cursor's Filtered property to True. In this project, the order of steps one and two are interchangeable.

The third step is to invoke the OnDataChange event handler of DataSource1. This invocation causes the cloned cursor to display its initial detail view.

As must be obvious from this discussion, the OnDataChange event handler actually creates the detail view. The following is the relevant code associated with this event handler:

```
var
  PartFld: TField;

procedure TForm1.DataSource1DataChange(Sender: TObject; Field:
TField);
begin
  PartFld := ClientDataSet1.FieldByName('PartNo');
  ClientDataSet2.SetRange([PartFld.AsString], [PartFld.AsString]);
  if not IncludeCurrentOrderCbx.Checked then
    ClientDataSet2.Filter := 'OrderNo <> ' +
      QuotedStr(ClientDataSet1.FieldByName('OrderNo').AsString)
  else
    ClientDataSet2.Filter := '';
end;
```

The var declaration declares a Field variable, which is used by the OnDataChange event handler. The first line of code in this event handler assigns a reference to the part number field of ClientDataSet1 to this Field variable. The value of this Field is then used to create a range on the cloned cursor. This produces a detail view that includes all records in the clone whose part number matches the part number of the current master table record.

The remainder of this event handler is associated with the inclusion or exclusion of the order for the master table's current record from the detail table. If the Include Current OrderNo checkbox is not checked, a filter that removes the master order number is assigned to the cloned cursor's Filter property (remember that Filtered is set to True). This serves to suppress the display of the master table's order number from the detail table. If Include Current OrderNo is checked, an empty string is assigned to the clone's Filter property.

That last piece of interesting code in this project is associated with the OnClick event handler of the Include Current OrderNo checkbox. This code, shown in the following method, simply invokes the OnDataChange event handler of DataSource1 to update the detail view:

```
procedure TForm1.IncludeCurrentOrderCbxClick(Sender: TObject);
begin
  DataSource1DataChange(Self, ClientDataSet1.Fields[0]);
end;
```

Although this project is really quite simple, I think the results are nothing short of fantastic.

Deleting a Range of Records

This next example further demonstrates how creative use of a cloned cursor can provide you with an alternative mechanism for performing a task. In this case, the task is to delete a range of records from a ClientDataSet.

Without using a cloned cursor, you might delete a range of records from a ClientDataSet by searching for records in the range and deleting them, one by one. Alternatively, you might set an index and use the SetRange method to filter the ClientDataSet to include only those records you want to delete, which you then delete, one by one.

Whether you use one of these approaches, or some similar technique, your code might also need to be responsible for restoring the pre-deletion view of the ClientDataSet, particularly if the ClientDataSet is being displayed in the user interface. For example, you would probably want to note the current record before you begin the range deletion, and restore that record as the current record when done (so long as the previous current record was not one of those that were deleted). Similarly, if you had to switch indexes in order to perform the deletion, you would likely want to restore the previous index.

Using a cloned cursor to delete the range provides you with an important benefit. Specifically, you can perform the deletion using the cloned cursor without having to worry about the view of the original ClientDataSet. Once you clone the cursor, you perform all changes to the ClientDataSet's view on the clone, leaving the original view undisturbed.

Note: The code project CDSDeleteRange is available from the code download. See Appendix A.

The following is the CDSDeleteRange function found in the CDSDeleteRange project:

```
function CDSDeleteRange(SourceCDS: TClientDataSet;
  const IndexFieldNames: String;
  const StartValues, EndValues: array of const): Integer;
var
  Clone: TClientDataSet;
begin
  //initialize number of deleted records
  Result := 0;
  Clone := TClientDataSet.Create(nil);
  SourceCDS.DisableControls;
  try
    Clone.CloneCursor(SourceCDS, True);
    Clone.IndexFieldNames := IndexFieldNames;
    Clone.SetRange(StartValues, EndValues);
    while Clone.RecordCount > 0 do
    begin
      Clone.Delete;
      Inc(Result);
    end;
  finally
    SourceCDS.EnableControls;
    Clone.Free;
  end;
end;
```

This function begins by creating a temporary ClientDataSet, which is cloned from the ClientDataSet passed to this function in the first parameter. The clone is then indexed and filtered using a range, after which all records in the range are deleted.

Figure 11-5 shows the running CDSDeleteRange project. This figure depicts the application just prior to clicking the button labeled Delete Range. As you can see in this figure, the range to be deleted includes all records in which the State field contains the value CA.

Note: While this example project includes only one field in the range, in practice you can have up to as many fields in the range as there are fields in the current index. For more information on SetRange, see Chapter 9, Filtering ClientDataSets.

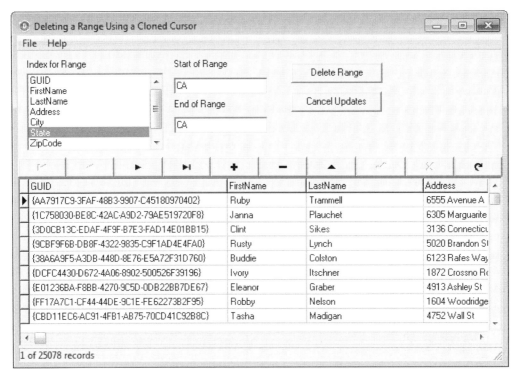

Figure 11-5: Prior to the deletion of records from the State CA, there were 25,078 records in the ClientDataSet

The following is the code associated with the OnClick event handler of the button labeled Delete Range. As you can see, the deletion is performed simply by calling the CDSDeleteRange:

```
procedure TForm1.DeleteRangeButtonClick(Sender: TObject);
begin
if (Edit1.Text = '') and (Edit2.Text = '') then
  begin
    ShowMessage('Enter a range before attempting to delete');
    Exit;
  end;
  Screen.Cursor := crHourGlass;
  try
    ShowMessage(IntToStr(CDSDeleteRange(ClientDataSet1,
```

```
      IndexListBox.Items[IndexListBox.ItemIndex],
      [Edit1.Text],[Edit2.Text])) + ' records were deleted');
  finally
    Screen.Cursor := crDefault;
  end;
end;
```

Figure 11-6 shows this same application immediately following the deletion of the range. Note that because the deletion was performed by the clone, the original view of the displayed ClientDataSet is undisturbed, with the exception, of course, of the removal of the records in the range. Also, because operations performed on the data store and change cache are immediately visible to all ClientDataSets using a shared in-memory dataset, the deleted records immediately disappear from the displayed grid, without requiring any kind of refresh.

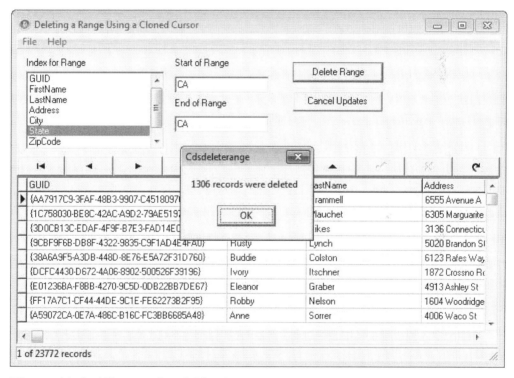

Figure 11-6: All records within the range were deleted by a cloned cursor, which precluded the need to change the current ClientDataSet index

Since all of the deletions remain in the change cache, it is also possible to restore those deleted records. The button labeled Cancel Updates can be used to clear the change cache, which restores any records that were deleted. The following code segment shows the OnClick event handler for the button labeled Cancel Updates:

```
procedure TForm1.CancelUpdatesButtonClick(Sender: TObject);
begin
  ClientDataSet1.DisableControls;
  try
    ClientDataSet1.CancelUpdates;
  finally
    ClientDataSet1.EnableControls;
  end;
end;
```

The use of the ClientDataSet's DisableControls and EnableControls methods in this event handler is necessary since the canceling of the change cache triggers the OnDataChange event handler once for each restored record, which is the event handler that updates the status bar record count indicator. Actually, this was a behavior that I did not expect, but you can easily see it if you comment out the DisableControls call in this event handler.

I have to admit, I really like this example. It is a nice demonstration of a cloned cursor being used to perform background tasks on a ClientDataSet with minimal impact on data-aware controls that might be displaying the contents of the data store. Keep in mind, however, that the point of this example is not about deleting records. The point is that a cloned cursor provides an attractive alternative mechanism for performing a task involving the data in a ClientDataSet.

In the next chapter you will learn how to create nested datasets.

Chapter 12
Using Nested DataSets

A nested dataset is what it sounds like — a dataset within a dataset. More specifically, a nested dataset is a Field of type DataSetField, and this Field can hold the row-column structure of a DataSet.

For example, imagine that you have a table that holds information about a company's employees. Such a table could have one field to hold the employee ID, another to hold their name, and another to hold their job title. Imagine further that you also want to keep track of each employee's dependants, possibly for health insurance reasons. One way to do that would be to add another field to the employee table of type DataSetField, and to store information about each employee's dependants in that field.

Since the DataSetField holds a DataSet, it can hold zero or more records with one or more columns (which are defined by Field instances). For example, the first column might be a StringField to hold the name of the dependant. The second column might be an IntegerField to hold a code that identifies the type of dependant (spouse, child, and so forth). A third DateTimeField might hold the dependant's date of birth. A nested dataset can have as many fields as any ClientDataSet, and may actually include one or more DataSetFields.

The DataSetField is special in that it is almost like each record of the Employee table has its own embedded table for holding the dependants' records. When you are on the record for a particular employee, the size of the nested dataset is based on how many dependants have been entered for that employee, and that number might be zero, or two, or whatever. If you navigate to the next employee record, the nested dataset for that record will have a structure identical to that in the preceding record, but the data will be different in that only the dependants' records for that employee will appear in the DataSetField.

If you are familiar with database design, you might raise objections to storing multiple pieces of information in a single field since this is normally frowned upon. Instead, you may prefer to have one table for employees and another for employee's dependants. Better still, you may have a single table that holds people, and that table may include all employees and their dependants, as well as any other individuals you need to store information about in your database. You then may have another table that stores the various relationships between the individuals who appear in your people table, such as supervisor-supervised, and employee-dependant.

But that is not the point. In most cases a nested dataset is not about the structure of your underlying database. (Most databases do not support the concept of a nested dataset field anyway.) Instead, a nested dataset is designed to store a related table of data in a single column of a record within a ClientDataSet (no other DataSets in Delphi can do this). For example, while you may actually store employees and their dependants in two separate tables (or a single table), that data can be loaded into a ClientDataSet in such a way that dependants appear in nested datasets.

Actually, there are two specific reasons for using nested datasets. The first applies when you want to use a ClientDataSet in MyBase applications, where the ClientDataSet is acting as a stand-alone database. In those cases, nested datasets permit you to store related data about numerous entities in a single ClientDataSet file.

The second reason is when you want to work with related data from an underlying relational database in a manner that permits the ClientDataSet to efficiently manage those relationships. For example, the data being loaded into a ClientDataSet may be associated with two or more related tables in your database, and those relationships can be embodied by nested datasets.

Once in memory, that related data can be edited. So long as the change cache is active, that data can subsequently be resolved back to the underlying database. Importantly, since nested datasets represent the master-detail association between related records in the underlying database, the ClientDataSet and its DataSetProvider can observe necessary rules for applying those changes back to the database.

For example, when a master record has been deleted, the DataSetProvider knows that all detail records associated with the nested dataset must be deleted before the master record can be deleted. However, inserted master records must be inserted prior to the insertion of the related child records. Fortunately, all of this can be done with a single call to ApplyUpdates on the ClientDataSet that contains the nested datasets. Furthermore, all rules associated with transactions and MaxErrors apply to both the ClientDataSet, as well as its nested datasets.

Loading data from multiple tables into a ClientDataSet using nested datasets has another benefit besides providing intelligent update resolution. The use of nested datasets makes it very easy to transfer and persist data associated with related tables. For example, a briefcase application may need to load related data from a database server before disconnecting. When nested datasets are used, this related data can be persisted to a single ClientDataSet file, and later restored from that file, with all data relationships intact. Briefcase applications were introduced in Chapter 3, *Saving Data with ClientDataSets and DataSetProviders.*

Similarly, when used in distributed applications, such as DataSnap applications, transferring data obtained from multiple tables in an underlying database between a server and a client using nested datasets not only increases efficiency of the transfer, but also perfectly maintains the relationships. That the change cache understands the relationships defined by nested datasets means that updates made to any data in such a ClientDataSet can be returned from the client to the server, and the server can then apply those updates efficiently and correctly, to the underlying tables.

Each ClientDataSet can support up to 15 nested datasets. Each of those nested datasets can support up to 15 additional nested datasets, and so on. There are two important aspects about these numbers. First, very complex relationships can be represented through the use of nested datasets. For example, a master-detail-subdetail relationship (three levels) can be handled easily. Second, when numerous nested datasets are involved, the memory requirements of the ClientDataSet can get large very fast. This is important because there is an upper limit to the amount of data that a given ClientDataSet can hold.

The remainder of this chapter focuses on the creation and use of nested datasets in ClientDataSets. In the first section, you will learn how to configure a ClientDataSet to create nested datasets automatically in response to loading master-detail data from a DataSetProvider. This section also discusses how to persist and navigate the contents of a nested dataset, though this information applies to any nested dataset, not just those obtained through a DataSetProvider.

The remaining sections in this chapter focus on creating the structure of ClientDataSets manually where you want to introduce one or more nested datasets. These sections demonstrate creating DataSetFields using either FieldDefs or Fields, both at design time and at runtime.

Nested DataSets and Dynamic Master-Detail Links

When a ClientDataSet obtains its data from a DataSetProvider, and that DataSetProvider points to a DataSet that represents the master table in a dynamic master-detail relationship, the detail tables are loaded into the ClientDataSet as nested datasets. If one or more of the detail tables in the dynamic relationship are themselves master tables to additional detail tables, those detail tables will be represented as nested datasets within nested datasets.

There are two ways in Delphi to define a master-detail relationship between two DataSets. If the detail table is similar to a Table (such as an ADOTable, an IBTable, a SQLTable, or even a ClientDataSet), you link it to a master table using the detail table's MasterSource and MasterFields properties.

MasterSource must point to a DataSource that in turn points to the master table. MasterFields defines which fields form the relationship between the master and the detail. Configuring dynamic master-detail relationships this way also requires that you set the detail table to use an index that orders the detail records according to the detail table's foreign key, the field or fields that represent the relationship between the tables. I will walk through an example of configuring a master-detail relationship using this technique a bit later in this section, so I won't go into any more detail right now.

If your detail DataSet supports an interface similar to a Query (such as an ADOQuery or a SQLQuery), the dynamic master-detail relationship is defined using a parameterized query. The query must include one or more named parameters, and each parameter name must match the name of the corresponding field in the master table on which the relationship is based. For example, if your detail table is the orders.db Paradox table, and the master table is the customer.db Paradox table, you can dynamically link a customer's orders to a customer by setting the detail DataSet's query to the following:

```
SELECT * FROM ORDERS WHERE CustNo = :custno
```

In this query, the named parameter is :custno. When the detail DataSet's DataSource property points to a DataSet that loads its data from customer.db, the :custno parameter will dynamically bind to the CustNo field of the customer.db table.

Once a dynamic master-detail link has been defined, and the master table is active, navigation in the master table will cause a dynamic filtering of the detail table. For example, using the customer.db and orders.db table, each time you navigate to a new customer, the detail DataSet is filtered to display only the orders for the current customer in the master DataSet.

Creating a Dynamic Master-Detail Link

Creating a dynamic master-detail link requires attention to detail, and when done using the MasterSource and MasterFields properties, it requires that your detail DataSet has an appropriate index. The use of a dynamic master-detail link is demonstrated in the MasterDetailLink project.

Note: The code project MasterDetailLink is available from the code download. See Appendix A.

The MasterDetailLink project is unlike many that you have encountered in this book in that it is a partially complete project. I describe a number of its characteristics here so it is a good idea if you open this project and follow the steps I describe later to make changes to this project.

When you first open this project (or compile and run it without changes), it shows you the results of a dynamic master-detail link. We will later use that dynamic master-detail link to create a nested dataset.

The main form of the MasterDetailLink project is shown in Figure 12-1. In this figure, the master table data is displayed in the upper DBGrid, and the detail table data is displayed in the lower DBGrid. Notice that the detail table is displaying only those orders for CustNo 1221.

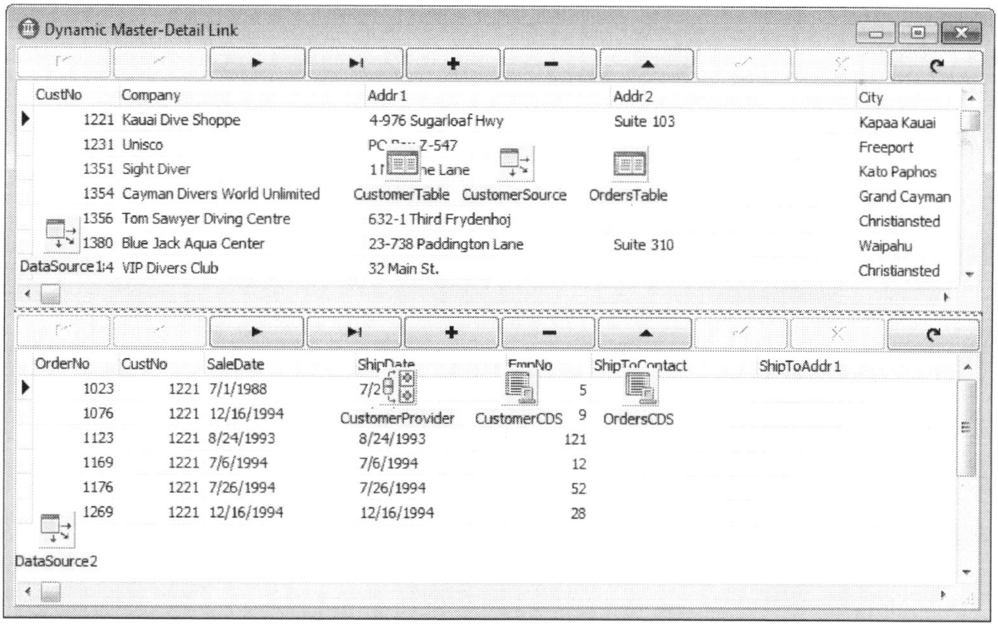

Figure 12-1: The results of a dynamic master-detail link

Let's begin by taking a closer look at the dynamic master-detail link. The Table named CustomerTable is associated with the customer.db Paradox table that ships with Delphi. DataSource1, the DataSource for DBGrid1, the upper DBGrid, points to CustomerTable. The Table named OrdersTable is associated with the orders.db Paradox table. DataSource2, the DataSource for DBGrid2, points to OrdersTable.

OrdersTable is the detail table of the dynamic master-detail link. The MasterSource property of OrdersTable points to CustomerSource (a DataSource), which in turn points to CustomerTable.

Note: You might be wondering why there are two different DataSources that point to CustomerTable when one would be enough. The answer is that DataSource1 and DataSource2 are being used to connect data-aware controls to DataSets. By comparison, CustomerSource is being used to link a detail table to a master table. Since these are different roles, I prefer to use two different DataSources.

While we're on this topic, in the real world I would have placed CustomerTable, CustomerSource, and OrdersTable in a data module. I would have then used that data module from this form. (CustomerProvider, CustomerCDS, and OrdersCDS would also have been placed on that data module, but we have not really discussed them yet.) In that case, it would make even more sense to use two different DataSources to point to CustomerTable. DataSource1, because it is related to the user interface, would remain on the main form, while CustomerSource would be moved to the data module.

The dynamic link from OrdersTable to CustomerTable also requires an appropriate index as well as a MasterFields definition. With Table DataSets, this is done with the Field Link Designer, shown in Figure 12-2. You display the Field Link Designer by selecting the MasterFields property of the detail Table and clicking the ellipsis button.

In this case, I selected the CustNo index. Once the index was selected, the Detail Fields list listed the one field associated with this index, which is CustNo. Next, I selected CustNo from Detail Fields and CustNo from Master Fields, and then clicked the Add button. Clicking Add defined the Joined Fields value. Once OK is clicked, just the name of the master field was entered into the MasterFields property (since the detail table field name is known by way of the index on the detail table).

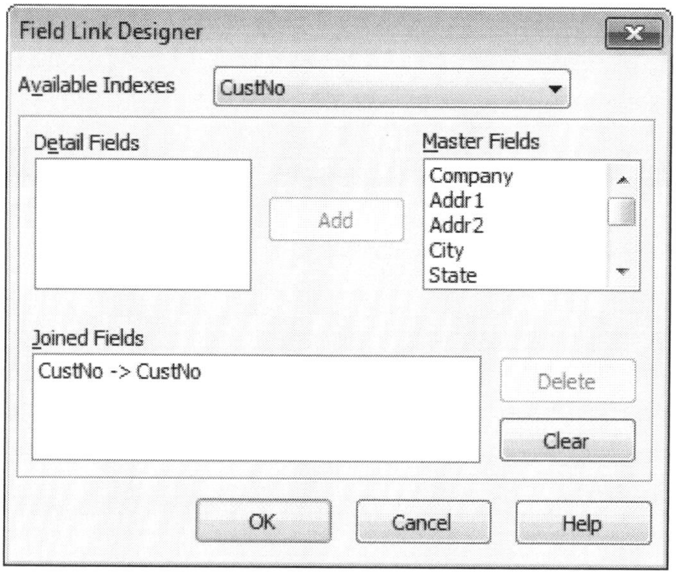

Figure 12-2: The Field Link Designer

Note: Not all DataSets support the Field Link Designer. For those that do not, you must first manually set IndexName to the appropriate index. Then, you enter the name of the field or fields of the master DataSet that map to the corresponding field or fields of the detail table, based on the fields defined in the selected index. If there are two or more fields in the link, separate them with semicolons.

Once these properties have been set, making these DataSets active produces the master-detail link you see in Figure 12-1. If you run this project, and then use the top DBNavigator to navigate the master table, you will see the detail table refreshing with only the associated orders as you move through the master table, as seen in Figure 12-3.

If you want to see the master-detail link in action from the design-time interface, double-click CustomerTable (or right-click it and select Fields Editor) to display the Fields Editor. Using the little navigator control at the top of the Fields Editor, you can navigate to the top or end of the associated active DataSet, as well as move forward and backward one record at a time. In Figure 12-4, the Fields Link Editor was used to navigate the master table to the third record, which caused the detail table to update, displaying only orders for CustNo 1351.

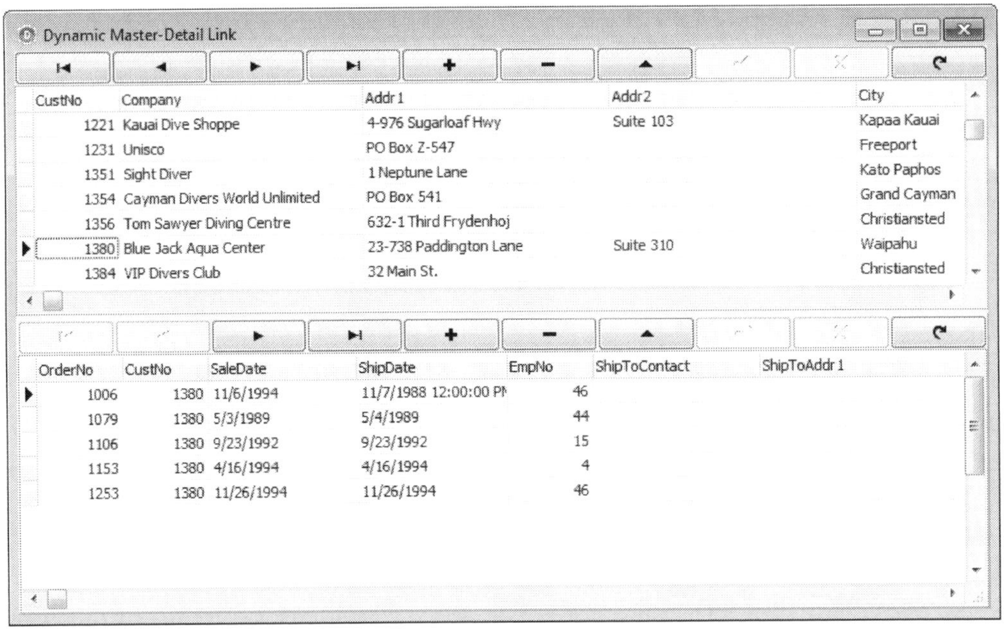

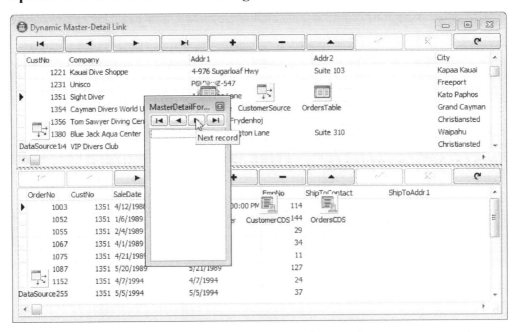

Figure 12-3: The dynamic master-detail link causes the detail table to update after each master table navigation

Figure 12-4: The Fields Editor includes a navigator that you can use to navigate at design time

Loading Master-Detail Links from a DataSetProvider

Now that you understand how dynamic master-detail links work, we will convert the MasterDetailLink project to use ClientDataSets and an automatically created nested dataset. While the following steps walk through the process of converting MasterDetailLink, the code disk includes a project named NestedFromMasterDetail that contains the finished project.

Note: *The code project NestedFromMasterDetail is available from the code download. See Appendix A.*

1. Begin by changing DataSource1 and DataSource 2 to point their DataSet properties to CustomerCDS and OrdersCDS, respectively. The DBGrids should now appear empty.

2. CustomerProvider is already pointing to CustomerTable in its DataSet property, and CustomerCDS is referring to CustomerProvider through its ProviderName property. As a result, all you need to do now is to open CustomerCDS by setting its Active property to True. The data of CustomerCDS is now visible in the top DBGrid.

The mere act of activating the ClientDataSet when its DataSetProvider points to the master table of a dynamic master-detail link is sufficient to create the nested dataset. This nested data appears as the last dynamic field in the CustomerCDS structure. This can be seen in Figure 12-5, which shows the CustomerCDS data displayed in the top DBGrid at design time. In this figure, the top DBGrid scroll bar was used to shift to the right-most (last) field in the DBGrid. This field, named OrdersTable, is the nested dataset.

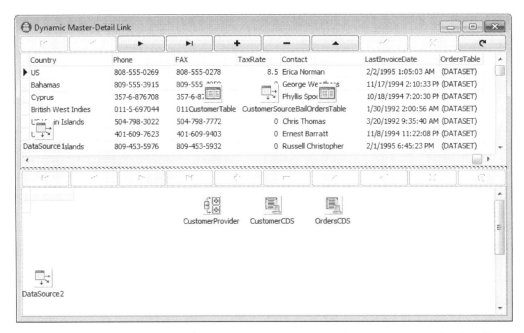

Figure 12-5: The DataSetField named OrdersTable was created by loading a ClientDataSet from a DataSetProvider that points to a master table of a dynamic master-detail link

The Default Nested DataSet Form

When a ClientDataSet includes one or more nested datasets, the DBGrid supplies a form that contains a grid that you can use to display the contents of, and even edit, the nested dataset. Use the following steps to demonstrate using this grid:

1. Run the project (either your modified version of MasterDetailLink or NestedFromMasterDetail).

2. Use the scroll bar or Tab key to display the right-most field in the top DBGrid. This field is named OrdersTable.

3. Click once to select this field, and then click once again to attempt to edit this field. After the second click on the field, an ellipsis appears:

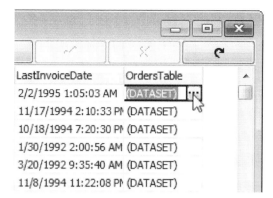

4. If you now click that ellipsis, a DBGrid-like form is created dynamically and displayed, as shown in Figure 12-6. This is the default nested dataset form.

OrderNo	CustNo	SaleDate	ShipDate
► 1005	1356	4/20/1988	1/21/1988 12:00:00 P
1059	1356	2/24/1989	2/25/1989
1072	1356	4/11/1989	4/12/1989
1080	1356	5/5/1989	5/6/1989
1105	1356	7/21/1992	7/21/1992
1180	1356	8/6/1994	8/6/1994
1266	1356	12/15/1994	12/15/1994
1280	1356	12/26/1994	12/26/1994

Figure 12-6: Nested datasets can be viewed and even edited with the default nested dataset form. Display this form by attempting to edit a DataSetField and then clicking the ellipsis

The default nested dataset form is limited, but has a few interesting properties. One of these is that you can leave this form open, and then go back to the DBGrid on which the nested dataset appears and navigate to another record. With each successful navigation, the contents of the default nested dataset form are updated with nested data associated with the new master record. Furthermore, if one of the fields in the nested dataset is a nested dataset, you can attempt to edit that field from the default nested dataset form and another default nested dataset form will open with that nested dataset's contents.

Customizing Nested DataSet Views

I repeatedly mentioned the limited capabilities of the default nested dataset form that DBGrids provide for editing nested datasets. If you refer back to Figure 12-6, you can see some of these limitations. To begin with, the form has no caption. It also has no navigator control.

As a result, most developers who want to provide users with access to nested datasets use an alternative approach. In short, there are two techniques that you can use. One is to include one or more data-aware controls on the same form on which the master DataSet is displayed, and display the nested data in those controls. The second approach is to display the nested dataset in a separate form, but with customizations not provided by the default nested datasets form. Both of these approaches require you to assign the data-aware controls to a DataSource, which in turn must point to the nested dataset from its DataSet property.

There are two ways to point a DataSource to a nested dataset. The easiest, and only way that you can achieve this at design time, is to employ an additional ClientDataSet for each of the nested datasets. You then associate each new ClientDataSet with the underlying DataSetField that exists for each of the nested datasets. This is done using the ClientDataSet DataSetField property.

Use the following steps to associate OrdersCDS with the nested dataset in the CustomerCDS table:

1. Begin by right-clicking CustomerCDS to display its context menu, and select Fields Editor.

2. Right-click in the Fields Editor and select Add All Fields. The ClientDataSet responds by creating persistent Fields for each of its columns, including one for the nested dataset, as seen here:

3. Next, select OrdersCDS. Using the Object Inspector, set DataSetField to CustomersCDSOrdersTable (the full name of the persistent DataSetField). Since DataSource2 is now pointing to OrdersCDS, the contents of the nested dataset appear in the lower DBGrid, as shown in Figure 12-7.

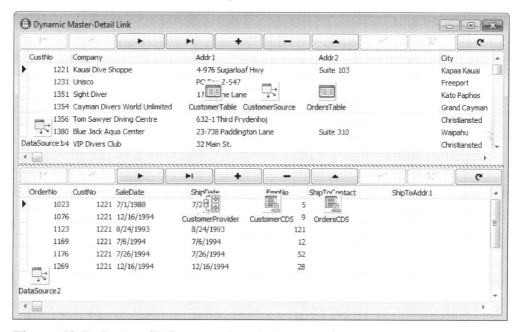

Figure 12-7: OrdersCDS now refers to the nested dataset through its DataSetField property, which can be set to a persistent DataSetField at design time

There is a second way to hook up a DataSource to a nested dataset, but this can only be done programmatically. Recall that a nested dataset is a field of a ClientDataSet of type DataSetField. DataSetFields have a property named NestedDataSet, and this property is of type TDataSet. In other words, the NestedDataSet property of a DataSetField can be assigned directly to the DataSet property of a DataSource.

The following code segment demonstrates how to make this assignment. If you want to test this code, begin by disassociating OrdersCDS from DataSource2. Then, add the following OnCreate event handler to the main form in the project you have been working with. After that, the nested dataset information will appear in the lower DBGrid at runtime.

```
procedure TMasterDetailForm.FormCreate(Sender: TObject);
begin
DataSource2.DataSet :=
 TDataSetField(CustomerCDS.FieldByName('OrdersTable')).NestedDataSet;
end;
```

Note: The preceding OnCreate event handler can be found in the NestedFromMasterDetail project. See Appendix A.

Nested DataSets and the Top-Level ClientDataSet

When using nested datasets, the top-level ClientDataSet serves a major role. In short, most of the major interactions that you have with ClientDataSets, such as saving them to a file, loading them from a file, calling ApplyUpdates, and even calling CreateDataSet, must only be performed on the top-level ClientDataSet. The top-level ClientDataSet in the MasterDetailLink project is named CustomerCDS.

When you call SaveToFile on a top-level ClientDataSet, the contents of the top-level ClientDataSet, as well as all nested datasets, are saved to that file. Likewise, if you call LoadFromFile on a top-level ClientDataSet, the top-level ClientDataSet is populated with both master table records as well as the nested datasets (and will recurse into any nested datasets contained within those nested datasets).

When using a ClientDataSet with a DataSetProvider, and nested datasets are involved, you only want to read the ChangeCount property of the top-level ClientDataSet. ChangeCount will return a positive number if there are any changes to the master table as well as changes to nested datasets. Similarly, you only call ApplyUpdates on the top-level ClientDataSet. As mentioned earlier in this chapter, calling ApplyUpdates applies updates to both the master table as well as to any nested datasets.

I am stressing this point because in many situations where nested datasets are involved, it is not uncommon to have two or more ClientDataSets referring to the data, where one ClientDataSet represents the top-level ClientDataSet, and additional ClientDataSets are associated with DataSetFields. For those additional ClientDataSets, you should not attempt to call SaveToFile or ApplyUpdates.

While there are a number of properties and methods that should only be used with the top-level ClientDataSet when nested datasets are involved, there are some methods that can be used with ClientDataSets associated with nested datasets. For example, you may often find it useful to programmatically navigate a ClientDataSet associated with a nested dataset. Likewise, you might want to filter a ClientDataSet associated with a nested dataset, or even set a range on one. But operations that affect the ClientDataSet as a whole should be reserved for the top-level ClientDataSet.

Creating Nested DataSets Explicitly

You learned in Chapter 4, *Defining a ClientDataSet's Structure,* how to configure the columns of a ClientDataSet both at design time as well as at runtime. You also learned that in most cases, you need to perform this task only when a ClientDataSet is not being populated through a DataSetProvider. (About the only time that you will define a ClientDataSet's structure for a ClientDataSet that will be populated from a DataSetProvider is when you need to define additional virtual fields, such as calculated fields. Doing so is a delicate process, as the structure defined for the ClientDataSet and that being loaded from the DataSetProvider must be compatible. This issue was discussed at length in Chapter 4.)

I deliberately avoided the topic of creating nested datasets in Chapter 4. The reason why is that defining a ClientDataSet's structure where one or more DataSetFields are involved can be a challenge. In fact, over the years, it is the one topic concerning ClientDataSets about which that I have received the most questions.

Most of the time, the question goes something like this: "I am trying to define a ClientDataSet with a nested dataset, but Delphi keeps raising an exception when I call CreateDataSet." I can sympathize. I have seen that message many times myself, and it can be frustrating to the point where you start to wonder if what you are trying to do is even possible.

Well, I am here to tell you that it is possible. You can add DataSetFields to a ClientDataSet using either FieldDefs or Fields. You can also add these DataSetFields at design time as well as at runtime.

But there is a little trick. All of your fields, both in the top-level ClientDataSet as well as in all nested datasets, must be defined before you can create the top-level ClientDataSet. In almost every occasion where defining a ClientDataSet with a nested dataset fails, there is at least one field that is undefined, set to an invalid field type for a ClientDataSet, or missing some other critical configuration.

Defining Nested DataSets at Design Time

This section will walk you through two examples of defining ClientDataSet structures that include nested datasets at design time. The first example uses FieldDefs, while the second employs Fields. For more details about design-time creation of FieldDefs and Fields, please refer to Chapter 4, *Defining a ClientDataSet's Structure.*

Before continuing, let me add a little warning. When you define the structure of a ClientDataSet at design time, always make sure to start with a fresh ClientDataSet. If there is any chance that your ClientDataSet already has one or more FieldDefs defined, IndexDefs defined, or persistent fields defined, any inconsistencies between those existing objects and the definition you are try to apply will make it impossible for Delphi to create the ClientDataSet structure.

Using FieldDefs at Design Time

You add a nested dataset to a ClientDataSet's structure at design time by adding at least one FieldDef of the data type ftDataSet to the top-level ClientDataSet. You then use the ChildDefs property of that added FieldDef to define the structure of the nested dataset. This is demonstrated in the following steps:

1. Create a new VCL Forms Application.

2. Add to the main form a DBNavigator, a DBGrid, a DataSource, and a ClientDataSet.

3. Align the DBNavigator to alTop, and the DBGrid to alClient. Also, set the DataSource properties of both the DBNavigator and the DBGrid to DataSource1.

4. Set the DataSource's DataSet property to ClientDataSet1.

5. Select the FieldDefs property of the ClientDataSet and click the ellipsis button to display the FieldDefs collection editor.

6. Using the FieldDefs collection editor, click the Add New button three times.

7. Select the first FieldDef in the FieldDefs collection editor and use the Object Inspector to set its DataType to ftString.

8. Select the second FieldDef and set its DataType to ftInteger.

9. Select the third FieldDef and set its DataType to ftDataSet. With the third FieldDef still selected, click the ChildDefs property in the Object Inspector, and then click the displayed ellipsis button to display the ChildDefs collection editor shown here:

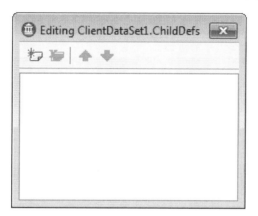

10. Using the ChildDefs collection editor, click the Add New button twice. Using the Object Inspector, set the DataType property of the first ChildDef to ftString, and the second ChildDef to ftDateTime. Close the ChildDefs collection editor when you are done. Also close the FieldDefs collection editor.

11. All of the FieldDefs have been defined. You can now create the ClientDataSet's structure in memory. To do this, right-click the ClientDataSet and select Create DataSet. Since DataSource1 is pointing to ClientDataSet1, and the DBGrid is pointing to DataSource1, the structure appears in the DBGrid, as shown in Figure 12-8.

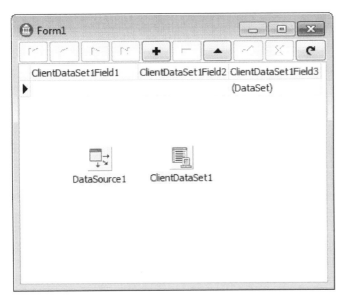

Figure 12-8: The newly created ClientDataSet structure includes a DataSetField. That nested dataset has two fields

If you had wanted the nested dataset in this example to include a nested dataset, you would have simply used the ChildDefs collection editor to add at least one ChildDef whose DataType you set to ftDataSet. You would then use the ChildDefs property of that new ChildDef to define the structure of that nested dataset.

Note: The code project DesigntimeNestedFieldDefs is available from the code download. See Appendix A.

Using Fields at Design Time

When you define a ClientDataSet using Fields, you are specifically defining persistent fields, with one data field for each field that the ClientDataSet can hold.

Use the following steps to define a ClientDataSet's structure that includes a nested dataset at design time using Fields:

1. Repeat steps 1 through 4 from the preceding demonstration to create a new project with a DBNavigator, DBGrid, DataSource, and ClientDataSet.

2. Right-click the ClientDataSet and select Fields Editor from the context menu.

3. Right-click the Fields Editor and select New Field.

4. Using the New Field dialog box, set Name to Field1, Type to String, Size to 20, and Field type to Data. Click OK to save the new field.

5. Right-click the Fields Editor and select New Field again.

6. Set Name to Field2, Type to Integer, and Field type to Data. Click OK to save this field.

7. Add one more field. This time set Name to Field3, Type to DataSetField, and Field type to Data. Click OK to continue.

8. At this point we have our structure for the top-level ClientDataSet, but Field3, being a DataSetField, needs to have structure as well. To define the structure for Field3 we need another ClientDataSet. Add a second ClientDataSet to the main form. This ClientDataSet should be named ClientDataSet2.

9. Select ClientDataSet2 and set its DataSetField property to ClientDataSet1Field3. This is the full name of the persistent field created by the designer when you created the nested dataset field.

10. Now, right-click ClientDataSet2 and select Fields Editor.

11. Using the Fields Editor, add a new field. Set Name to Field1, Type to String, Size to 20, and Field type to Data. Click OK to continue.

12. Create another new field. Set Name to Field2, Type to DateTime, and Field type to Data. Click OK one last time.

13. You have now completed the structure. Right-click ClientDataSet1 and select Create DataSet. The ClientDataSet structure is created, and the form now looks like that shown in Figure 12-9.

If we wanted to add a nested dataset to the nested dataset, we could have easily done this by adding a DataSet field to the ClientDataSet2 structure. We would then have to add another ClientDataSet to the form, set its DataSetField to point to the ClientDataSet2 DataSetField, and then use this new ClientDataSet to define the structure of this nested dataset. It's important to note that all of this must be done before the top-level ClientDataSet is created.

Note: The code project DesigntimeNestedFields is available from the code download. See Appendix A.

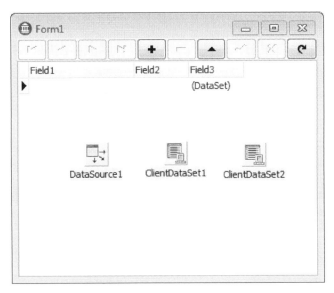

Figure 12-9: A ClientDataSet with a nested dataset has been created using persistent Fields

Defining Nested DataSets at Runtime

Creating ClientDataSet structures that support nested datasets at runtime can be performed using both FieldDefs and Fields, just as this task can be performed manually at design time. The trick to writing the runtime code is to mimic exactly the steps that you take when you configure a ClientDataSet manually, and in the same order. So long as you get that right, your code should work fine.

Unfortunately, writing code that repeats the steps that you take manually is not as easy as it sounds. As a result, the two example projects that we are going to look at in the following sections are a bit more complicated than their design-time counterparts, in that they both create a nested, nested dataset — a top-level ClientDataSet that contains one nested dataset which in turn contains another nested dataset.

Using FieldDefs at Runtime

Defining a ClientDataSets structure to include nested datasets at runtime using FieldDefs is demonstrated in the RuntimeNestedFieldDefs project. The main form of this project is shown in Figure 12-10.

Note: The code project RuntimeNestedFieldDefs is available from the code download. See Appendix A.

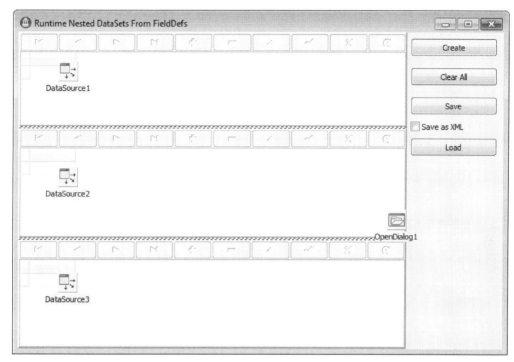

Figure 12-10: The main form of the RuntimeNestedFieldDefs project

The actual creation of the ClientDataSet structure is performed in a method named CreateNestedDataSets. This method is called from the OnClick event handler of the button labeled Create. The CreateNestedDataSets method is shown in the following code segment:

```
procedure TForm1.CreateNestedDataSets;
begin
  TopLevelCDS := TClientDataSet.Create(Self);
  MidLevelCDS := TClientDataSet.Create(TopLevelCDS);
  ThirdLevelCDS := TClientDataSet.Create(TopLevelCDS);

  with TopLevelCDS.FieldDefs do
  begin
    Add('TopID', ftInteger);
    Add('TopName', ftString, 40);
    Add('TopComments', ftMemo);
    Add('TopDateInitiated', ftDate);
  end;
  with TopLevelCDS.FieldDefs.AddFieldDef do
  begin
    Name := 'TopNested';
```

```
    DataType := ftDataSet;
    with ChildDefs do
    begin
      Add('MidID', ftInteger);
      Add('MidName', ftString, 30);
      with AddChild do
      begin
        Name := 'MidNested';
        DataType := ftDataSet;
        with ChildDefs do
        begin
          Add('ThirdID', ftInteger);
          Add('ThirdName', ftString, 25);
          Add('ThirdActive', ftBoolean);
        end;
      end;
    end;
  end;
  //Create the ClientDataSet and its nested datasets
  TopLevelCDS.CreateDataSet;
  //Hook up the other ClientDataSets
  MidLevelCDS.DataSetField :=
    TDataSetField(TopLevelCDS.FieldByName('TopNested'));
  ThirdLevelCDS.DataSetField :=
    TDataSetField(MidLevelCDS.FieldByName('MidNested'));
  //Configure the DataSources
  DataSource1.DataSet := TopLevelCDS;
  DataSource2.DataSet := MidLevelCDS;
  Datasource3.DataSet := ThirdLevelCDS;
end;
```

As you can see from this code, after creating the three ClientDataSet objects, five FieldDefs are added to the top-level ClientDataSet using the FieldDefs Add and AddFieldDef methods. These methods were discussed in detail in Chapter 4.

Once the structure of the top-level ClientDataSet has been defined, each of the nested dataset structures needs to be defined. After completing all of the necessary FieldDef configurations, CreateDataSet is called for the top-level ClientDataSet, which creates both the top-level ClientDataSet and the nested datasets.

Finally, this code hooks up the second-tier and third-tier ClientDataSets to their appropriate DataSetFields. Figure 12-11 shows the main form of the RuntimeNestedFieldDefs project at runtime, after the Create button has been clicked.

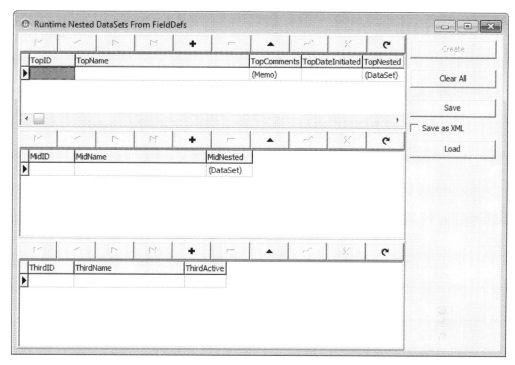

Figure 12-11: A three-tier nested ClientDataSet structure has been created at runtime using FieldDefs

Another interesting aspect of this project, one that it shares with the project covered in the next section, is that it permits the three tier ClientDataSet to be saved to disk as well as loaded from a previously save ClientDataSet. Figure 12-12 displays the contents of one of these saved ClientDataSets. In this image, the data was saved using the XML format and is being displayed in Internet Explorer.

Figure 12-12: When a ClientDataSet includes nested datasets, saving the ClientDataSet saves the nested metadata, data, and change cache

Using Fields at Runtime

Defining a ClientDataSet's structure to include nested datasets at runtime using persistent Fields is demonstrated in the RuntimeNestedFields project. The main form of this project looks exactly like the one shown for the RuntimeNestedFieldDefs project shown in Figure 12-10. In fact, the only different between these two projects is the code found on the CreateNestedDataSets method.

The following code is from the CreateNestedDataSets method found in the
RuntimeNestedFields project:

```
procedure TForm1.CreateNestedDataSets;
begin
  TopLevelCDS := TClientDataSet.Create(Self);
  MidLevelCDS := TClientDataSet.Create(TopLevelCDS);
  ThirdLevelCDS := TClientDataSet.Create(TopLevelCDS);

  with TIntegerField.Create(Self) do
  begin
    Name := 'TopID';
    FieldKind := fkData;
    FieldName := 'ID';
    DataSet := TopLevelCDS;
    Required := True;
  end;
  with TStringField.Create(Self) do
  begin
    Name := 'TopName';
    FieldKind := fkData;
    FieldName := 'Name';
    Size := 40;
    DataSet := TopLevelCDS;
  end;
  with TMemoField.Create(Self) do
  begin
    Name := 'TopComments';
    FieldKind := fkData;
    FieldName := 'Comments';
    DataSet := TopLevelCDS;
  end;
  with TDateField.Create(Self) do
  begin
    Name := 'TopDateInitiated';
    FieldKind := fkData;
    FieldName := 'Date Initiated';
    DataSet := TopLevelCDS;
  end;
  //Note: For TDataSetFields, FieldKind is fkDataSet by default
  with TDataSetField.Create(Self) do
  begin
    Name := 'TopNested';
    FieldName := 'NestedDataSet';
    DataSet := TopLevelCDS;
  end;

  //MidLevelCDS
  MidLevelCDS.DataSetField :=
TDataSetField(FindComponent('TopNested'));
```

```
with TIntegerField.Create(Self) do
begin
  Name := 'MidID';
  FieldKind := fkData;
  FieldName := 'MidID';
  DataSet := MidLevelCDS;
  Required := True;
end;
with TStringField.Create(Self) do
begin
  Name := 'MidName';
  FieldKind := fkData;
  FieldName := 'MidName';
  DataSet := MidLevelCDS;
  Size := 30;;
end;
with TDataSetField.Create(Self) do
begin
  Name := 'MidNested';
  FieldName := 'NestedNestedDataSet';
  DataSet := MidLevelCDS;
end;

//Third Level
ThirdLevelCDS.DataSetField :=
  TDataSetField(FindComponent('MidNested'));
with TIntegerField.Create(Self) do
begin
  Name := 'ThirdID';
  FieldKind := fkData;
  FieldName := 'ThirdID';
  DataSet := ThirdLevelCDS;
  Required := True;
end;
with TStringField.Create(Self) do
begin
  Name := 'ThirdName';
  FieldKind := fkData;
  FieldName := 'ThirdName';
  DataSet := ThirdLevelCDS;
  Size := 25;
end;
with TBooleanField.Create(Self) do
begin
  Name := 'ThirdActive';
  FieldKind := fkData;
  FieldName := 'ThirdActive';
  DataSet := ThirdLevelCDS;
end;
//Create the ClientDataSet and its nested datasets
TopLevelCDS.CreateDataSet;
//Configure the DataSources
DataSource1.DataSet := TopLevelCDS;
(**)
DataSource2.DataSet := MidLevelCDS;
Datasource3.DataSet := ThirdLevelCDS;
```

```
(**)
(*
DataSource2.DataSet :=
  DataSetField(FindComponent('TopNested')).NestedDataSet;
Datasource3.DataSet :=
  TDataSetField(FindComponent('MidNested')).NestedDataSet;
(**)
end;
```

There are two rather slight differences between this code and the corresponding method in the RuntimeNestedFieldDefs project. One is that the DataSetField properties of the MidLevelCDS and ThirdLevelCDS components are assigned prior to defining the structure of those ClientDataSets. This step is required earlier in the code since each persistent Field that you create must specifically be assigned to a ClientDataSet, and that must be a valid ClientDataSet at the time CreateDataSet is called on the top-level ClientDataSet.

The second difference is that this code calls the constructors of Field descendants, such as IntegerField, StringField, and DataSetField. The use of those constructors is more verbose than the Add methods associated with FieldDefs and ChildDefs. As a result, this version of the method is much longer than the previous one.

Figure 12-13 shows what this project looks like when it is running and the Create button has been clicked. As you can see, there is no real discernable difference between what you see in this figure and what is shown in Figure 12-11.

Final Thoughts About Nested DataSets

Nested dataset are powerful and useful. On the other hand, they introduce limits on how you can work with your data when compared to those situations where you load data from related tables into two or more separate ClientDataSets.

The primary limit introduced by nested datasets is that they make searching for data across master table records slow and inconvenient. For example, imagine that you have written a contact management system using MyBase (a ClientDataSet as a stand-alone database), and want to employ a master-detail relationship between contacts and their various phone numbers.

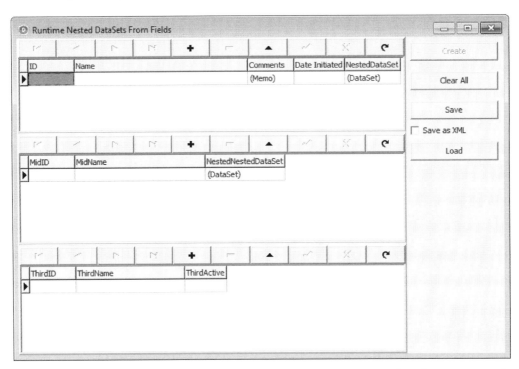

Figure 12-13: A three-tier nested ClientDataSet structure has been created at runtime using persistent Fields

One way to do this would be to utilize two tables, one for contacts, and one for contact phone numbers. Your application would then have to separately load contacts and contact phone numbers into two separate ClientDataSets, and employ user interface techniques (such as dynamic master-detail links or filters or ranges) to display the master-detail relationship between a given contact and their phone numbers.

An alternative would be to create a single contacts ClientDataSet, and include a nested dataset for contact phone numbers. The advantage of this approach is that you can easily create master-detail views that limit the display of a contact's phone numbers automatically.

The drawback to this second technique involves your options for working with the nested data. For example, imagine that you get a phone bill and want to know which contact is associated with a rather expensive call that appears on that bill. If you loaded contact phone numbers into a separate ClientDataSet, you can use one of the search techniques described in Chapter 8, *Searching ClientDataSets,* to locate the phone number in the contact phone numbers table, which will quickly reveal the contact associated with that phone number.

By comparison, if you have embedded contact phone numbers as a nested dataset in the contacts table, no global search is possible. Your only solution is to navigate (scan) record by record through the contacts table, performing a separate search on each nested dataset. Such a search would be significantly slower, on average, than a search on a separate contact phone numbers table.

Does this affect your decision to employ nested datasets or not? The answer is that it depends on what you are using nested datasets for. In most cases, nested datasets are used to manage relational data obtained from a DataSetProvider, in which case, any search for a particular phone number would be performed directly on the underlying database rather than using the cached data stored in a ClientDataSet. Nonetheless, I wanted to bring up this issue because it makes a difference in some cases.

The remaining three chapters of this book show you how to use ClientDataSets with Delphi's multi-tier DataSnap technology.

Chapter 13
ClientDataSets and DataSnap Servers

DataSnap (formerly known as MIDAS, the Multi-tier Distributed Application Services Suite) is a framework that allows you to quickly and easily built multi-tier applications. In most cases, a multi-tier environment consists of at least three parts: A data source, an application server, and one or more application clients.

In most cases, the data source is a database server, such as Oracle, Microsoft SQL Server, or Advantage Database Server, to name a few. These servers, and others like them, are standalone applications that store and manipulate data, typically in a highly optimized and stable fashion.

In some cases, the data source is something a little less formal. For example, it could be a file server database, such as Paradox, dBase, or MS Access. Or, it could be based on MyBase, where a ClientDataSet works as a simple database. But because database servers are stable, reliable, and fast, they are nearly always used as the data source.

The application server in DataSnap is a Delphi application that communicates with both the data source and the client applications. The role of the application server is to retrieve data from the data source and provide it to the application clients, receive data updates from the application clients and apply them back to the data source, as well as expose methods that serve the needs of the application clients.

DataSnap clients are applications that connect to one or more DataSnap servers to execute their exposed methods. Client applications obtain most, if not all, of their data from the application server. If that data needs to be changed, the client application makes the change and then returns the data to the application server, and the server is responsible for applying those changes.

One of the identifying characteristics of client applications is that they do not directly communicate with a database, and therefore, do not require any sort of client application programming interface (API) related to data access. For example, even though the application server is retrieving its data from an Oracle database, the client application does not communicate with the Oracle server directly. As a result, the computer on which the client is running does not require the Oracle client to be installed (at least not for the client application's use). Since these clients have fewer installation requirements, they are often referred to as *thin clients*.

Figure 13-1 depicts the relationship between these three tiers.

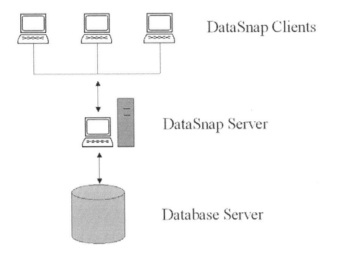

Figure 13-1:The three tiers in a typical DataSnap application

Note: DataSnap is not available in the Professional version of Delphi. In order to use DataSnap, you must be using the Enterprise or Architect edition.

This chapter is designed to introduce you to DataSnap servers, specifically those that interact with ClientDataSets in DataSnap clients. This discussion begins with an overview of DataSnap, past and present.

Overview of DataSnap

There are several aspects to DataSnap that make it an important technology for database application development. As mentioned earlier in this chapter, one of these is that DataSnap supports thin clients. Thin clients have minimal installation requirements, which is especially valuable when you need to install a large number of client applications.

A number of years ago, one of my customers had to install over 200 client applications. Those applications were thick clients, in that they required the installation of the Oracle client API. Each installation took more than one hour, and the entire installation process extended over a two month period. By switching to DataSnap, client installations shortened to less than two minutes per workstation, and could be automated.

The second benefit of DataSnap is that business rules can be defined on the application server. These, in turn, are enforced on those requests coming from client applications. There are a number of benefits gained from separating the business rules from both the client applications and the database server. Rather than implementing business rules in your database using stored procedures, you can implement those business rules in the DataSnap server. Doing so permits you to more easily replace your database server, if the need ever arises, without having to rewrite the business rules.

A second benefit of implementing business rules in the DataSnap server is that you can enhance, extend, or modify those rules simply by updating and redeploying your DataSnap server or servers. If the business rules were implemented in the client applications, updating business rules would require redeployment of all client applications. It also avoids the possibility that client-side business rules might be implemented inconsistently in different clients.

Another benefit of implementing business rules in the middle tier is that the processing of business rules can be distributed. Business rules can be process intensive. If those rules are applied by the database server, this processing can interfere with all applications that access data using that server. The middle tier, however, can be distributed across many machines, eliminating the bottleneck created by a single point of processing.

That client applications can be served by one of a number of application servers not only permits load balancing in the middle tier, but fail-over as well. Specifically, if you are running multiple DataSnap servers and the server used by one of the client applications crashes, your code can attempt to make a new connection to a different DataSnap server. (In old-style DataSnap applications, support for fail-over is provided by the SimpleObjectBroker component. In the latest revisions of DataSnap, you have to create your own fail-over mechanism programmatically.)

In the earliest versions of DataSnap (going back to Delphi 3), DataSnap employed COM (the component object model), a Windows technology for interprocess communication. In the newest incarnation of DataSnap, client-server communication employs TCP/IP (transmission control protocol/Internet protocol) or HTTP (hypertext transfer protocol). In order to simplify this discussion, I will refer to DataSnap that employs COM as being COM-based, and the version that supports TCP/IP and HTTP as being IP-based.

While DataSnap provides a variety of mechanisms for communicating between the application server and client applications, and in the most recent versions, supports REST (REpresentational State Transfer) the focus of this chapter is on ClientDataSets. In this scenario, a DataSnap server employs one or more DataSetProviders, which are used to obtain data from, and apply updates to, the underlying data source.

The clients of these DataSnap servers are Delphi applications that include one or more ClientDataSets that obtain their data from, and return updates to, those DataSetProviders on the application server. Other types of DataSnap clients are not necessarily Delphi applications, but those cannot employ ClientDataSets, so they don't apply to this discussion.

This chapter begins with a look at DataSnap servers, including how to create them and some of the options you have for their configuration. Chapter 14, *ClientDataSets and DataSnap Clients,* demonstrates how to create the client applications for these servers.

DataSnap Servers

DataSnap servers consist of a mechanism for interprocess communication, in conjunction with an object, typically a type of DataModule, that implements methods that can be called by client applications. This section begins with a look at creating a DataSnap server using COM technology. A later section introduces IP-based DataSnap server creation.

COM-Based DataSnap Servers

COM has proven to be a resilient technology, and it still forms the backbone of many of the APIs (application programming interfaces) in the Windows operating system. It has its limitations, however. It only runs on the Windows operating system, and it carries the burden of requiring COM registration of all COM servers.

On the other hand, COM's strength lies in it being an interface-based, language-independent mechanism for exposing methods and properties of objects. When used in conjunction with DCOM (distributed COM), which has been universally available in all recent versions of the Windows operating systems, a COM client can communicate with a COM server across a network.

The key to a COM-based DataSnap server is its support for IAppServer, an automation interface. This interface exposes methods that permit a client to retrieve a list of DataSetProviders available on the server, request data, send data, and so forth. This can be seen in the following code listing taken from the MIDAS unit, which displays the IAppServer interface declaration:

```
IAppServer = interface(IDispatch)
  ['{1AEFCC20-7A24-11D2-98B0-C69BEB4B5B6D}']
  function  AS_ApplyUpdates(const ProviderName: WideString;
    Delta: OleVariant; MaxErrors: Integer;
    out ErrorCount: Integer;
    var OwnerData: OleVariant): OleVariant; safecall;
  function  AS_GetRecords(const ProviderName: WideString;
    Count: Integer; out RecsOut: Integer; Options: Integer;
    const CommandText: WideString; var Params: OleVariant;
    var OwnerData: OleVariant): OleVariant; safecall;
  function  AS_DataRequest(const ProviderName: WideString;
    Data: OleVariant): OleVariant; safecall;
  function  AS_GetProviderNames: OleVariant; safecall;
  function  AS_GetParams(const ProviderName: WideString;
    var OwnerData: OleVariant): OleVariant; safecall;
  function  AS_RowRequest(const ProviderName: WideString;
    Row: OleVariant; RequestType: Integer;
    var OwnerData: OleVariant): OleVariant; safecall;
  procedure AS_Execute(const ProviderName: WideString;
    const CommandText: WideString; var Params: OleVariant;
    var OwnerData: OleVariant); safecall;
end;
```

Fortunately, Delphi provides a special DataModule class, called RemoteDataModule, that provides a design surface as well as a concrete implementation of the IAppServer interface. Once you've created your basic DataSnap application, all you need to do is add DataSetProviders and other DataSets to this RemoteDataModule, and possibly add methods and/or properties to the exposed interface.

The project that you create can either be an application or a DLL. However, nearly all DataSnap servers are based on applications, since they run in their own process space. A DLL is designed to run in the process space of an application. Unless you are creating your DataSnap server as a ActiveX DLL designed to be executed in the COM + runtime environment (previously referred to as Microsoft Transaction Server), a DataSnap server DLL would have to be loaded by the DataSnap client, in which case most of the benefits of DataSnap are lost.

Note: The code project COMDataSnapServer is available under the COMDataSnap folder in the code download. See Appendix A.

There are two projects in the code download that demonstrate basic COM-based DataSnap. In this section, we are going to concern ourselves with the

COMDataSnapServer project. The other project is a client for this server, and it is discussed in the next chapter.

While you can create an IP-based DataSnap server using one of several project wizards in the Object Repository, a COM-based DataSnap project has to be created manually. Fortunately, once a basic project has been created, you can use one of two module wizards in the Object Repository to add a RemoteDataModule to the project.

Creating a Basic COM-Based DataSnap Server

The following steps describe how the COMDataSnapServer project was created. You can following along with these steps if you like. Otherwise, you can use these steps later as a guideline for creating your own COM-based DataSnap server:

1. Begin by creating a new project. Select File | New | VCL Forms Application to create a new application. Before continuing, save this project using meaningful name, such as COMDataSnapServer.

2. You are now ready to add the RemoteDataModule. Select File | New | Other. Expand Delphi Projects and select the Multitier node. Double click the Remote Data Module icon to display the Remote Data Module Wizard shown in Figure 13-2.

3. You use the Remote Data Module Wizard to provide a name for your RemoteDataModule, as well as fine-tune its COM implementation. In this case, set CoClass Name to DSCOMServer and Description to COM-based DataSnap server. Leave all other options set to their default values and click OK to continue.

The Remote Data Module Wizard adds both a COM type library and a special data module to your project. The type library defines a new COM interface whose name is based on the name of your coclass. This interface, which is named IDSCOMServer in this project, descends from IAppServer, which means that any object that implements this new interface must also implement the methods of IAppServer.

The data module class, named TDSCOMServer, implements this interface. Importantly, TDSCOMServer itself descends from TRemoteDataModule, from which it inherits a concrete implementation of IAppServer.

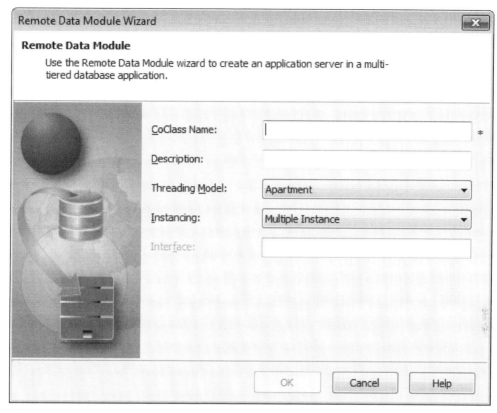

Figure 13-2: The Remote Data Module Wizard

You now have a basic project that supports DataSnap communication over COM. This server, however, is bare bones in that it supports communication but does not have anything to communicate about. In most cases, you will add one or more DataSetProviders to the RemoteDataModule. You might also add one or more properties or methods to your COM interface, or even add entirely new COM interfaces to your project. Adding methods to a COM-based DataSnap server is beyond the scope of this chapter.

Exposing DataSetProviders from a COM-Based DataSnap Server

Because of the IAppServer interface, any DataSetProvider placed on the RemoteDataModule will be available from a DataSnap client configured to use your DataSnap server. The following steps demonstrate how to expose data from a COM-based DataSnap server using a DataSetProvider:

1. Select the RemoteDataModule.

2. Place a DataSetProvider from the Data Access tab of the Tool Palette and a Query from the BDE tab of the Tool Palette onto your RemoteDataModule.

3. Set the DataSetProvider's DataSet property to Query1.

4. With the Query selected, set its DatabaseName property to DBDEMOS and its SQL property to SELECT * FROM CUSTOMER. Your RemoteDataModule will now look something like that shown here:

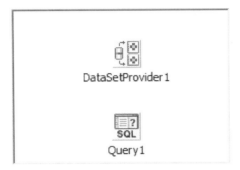

Registering a COM-Based DataSnap Server

Before a DataSnap client can access a COM-based DataSnap server, the server must be registered on the machine on which it will reside. (It must also be registered on a machine on which the client resides if the client is using DCOM to communicate with the server.) If you want to register your COM server on the same machine on which you are running Delphi, registration is a simple process. Registering a COM server on another machine is only slightly more involved.

To run your COM server on the machine on which you built it, use the following step to make your server available:

1. With your COM-based DataSnap server open in Delphi, select Run | ActiveX Server | Register. Delphi will now compile your project and display a message similar to the one here:

If Delphi cannot compile the project, no registration will take place. In that case, fix any errors and then repeat step 1.

Note: Some earlier versions of Delphi, such as Delphi 7, do not support the registration of standalone automation servers from its menus. Only DLL-based COM servers can be registered this way in those versions (which is technically accurate since ActiveX servers are DLLs). For those versions, you use one of the following techniques to register your standalone automation sever.

If you cannot register your COM-base DataSnap server from Delphi's menu, whether its because you are registering the server on a machine on which Delphi is not installed, or you are using an older version of Delphi, you have additional options.

If your server is a standalone application, as opposed to being a DLL, you can register the server from the command line by passing it the /RegServer parameter. For example, if you launch the command prompt (with Administrative privileges), and then navigate to the directory in which your standalone server has been copied, entering a command line similar to the following will register the COM server:

```
COMDataSnapServer.exe /RegServer
```

If you need to subsequently unregister the COM server, pass the /UnRegServer parameter, as shown here:

```
COMDataSnapServer.exe /UnRegServer
```

When you are using /RegServer or /UnRegServer, the COM-based server is installed silently. In other words, no message or dialog box is generated, and the application actually shuts itself down as soon as it has completed its registration. This means that an installation program, which must be run using Administrative privileges, can be used to install your COM server using this technique.

Note: It is also possible to register a COM server using its type library and the TRegSvr.exe application that ships with Delphi in its bin directory. See Delphi's Help for more information.

If you are registering a DLL-based DataSnap server on a machine on which Delphi is not installed, you can use the RegSvr32 console application that ships with Windows. To register the server, call RegSvr32, passing the name of the DLL as a command-line argument. For example, to register an ActiveX named

MyDataSnap.dll use the following command line (from a command prompt with Administrative privileges):

```
RegSvr32.exe MyDataSnap.dll
```

To unregister that same server, use the following:

```
RegSvr32.exe /u MyDataSnap.dll
```

If you are performing the registration from an installation program, you can pass the optional /s parameter to perform a silent installation.

Note: When you initially created this project, you were asked to save it with a meaningful name. The name of the project is important in that when you register its COM interface, the project name becomes part of the ProgID, a string-based identifier for the COM interface. This is why it is important to give your project name a meaningful name prior to the first time you register its COM interface.

The RemoteDataModule and Concurrency

The RemoteDataModule is the centerpiece of a COM-based DataSnap server. As you learned earlier, due to the IAppServer interface implemented by the RemoteDataModule, any DataSetProvider that you place on the RemoteDataModule will be available to a COM-based DataSnap client.

DataSnap clients use COM to request a reference to the RemoteDataModule, after which the client can call the methods and work with the properties of the requested object. Each request is supplied by a COM object factory in the DataSnap sever, which creates a separate RemoteDataModule for each client. When a given client no longer needs the RemoteDataModule, it stops referencing it (the connection is closed), which results in the automatic destruction of the RemoteDataModule.

Because the client uses COM to connect to the DataSnap server, the DataSnap server uses the threading model and instancing that you selected when you created the RemoteDataModule. In the preceding steps, you left Threading Model set to Apartment and Instancing set to Multiple Instance.

When Threading model is set to Apartment, the RemoteDataModule uses the single-threaded apartment model. The single-threaded apartment model accepts all calls from a given client on a single thread (only one request from a given client is handled at any given time). Since different clients communicate with separate instances of the RemoteDataModule, and each RemoteDataModule handles only one request at time, instance data within the

RemoteDataModule is thread-safe. Only global data that is accessible to two or more instances of the RemoteDataModule need to be protected using synchronization objects such as critical sections.

Instancing refers to the mechanism used by a COM server to affect what it does when its object factory returns its interfaced object (the RemoteDataModule). If a client requests a RemoteDataModule from the DataSnap sever, and that server is not currently running, Windows launches the server. If the server is already running, and has not already produced a RemoteDataModule in response to another client request, that server handles the request.

When Instancing is set to Single Instance, once the object factory has created the RemoteDataModule and returned a reference of it to the client, the server becomes unavailable for new client requests. As a result, if another client requests a copy of the RemoteDataModule, another instance of the server is launched and its object factory creates the RemoteDataModule whose reference is returned to the client, after which this instance of the sever becomes unavailable.

By comparison, when Instancing is set to Multiple Instance, only one instance of the server is launched through COM. If the server is not already running when a client attempts to connect, the server is launched, and that server creates an instance of the RemoteDataModule which is returned to that client. If the server is already running, that server creates a new RemoteDataModule and returns it to the client.

Importantly, after returning the interfaced object in response to the client request, a multiple instance server remains available. If a second client requests a RemoteDataModule, that server creates a new RemoteDataModule, a reference to which it returns to the client.

In a confusing irony of naming conventions, this means that Single Instancing may result in multiple instances of your server running, while Multiple Instancing reuses a single instance of the server to create the RemoteDataModules.

By choosing the Apartment threading model, and an Instance value of Multiple Instance, we are producing thread safety on each RemoteDataModule through serialization, and are avoiding the overhead of having to create a new process for each RemoteDataModule. Unfortunately, a further discussion of COM threading models is beyond the scope of this book.

Before leaving the topic of COM-based DataSnap servers, I want to briefly talk about the Transaction Data Module, which is the second icon on the

Multitier tab of the Object Repository. The Transaction Data Module Wizard is used to add a RemoteDataModule to a transactional ActiveX library. To create such a project in Delphi, you start by creating an ActiveX library. You then add a Transactional Object to this library. Only then can you add a Transaction Data Module.

Adding a Transaction DataModule to a transactional ActiveX library permits you to implement a DataSnap server that runs under MTS (Microsoft Transaction Services) which was subsequently renamed the COM + runtime environment. While Microsoft was promoting these technologies in the past, nowadays these technologies have been largely supplanted by Web services, REST servers, and other similar technologies.

IP-Based DataSnap Servers

A new style of DataSnap was released beginning with Delphi 2009. This DataSnap does not rely on COM, but instead uses socket connections over IP. Each subsequent release of Delphi has expanded on this model, adding major enhancements such as compression and encryption, communication over HTTP, REST (REpresentational State Transfer), and WebBroker integration.

The improvements to DataSnap are changing the way that distributed applications can be built, and DataSnap will likely continue to play an important role in future versions of Delphi. Nonetheless, this is a ClientDataSet book, and from that perspective, we are interested in a subset of these DataSnap topics. Specifically, we are interested in those DataSnap classes that permit a ClientDataSet on a thin client to access DataSetProviders on the DataSnap server.

Note: The code project IPDataSnapServer is available under the IPDataSnap folder in the code download. See Appendix A.

The latest versions of Delphi include a collection of wizards that create a variety of different DataSnap projects, making the creation of an IP-based DataSnap server easier than the corresponding COM-based DataSnap server. For our purposes, there are two wizards that we are interested in. Specifically, the DataSnap Server Wizard and the DataSnap WebBroker Application Wizard, located on the DataSnap Server tab of the Object Repository, as shown in Figure 13-3.

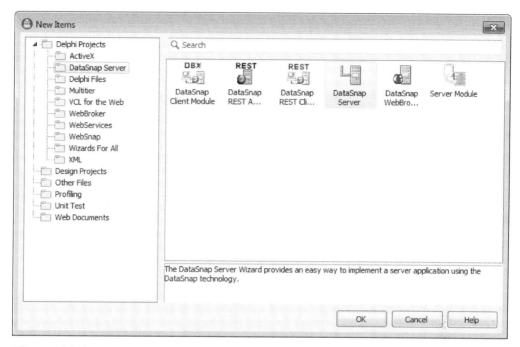

Figure 13-3: The DataSnap Server Wizard is selected on the DataSnap Server tab of the Object Repository

What differentiates these wizards from the others is that each can create a specialized class called DSServerModule. The DSServerModule is similar to RemoteDataModule, though the way that it is instantiated and used is very different. On the other hand, both expose the DataSetProviders that appear on the DataModule. None of the other wizards on the DataSnap tab can produce a DSServerModule.

The following example uses the DataSnap Server Wizard. Although we could also have created a DSServerModule using the DataSnap WebBroker Application Wizard, that wizard specifically creates a Web application, which introduces significant complexities that are unrelated to our discussion of ClientDataSets.

Creating an IP-Based DataSnap Server

The following steps describe how the IPDataSnapServer project was created. You can follow along with these steps if you like. Otherwise, you can use these steps later as a guideline to creating your own IP-based DataSnap server:

1. Close any open projects. Then, select File | New | Other from Delphi's main menu.

2. Select the DataSnap Server tab under the Delphi Projects tab.

3. Double-click the DataSnap Server icon to launch the DataSnap Server Wizard, shown in Figure 13-4.

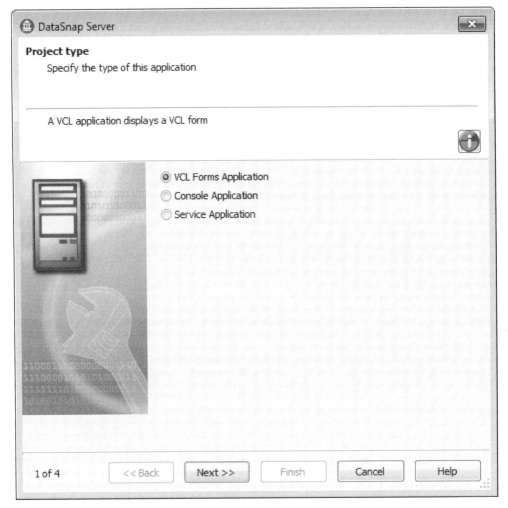

Figure 13-4: The DataSnap Server Wizard

4. This first form offers to create one of three types of applications. A VCL Forms Application is a standalone Windows application. This is the easiest type of DataSnap server to create, but is not terribly practical when deployed. You can also create a DataSnap server as a Console Application, which has no user interface, or as a Windows Service. I'll discuss the Windows Service Application option a little later in this chapter, since that is the type you will ultimately want to use, but for this example, select VCL Forms Application. Click OK

to continue onto page 2, shown in
Figure 13-5.

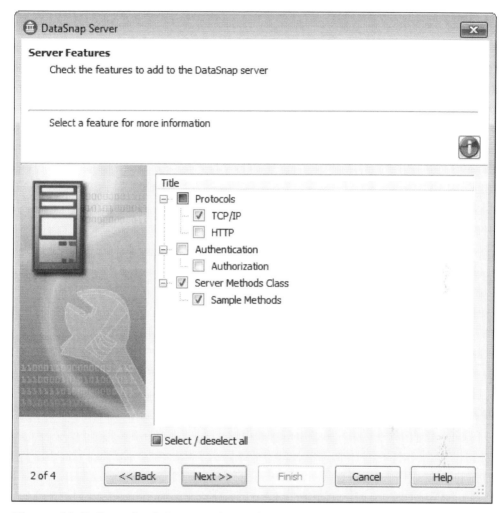

Figure 13-5: Page 2 of the DataSnap Server Wizard

5. You use page 2 of the DataSnap Server Wizard to define the features
    for your DataSnap server. Under Protocols, you can select TCP/IP,
    HTTP, or both. TCP/IP is faster, but firewalls tend to be a little more
    lenient with HTTP traffic. This page also permits you to add
    authentication and authorization support. Finally, this page permits
    you to expose server methods from your DataSnap server (and offers
    to provide you with some samples). Leave this page set to the default
    settings and click Next to advance to Page 3 of the DataSnap Server
    Wizard, shown in Figure 13-6.

Figure 13-6: Page 3 of the DataSnap Server Wizard

6. You use page 3 of the DataSnap Server Wizard to define the port on which the DataSnap server will listen for client connections, depending on the protocols that you selected to support on Page 2 of the DataSnap Server Wizard. The default port for TCP/IP connections is 211 and the default port for HTTP is 8080.

You can accept the default settings, provide your own, or click Find Open Port to have the DataSnap Server Wizard test for an open port, which upon finding one, will assign that port number to the port field. (Recall that only one server can listen on a given port. If a second server tries to listen on a port already in use, an exception is raised.) Click Test Port to verify that the offered port is available. If not, click Find Open Port or manually enter a port you want to use (after which you should test its availability). When you have a port selected, click next to advance to page 4 of the DataSnap Server Wizard, shown in Figure 13-7.

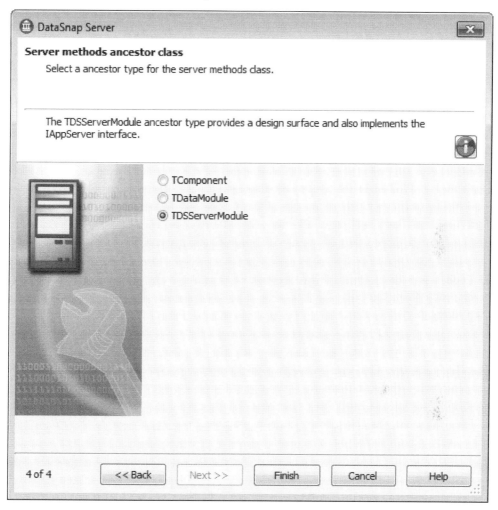

Figure 13-7: Page 4 of the DataSnap Server Wizard

7. On this final page of the DataSnap Server Wizard you get to select the type of class to use to implement the server methods and associated objects that you will expose through the DataSnap interface. There is only one selection that will serve us on this page, and that is TDSServerModule. Select the TDSServerModule and click Finish.

The DataSnap server created using these steps contains three primary units. One is the main form of the VCL Forms application. This unit is absent when you create a DataSnap server based on a console application or a Windows service application.

The second unit is the server methods module, and it is a DSServerModule. You extend the DSServerModule in order to expose DataSetProviders and custom methods.

The third unit is called the server container, and it is a DataModule that holds several critical components that manage the lifecycle of the DSServerModule and enables the interaction between your DataSnap server and DataSnap clients. Also, depending on features you selected when you were using the DataSnap Server Wizard, this DataModule might also contain components to support authentication and HTTP communication. (If you had created a Windows service application using the DataSnap Server Wizard, the server container would be based on a Service object instead of a DataModule.)

Exposing DataSetProviders from an IP-Based DataSnap Server

Because of methods inherited by the DSServerModule, any DataSetProvider placed on the DataModule will be available to an IP-based DataSnap client configured to use your DataSnap server.

The steps you take to expose a DataSetProvider from an IP-based DataSnap server are the same as those you use to build a COM-based DataSnap server. The only difference is that you are placing the DataSetProvider on a DSServerModule, as opposed to a RemoteDataModule. For convenience, these steps are repeated here:

1. Open the DSServerModule.

2. Place a DataSetProvider from the Data Access tab of the Tool Palette and a Query from the BDE tab of the Tool Palette onto the design surface of your DSServerModule.

3. Set the DataSetProvider's DataSet property to Query1.

4. With the Query selected, set its DatabaseName property to DBDEMOS and its SQL property to SELECT * FROM CUSTOMER.

Installation of an IP-Based DataSnap Server

Since IP-based DataSnap servers do not make use of COM, they have minimal installation requirements. All you really need to do is to ensure that you have installed any necessary APIs required by your DataSnap server, and provide a mechanism for launching your DataSnap server.

The client API that DataSnap servers most often require is associated with the data access mechanism being used. The IPDataSnapServer project, for instance, requires the BDE. As a result, if you wanted to install that server on a new machine on your network, you must ensure that you also install the BDE if it is not already installed.

Providing for the launching of your DataSnap server is another thing. A COM-based DataSnap server is automatically launched if it is not already running, through COM. Since an IP-based DataSnap server is not a COM server, you need to take other steps. To put it simply, if an IP-based DataSnap server is not running, any attempt by a DataSnap client to contact it will fail.

One of the traditional ways to ensure that a process is highly available is to implement it as a Windows service that starts automatically. In short, a Windows service that is configured to start automatically will restart if the server on which it is installed reboots. More importantly, the service will start even if there is no user around to log in.

While DataSnap servers implemented as Windows services are great when it comes to launching the server and ensuring high availability, they are rather difficult to debug. Fortunately, there is a middle ground solution that you can implement. Create and debug the DataSnap server as a VCL Forms application and then convert it to a Windows service.

There are two differences between a DataSnap server created as a VCL Forms application and a Windows service. The first is the project source (and associated configuration files). The project source for a VCL Forms application includes the main form unit in its uses clause, and instantiates both the main form and the server container. By comparison, the Windows service project source has some additional code and comments that give you some insight into additional steps that you might have to take if your DataSnap server employs COM. It also instantiates the server container.

These differences are rather minor. The biggest difference between these types of projects is that the server container does not descend from DataModule in a Windows service DataSnap server. Instead, it descends from TService, the class in Delphi that you use to create Windows service applications. (As described earlier, the VCL Forms application server container descends from TDataModule.)

In most DataSnap servers, the bulk of your core DataSnap server functionality is located on the server methods module, and these modules are initially identical between a DataSnap server created as a VCL Forms application and one created as a Windows service. As a result, with a little finesse, you can create a DataSnap Windows service from an existing DataSnap VCL Forms application.

Here is what you do. Build your application using the DataSnap Server VCL Forms application. As you build the application, try to keep the customization to the server container to a minimum.

Once your DataSnap server is debugged and ready to deploy, create a New DataSnap server using the DataSnap Server Wizard, this time creating a Windows service. Save the Windows service project in a directory separate from the one in which the VCL Forms application was created. Once saved, remove the new DSServerModule unit from the Windows service application, and add the DSServerModule unit from the VCL Forms application.

The hardest part is synchronizing the new service-based server container with the one from the VCL Forms project. One way to do this is to simply copy the properties from the components on the DataModule version over to the Service version. Any new methods or event handlers that you added to the VCL Forms application server container have to be moved over as well.

When you are done you are ready to compile and install your Windows service. And, since the same DSServiceModule is used by both projects, you can return to using the VCL Forms application if you later need to enhance or debug your DataSnap server with respect to the features implemented on the DSServiceModule.

Note: The code project IPDataSnapWindowsService is available under the IPDataSnap folder in the code download. This project implements a Windows service that uses the DSServerModule that is also used by the IPDataSnapServer project. See Appendix A.

If you are willing to do a little more work, instead of copying the properties and methods over from the VCL Forms application server container to the Windows service server container, you can use IFDEF compiler directives to merge the two modules so that a single server container is used in both the VCL Forms and Windows service versions of the application.

If you do this carefully, you will end up with a common server container and server methods module for both projects. When compiled using the Windows service project, the server container will be a Service. When compiled using the

VCL Form project, the server container will be a DataModule. You can now maintain and deploy your DataSnap server with ease.

The following code segment should give you some insight into how you can create a merged server container. In this segment, the server container will be a DataModule when compiled from the VCL Forms application DataSnap server and a Service when compiled by the Windows service DataSnap server. This code segment assumes that the VCL Forms application includes a VCLFORMS define and the Windows service project includes a WINSERVICE define. (You specify a define for a project from the Directories and Conditionals tab of the Project Options dialog box.) A number of additional IFDEFs are necessary in the server container unit for this to work properly, but you can discover these by comparing the differences between the server containers created for the two types of DataSnap servers.

```
type
  {$IFDEF WINSERVICE}
  TMyServerContainer = class(TDataModule)
  {$ENDIF}
  {$IFDEF VCLFORMS}
  TMyServerContainer = class(TService)
  {$ENDIF}
```

Once you have created your IP-based DataSnap server installing as a Windows service, you must install and run it. You install a Windows service by executing it from the command prompt (with Administrative privileges in Vista and Windows 7), passing to it the /install command-line parameter. (You subsequently uninstall a Windows service by passing the /uninstall command line parameter.) For example, if your Windows service is named IPDataSnapWindowsService, you install it using the following command:

```
IPDataSnapWindowsService.exe /install
```

While this command installs the service, it still needs to be started. Either reboot the machine on which you installed the service, or open the Services applet in Administrative Tools and manually start the service.

DSServerModules and Concurrency

The DSServerModule of your IP-based DataSnap server plays a role very similar to a RemoteDataModule in a COM-based DataSnap server. The biggest difference is how they are instantiated. Instead of being created by an object factory through a COM request, a DSServerModule is created by the DSServerClass component on the server container in response to a request received from a DataSnap client.

You learned earlier in this chapter about the complexities of COM threading models, and the impact they have on whatever synchronization you need to employ to ensure thread safety. The situation is different using IP-based DataSnap. Fortunately, it is simpler.

IP-based DataSnap servers employ Internet Direct (Indy) socket components, specifically the IdTCPServer and IdHTTPServer components, to accept socket connections from DataSnap clients. Upon accepting a connection, the DSServerClass provides the client with access to a DSServerModule instance. How the DSServerClass does this depends on the value assigned to the LifeCycle property of the DSServerClass.

LifeCycle can be one of three values: Server, Session, or Invocation.

When LifeCycle is set to Server, the DSServerClass will create on instance of the DSServerModule, and this DSServerModule will be used to manage all requests. Since Internet Direct servers can handle client requests concurrently, and the DSServerModule created by the DataSnap Server Wizard implements no thread safety, you will need to implement thread synchronization within your DSServerModule if you set LifeCycle to Server.

For example, you may need to acquire a critical section before continuing with the execution of any of the server methods you expose on the DSServerModule. Likewise, you may have to acquire (and release) that same critical section in one or more of the DataSetProvider event handlers. The purpose of this synchronization would be to ensure that two or more client requests received concurrently will not interfere with each other.

Setting LifeCycle to Session causes the DSServerClass to generate an instance of the DSServerModule upon each client connection. That one instance then serves all requests by that client until the client disconnects, at which the time that instance of the DSServerModule is freed.

There are two advantages of setting LifeCycle to Session. First, minimal thread synchronization is required, so long as each DSServerModule uses its own connection to its underlying database and shares no global resources with other instances of DSServerModules that might be working for other client connections.

Because each client connection works with its own copy of DSServerModule, a second advantage is realized. Basically, the DSServerModule can maintain state between requests. For example, you learned in Chapter 2, *Loading Data with ClientDataSets and DataSetProviders,* that when PacketRecords is set to a positive integer, a DataSetProvider will not close its associated DataSet until it has fetched the last record from that DataSet for the requesting ClientDataSet. This record position in the DataSet is information that permits a subsequent fetch (or GetNextPacket) request from the ClientDataSet to continue retrieving records from the previous position. If several DataSnap clients are simultaneously fetching less than all records from their DataSetProviders, the corresponding DataSets from which the DataSetProviders are retrieving data will maintain their own current record position separately from one and other.

While a LifeCycle of Session is thread-safe, as far as individual client connections are concerned, a problem could arise if you attempt to use a client connection in a given DataSnap client from more than one thread. If two or more threads in a given client attempt to use a common connection, those invocations could occur concurrently, and serious problems could result. If a DataSnap client needs to access the DataSnap server from more than one thread, you should create a separate connection for each thread. Doing so will ensure that each thread is working with a different instance of the DSServerModule.

Setting LifeCycle to Invocation causes the DSServerClass to create an instance of DSServerModule for each and every request. Once a given request has been satisfied, the corresponding DSServerModule is freed.

So long as each DSServerModule uses its own connection to its underlying database and shares no global resources with other instances of DSServerModules, a LifeCycle of Invocation gives the ultimate in thread safety. There are two drawbacks, however, to Invocation. First, if a DSServerModule connects to a database, an Invocation LifeCycle incurs a great deal of overhead, having to connect to and disconnect from the database on each and every request. By comparison, when LifeCycle is Session, a connection to the database is made upon the first client request, and is used for the remaining requests by that client until the client disconnects.

This problem can be mitigated if you employ a connection pool, but doing so introduces another level of complexity to your server's architecture.

The second drawback is that you cannot easily provide server-side state management when LifeCycle is Invocation. Since each request is handled by a different instance of the DSServerModule, there is no convenient place to save data.

This problem can also be overcome, but again at the expense of simplicity. If you want to maintain state while using a LifeCycle of Invocation, you can do so by sending any information that you want to persist for the client to the client in each and every response. The client then needs to return this

information along with any subsequent requests, permitting the
DSServerModule to understand the continuing context of the request.

A technique for passing data between a DSServerModule and a DataSnap
client is demonstrated in Chapter 15, *Remote ClientDataSet-DataSetProvider
Interaction.*

In the next chapter you will learn how to create DataSnap clients for the
DataSnap servers introduced in this chapter.

Chapter 14
ClientDataSets and DataSnap Clients

DataSnap clients are applications that connect to, and interact with, DataSnap servers. When those DataSnap servers support HTTP, the client can be almost any kind of application written in any language that supports HTTP. In the context of this chapter, however, we are specifically interested in DataSnap servers that expose DataSetProviders. In those cases, the clients are Delphi applications, since ClientDataSets are a Delphi feature.

The interaction between a ClientDataSet in a DataSnap client and a DataSetProvider in a DataSnap server is nearly identical to their interaction when the two components appear on the same form in an application. There is one difference, however. The ClientDataSet needs help connecting to the DataSetProvider.

DataSnap Clients

A DataSnap client can be any type of application. For example, it can be a VCL Forms application, a console application, a Windows service, a Web service, a WebBroker application, or even a DLL (dynamic link library). All that is required is that the DataSnap client makes use of one or more components that enable the ClientDataSet to communicate with a DataSetProvider on a DataSnap server.

The following sections describe how to create DataSnap clients that communicate with the DataSnap servers introduced in Chapter 13, *ClientDataSets and DataSnap Servers*. As we did in that chapter, we will begin this discussion by looking at DataSnap clients for COM-based DataSnap servers.

COM-Based DataSnap Clients

COM-based DataSnap clients makes use of one of three components to connect to a DataSnap server. The most commonly used component is the DCOMConnection, and it is designed to connect directly to a DataSnap server using COM or DCOM.

Sometimes the DataSnap server is not on the same network as the DataSnap client, in which case a direct connection to the DataSnap server may not be possible. For those cases, Delphi provides two alternatives.

The first is SocketConnection. SocketConnection uses TCP/IP (transmission control protocol/Internet protocol) to connect to a server installed on another machine on the network, intranet, or even the Internet. That machine must have a running copy of ScktSrvr.exe, which is a Windows service. This program can be found in the bin directory under your Delphi installation.

Because ScktSrvr is a Windows service, you must install and run it before it is available on the machine on which it is installed. You install ScktSrvr from a command prompt (using Administrative privileges under Windows Vista and Windows 7) using the following command:

```
ScktSrvr.exe /install
```

Once installed, you need to run it. Under Administrative Tools, select Services, select the service named Borland Socket Server, and then click Start. Alternatively, simply reboot the server on which ScktSrvr is installed. Once installed, ScktSrvr runs automatically each time the server reboots.

ScktSrvr is both a TCP/IP server and a COM client. When it receives a request from a DataSnap client over TCP/IP, ScktSrvr turns around and connects to the DataSnap server through COM, returning any results to the requesting DataSnap client using TCP/IP.

The second alternative is somewhat similar to SocketConnection, and it is called WebConnection. Like SocketConnection, WebConnection connects to a server on another machine. The difference is that WebConnection connects to a Web server using HTTP (hypertext transfer protocol).

The request sent by WebConnection is directed to a Web server extension, named HttpSrvr.dll. HttpSrvr.dll must be installed on the machine on which the Web server is running and from which the DataSnap server is accessible. The Web server must also be configured to enable calls to HttpSrvr.dll.

When a request is received by the Web server extension, a COM connection is made to the DataSnap server. (Like ScktSrvr.exe, HttpSrvr.dll can be found in Delphi's bin directory.) Similar to its TCP/IP counterpart, HttpSrvr.dll provides the interface between the DataSnap client and the COM-based DataSnap server.

Since the COM-based DataSnap client example described in this chapter will run on the same machine as the COMDataSnapServer project, DCOMConnection is the most straightforward of the connection components, requiring no additional configuration or installation, other than the required registration of the COM-based DataSnap server. As a result, this DCOMConnection component is used by the DataSnap client.

Note: The code projects COMDataSnapServer and COMDataSnapClient are available under the COMDataSnap folder in the code download. See Appendix A.

Creating a COM-Based DataSnap Client

Before continuing, you must ensure that the COMDataSnapServer project, or a similar one that you have created, is compiled and registered as a COM server on your machine. This project does not have to be running. Registering your COM-based DataSnap server is discussed in Chapter 13, *ClientDataSets and DataSnap Servers.*

The following steps describe how the COMDataSnapClient project was created. You can following along with these steps if you like. Otherwise, you can use these steps later as a guideline to creating your own IP-based DataSnap client:

1. Begin by creating a new VCL Forms application by selecting File | New | VCL Forms Application - Delphi.

2. Add to this form a DataSource and a ClientDataSet from the Data Access tab of the Tool Palette.

3. Next, add a DBNavigator and a DBGrid from the Data Controls tab of the Tool Palette.

4. Now add a DCOMConnection from the DataSnap Client tab of the Tool Palette.

5. Set the DataSource property of the DBNavigator and DBGrid to DataSource1, and the DataSet property of the DataSource to ClientDataSet1.

6. Arrange your DBNavigator and DBGrid so that they present a nice user interface. Your screen might now look something like that shown in Figure 14-1.

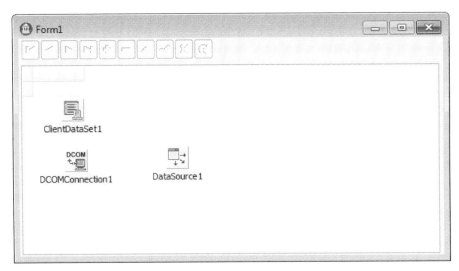

Figure 14-1: A basic form that will be used as a COM-based DataSnap client

Adding COM-Based DataSnap Server Connectivity

You connect to the DataSnap server using one of the connection components described in the preceding section. In this case, you will use the DCOMConnection component. Once you do this, you can associate the ClientDataSet with the DCOMConnection, after which the ClientDataSet can connect to any of the DataSetProviders available on the RemoteDataModule.

Use the following steps to add COM-based DataSnap server connectivity to the application:

1. Select the DCOMConnection component. If your DataSnap server is not on your computer, enter the computer name on which it is installed in the ComputerName property using the Object Inspector. In this case, the server is registered on your current machine, so you can ignore this property.

2. Next, select the ServerName field in the Object Inspector and use the dropdown list to select your server name. The name of the DataSnap server is its ProgID, and typically resolves to the name of the project and the COM coclass, separated by a period. For example, if you saved your server using the name COMDataSnapServer, and your coclass is named DSCOMServer, your server name (and its ProgID) will be COMDataSnapServer.DSCOMServer.

3. Once you select the ServerName property, the ServerGuid property will fill in automatically. (If the ServerName dropdown list does not include your server, it is probably not registered. Register your DataSnap server and try setting ServerName again.)

4. Now select the ClientDataSet. Set its RemoteServer property to DCOMConnection1.

5. Next, select the ProviderName property and open the dropdown list. All DataSetProviders that appear on the RemoteDataModule from the COMDataSnapServer project will appear in this list. Select DataSetProvider1:

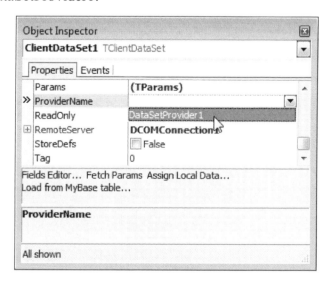

6. You can now activate the ClientDataSet. Set the ClientDataSet's Active property to True. Your form should look something like that shown in Figure 14-2.

Something that you may or may not have noticed is that the DataSnap server launched when you first expanded the ProviderName property dropdown list. The DCOMConnection had to connect to this server in order to ask it for the names of its DataSetProviders.

Figure 14-2: The ClientDataSet is getting its data from a DataSnap server at design time

The COMDataSnapClient Example

The code download includes a sample DataSnap client called COMDataSnapClient. This project is designed to interface with the COMDataSnapServer project. Figure 14-3 shows the main form of this project after it has been run and File | Open has been selected.

Figure 14-3: The main form of the COMDataSnapClient application

The following is the code that appears on the OnClick event handler for the File | Open menu item. Notice that after closing the ClientDataSet, the DCOMConnection is closed as well. If this is the only client attached to the DataSnap server, the server will shutdown when the DCOMConnection is closed.

```
procedure TForm1.Open1Click(Sender: TObject);
begin
  if not ClientDataSet1.Active then
  begin
    ClientDataSet1.Active := True;
    Open1.Caption := 'Close';
  end
  else
  begin
    ClientDataSet1.Active := False;
    DCOMConnection1.Close;
    Open1.Caption := 'Open';
    ApplyUpdates1.Enabled := False;
  end;
end;
```

This File menu also includes an Apply Updates menu item. The following is the OnClick event handler of this menu item:

```
procedure TForm1.ApplyUpdates1Click(Sender: TObject);
begin
  ClientDataSet1.ApplyUpdates(0);
  ApplyUpdates1.Enabled := False;
end;
```

The call to ApplyUpdates looks no different than it would have looked if the DataSetProvider had been in the same process as this ClientDataSet. Nonetheless, it works the same. If you make a change to a record, post that change, and then select File | Apply Updates, the update will be applied, barring any invalid data.

You can test this yourself by posting a change and then selecting File | Apply Updates. After saving an update, you can verify that the update was successfully persisted by selecting File | Close and then File | Open. When the ClientDataSet reopens, it will retrieve the current values from the underlying database, which will include the updated data.

There is only one more event handler on this form that is of interest, and it is associated with the OnDataChange event handler of the DataSource. This event handler enables or disables the Apply Updates menu item, depending on whether or not the ClientDataSet has any changes in its change cache. This event handler is shown here:

```
procedure TForm1.DataSource1DataChange(Sender: TObject;
  Field: TField);
begin
  ApplyUpdates1.Enabled := ClientDataSet1.ChangeCount > 0;
end;
```

IP-Based DataSnap Clients

There are only a few differences between creating a COM-based DataSnap client and an IP-based DataSnap client. Instead of having a single component like DCOMConnection, which you used in the preceding example to connect to the DataSnap server and enumerate its DataSetProviders, an IP-based DataSnap client has two components. One of these is SQLConnection, the component that you use to access database servers using dbExpress drivers. The second is DSProviderConnection, and it takes responsibility for enumerating the DataSetProviders on the server.

That IP-based DataSnap clients communicate to their servers using a dbExpress driver introduces some interesting configuration options. Specifically, you can either configure the connection to the DataSnap server using the DriverName and Params properties of the SQLConnection component, or you can create a reusable DataSnap connection with Delphi's Data Explorer.

The steps given in the next section describe how to configure a SQLConnection using its DriverName and Params properties. As a result, the following steps demonstrate how to create a reusable connection in the Database Explorer.

1. Before starting, ensure that the DataSnap server for which you are configuring this connection is running. If your DataSnap server is a VCL Forms application, and you are running Windows Vista or Windows 7 (or later), you might have to run your DataSnap server with administrative privileges.

2. Next, open the Data Explorer, shown here. By default, the Data Explorer is available as a tab in the same pane as the Project Manager. If you do not see this tab, you can click the right arrow at the lower right corner of this pane until you see the Data Explorer tab, after which you should click this tab. Alternatively, you can select View | Data Explorer from Delphi's main menu to display the Data Explorer.

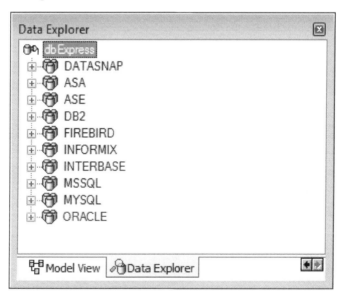

3. If you expand the DATASNAP node of the Data Explorer, you should find an existing connection named DATASNAPCONNECTION. If you want, you can modify this connection. In most cases, however, you will want to create a new DataSnap connection. To do this, right-click the DATASNAP node and select Add New Connection to display the Add New Connection dialog box shown here.

4. Make sure that Provider Name is set to DATASNAP, and enter the name of your connection in the Connection Name field. In the preceding image, the name IPDataSnapServer has been entered. Click OK when you are done.

5. You are ready to configure your new connection. Expand the DATASNAP node in the Data Explorer, right click IPDataSnapServer, and select Modify Connection.

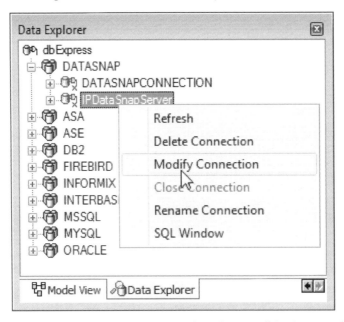

6. You configure the connection using the Modify Connection dialog box shown in Figure 14-4. Set Protocol to the protocol (tcp/ip or http) that your DataSnap server supports, and Port to the port on which your server listens for client connections. For the IP-based

DataSnap server created in Chapter 13, Protocol should be set to tcp/ip and Port should be set to 211. Set Host to the IP address of the machine on which your DataSnap server is running. In this case you can use localhost (or the 127.0.0.1 loopback IP address). If you are using authentication, you can also supply a User name and a Password in the Authentication section of the Modify Connection dialog box.

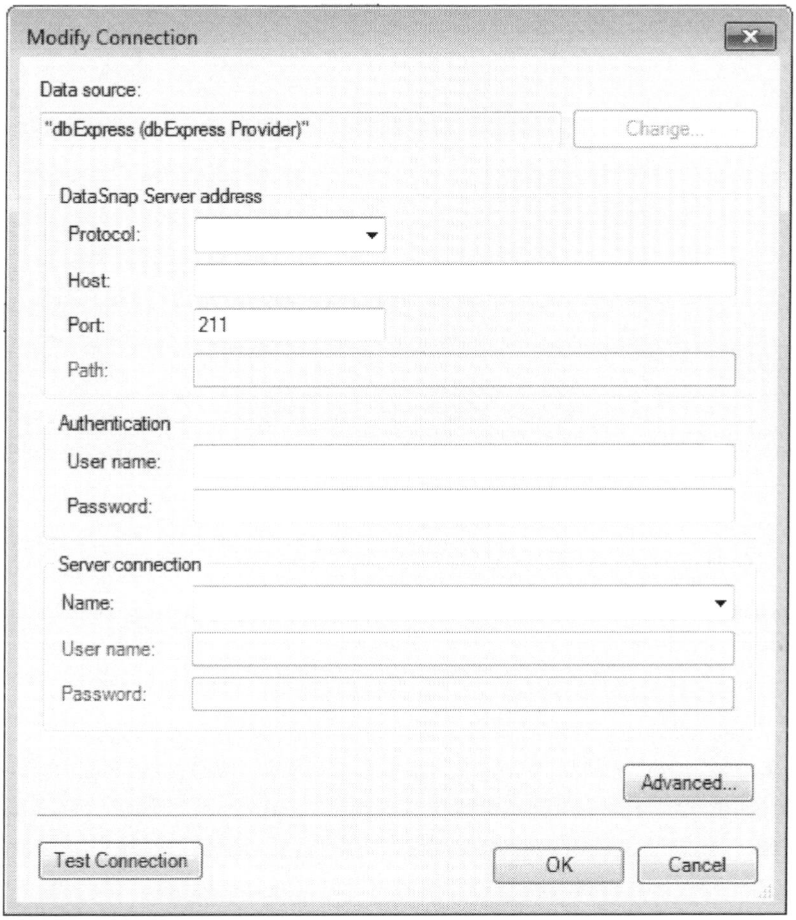

Figure 14-4. Use the Modify Connection dialog box to configure a dbExpress connection

7. You can now test your connection (as long as you are not using HTTPS). To test the connection, click the Test Connection button. If your configuration is correct, and your DataSnap server is running, a successful connection displays the following dialog box. Click OK to continue.

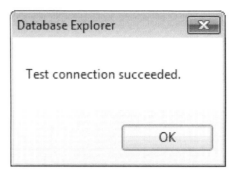

8. If you click Advanced, you will see the generic dbExpress Advanced Properties dialog box. This dialog box permits you to configure many different parameters of a dbExpress connection. While you can use this dialog box, the Modify Connection dialog box contains those settings that apply most often to DataSnap connections. As a result, you will probably not need the Advanced Properties dialog box. When you are through configuring your DataSnap connection, click OK on the Modify Connection dialog box to return to the Data Explorer.

Using a configured DataSnap connection is discussed in the following section, which walks you through the creation a DataSnap client for IP-based DataSnap servers.

Note: The code projects IPDataSnapServer and IPDataSnapClient are available under the COMDataSnap folder in the code download. See Appendix A.

Creating an IP-Based DataSnap Client

While COM was responsible for launching the COM-based DataSnap server, you are responsible for launching the IP-based DataSnap server. If you have implemented your DataSnap server as a VCL Forms application, you must run it before you use the following steps. If you have implemented it as a Windows service, that service must be installed and running.

The following steps describe how the IPDataSnapClient project was created. You can following along with these steps if you like. Otherwise, you can use these steps later as a guideline to creating your own IP-based DataSnap client:

1. Before starting, ensure that the DataSnap server for which you are configuring this connection is running. If your DataSnap server is a VCL Forms application, and you are running Windows Vista or

Windows 7 (or later), you might have to run your DataSnap server with administrative privileges.

2. Next, create a new VCL Forms application by selecting File | New | VCL Forms Application - Delphi.

3. Add to this form a DataSource and a ClientDataSet from the Data Access tab of the Tool Palette.

4. Next, add a DBNavigator and a DBGrid from the Data Controls tab of the Tool Palette.

5. Now add a SQLConnection from the dbExpress tab of the Tool Palette.

6. Next, add a DSProviderConnection from the DataSnap Client tab of the Tool Palette.

7. Set the DataSource properties of the DBNavigator and DBGrid to DataSource1, and the DataSet property of the DataSource to ClientDataSet1.

8. Arrange your DBNavigator and DBGrid so that they present a nice user interface. Your screen might now look something like that shown back in Figure 14-1.

Adding IP-Based DataSnap Server Connectivity

You connect to the DataSnap server using the SQLConnection and DSProviderConnection components. Once these components have been configured, you can associate the ClientDataSet with the DSProviderConnection component, after which the ClientDataSet can be associated with any of the DataSetProviders available on the DSServerModule of the DataSnap server.

Use the following steps to add IP-based DataSnap server connectivity to the application:

1. Select the SQLConnection component.

2. If you have previously configured a DataSnap connection using the Data Explorer, and that connection has been configured for your DataSnap server, you can set ConnectionName to the name of that connection. Doing so will set the DriverName property, and the Params property will load with the parameters defined for the selected DataSnap connection.

Using a DataSnap connection from the Data Explorer to configure a SQLConnection simply loads the current configuration from the selected connection, but does not maintain a relationship with that connection. Specifically, future changes to a DataSnap connection will not affect those SQLConnections in which that connection appears in their ConnectionName properties. If you want to update a SQLConnection to use the current settings of a Data Explorer connection, you must clear the ConnectionName property and then reset it to the connection, at which time the current connection parameters will be reloaded into the Params property of the SQLConnection.

If you are not using a configured Data Explorer connection to configure your SQLConnection, set DriverName to DataSnap. This will initialize parameters to default parameters.

3. Set LoginPrompt to False.

4. If you did not load the Params property from a Data Explorer connection, select the Params property and click the ellipsis that appears. This will bring up the Value List Editor shown in Figure 14-5. Ensure that the Port, HostName, and CommunicationProtocol shown in the Value List Editor matches what you have set for the DataSnap server. Close the Value List Editor when you are done.

5. Select the DSProviderConnection component, and set its SQLConnection property to SQLConnection1.

6. Set the ServerClassName to the name of the class that implements the DSServerModule. In the IPDataSnapServer application, this name was the default class name that the DataSnap Server Wizard created, which was TServerMethods1.

7. Select the ClientDataSet, and set its RemoteServer property to DSProviderConnection.

8. Select the ClientDataSet's ProviderName property and open the dropdown list. The DataSetProvider from the IPDataSnapServer project will appear in this list. Select it.

9. You can now activate the ClientDataSet. Set the ClientDataSet's Active property to True. Your form should look something like that shown in Figure 14-6.

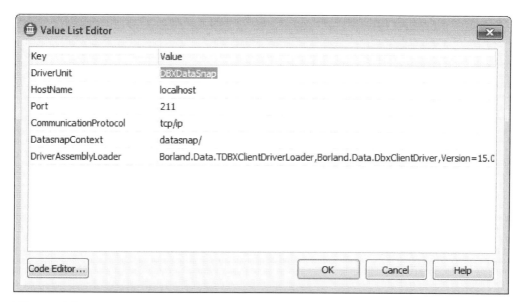

Figure 14-5: The Value List Editor displays the Params property of the SQLConnection

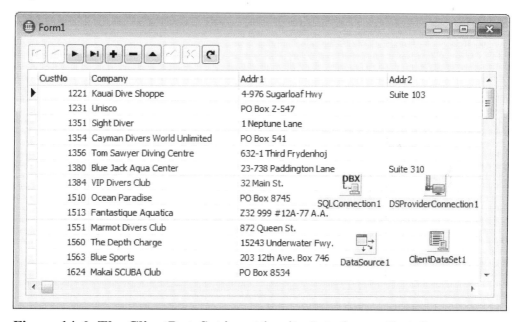

Figure 14-6: The ClientDataSet is getting its data from a DataSnap server at design time

The IPDataSnapClient Example

The code download includes a sample DataSnap client called IPDataSnapClient. This project is designed to interface with the IPDataSnapServer and IPDataSnapWindowsService projects.

The IPDataSnapClient project is a mirror image of the COMDataSnapClient project described earlier in this chapter. The only differences between these two projects are the captions on the main form and the components used to access the server from which the project obtains its data. Both projects have the same set of event handlers for connecting to and disconnecting from the server, as well as for applying updates back to the server and enabling the Apply Updates menu item. If you want to review those event handlers, please refer to the section "The COMDataSnapClient Example" found earlier in this chapter.

In the next and final chapter of this book, you will learn how to enable communication between a ClientDataSet in a DataSnap client and a DataSetProvider in a DataSnap server.

Chapter 15
Remote ClientDataSet-DataSetProvider Interaction

Throughout this book, I have focused on the features and capabilities of ClientDataSets. Those same features and capabilities are available when the ClientDataSet appears in a DataSnap client application. For example, after retrieving data from the DataSnap server, you can save that data to a file or stream, search or filter the data, and clone cursors from the ClientDataSet. In addition, if the DataSetProvider to which your ClientDataSet points is itself pointing to a master DataSet of a dynamic master-detail relationship, the ClientDataSet in the DataSnap client will include nested datasets.

So let me repeat this point again for emphasis. A ClientDataSet in a DataSnap client is no different than any other ClientDataSet, with the exception of where it gets its data. Furthermore, all ClientDataSet techniques described in the earlier chapters of this book apply equally to ClientDataSets used in DataSnap client applications.

There are, however, some ClientDataSet features that really only make sense when the ClientDataSet appears in a DataSnap client. These are primarily related to the fact that the ClientDataSet and its DataSetProvider reside not only in a different process, but in most cases, on entirely different computers.

When a ClientDataSet and its DataSetProvider are located in the same application, code that you write for that application can freely modify the DataSetProvider, assuming that it is within scope. So, for example, if you want to change which DataSet from which the DataSetProvider will load its data, or modify a query for the DataSet to which the DataSetProvider points, no problem. Your code can make those changes.

On the other hand, when the DataSetProvider is not within the scope of the ClientDataSet, which is the case in DataSnap client applications, those types of changes simply cannot be made programmatically. Sure, the ClientDataSet has the name of the DataSetProvider in its ProviderName property, but that is a string property. Furthermore, that string value was obtained either from the IAppServer interface of a COM-based DataSnap server or the DSServerModule of an IP-based DataSnap server. It is simply not possible to programmatically control a DataSetProvider in a DataSnap server from a DataSnap client.

That being said, it *is* possible to communicate between a ClientDataSet and its associated DataSetProvider. Specifically, some properties of the ClientDataSet can affect what a DataSetProvider does, and some event handlers provide a mechanism for passing arbitrary data between the ClientDataSet and the DataSetProvider.

We have already discussed some techniques for controlling a DataSetProvider from a ClientDataSet in earlier chapters in this book. For example, in Chapter 2, *Loading Data with ClientDataSets and DataSetProviders,* you learned that you could set a ClientDataSet's PacketRecords property to limit how many records a DataSetProvider will return on a given request. The FetchOnDemand property and GetNextPacket method were also discussed. As a result, I will not repeat those descriptions here. Instead, I will focus on controlling the type of data returned, as opposed to how much.

This chapter focuses on three powerful techniques for influencing a DataSetProvider in a DataSnap server from a ClientDataSet in a DataSnap client. In the first technique, you will learn how to pass parameters to a DataSetProvider, which in turn will bind these parameters to the DataSet from which it gets its data. In the second technique, you will learn how to pass commands from a ClientDataSet to a DataSetProvider. Finally, you will learn how to pass arbitrary data between a ClientDataSet and a DataSetProvider.

These techniques do not depend on the type of DataSnap server you are using. They can be used, exactly as described here, on both COM-based and IP-based DataSnap applications. In addition, these techniques can be freely used in non-DataSnap applications, though as mentioned earlier, they really only make sense when the ClientDataSet and DataSetProvider cannot interact directly.

The examples described in the following sections make use of IP-based DataSnap clients and servers. These techniques, however, are no different when implemented in COM-based DataSnap clients and servers. If you are interested in COM-based versions of these same examples, you should inspect the COM-based examples that are included in the code download.

Passing Query Parameters to the DataSnap Server

If the DataSetProvider points to a DataSet that supports parameters, you can pass data to be bound to those parameters from the ClientDataSet. This is done using the ClientDataSet's Params property.

When a ClientDataSet becomes active and creates its request for data from the DataSetProvider, it can include in that request any parameters that have been assigned to the ClientDataSet's Params property. Before the DataSetProvider opens the DataSet to which it points, it will bind the values of those passed parameters to the associated parameters of the query or stored procedure of the DataSet.

Note: The code for the client and server applications for this example can be found in the IPDataSnapParameters folder of the code download. The COM-based version of these projects can be found in the COMDataSnapParameters folder. See Appendix A.

The DSServerModule of the IPDataSnapParametersServer project is almost as simple as that for the IPDataSnapServer project described in Chapter 13. The only difference is that the Query to which DataSetProvider1 points contains a parameterized query, one employing a named parameter in this example. The following is this query:

```
SELECT * FROM Orders
   WHERE CustNo = :cust
```

Other than the query being a parameterized query, there are no other differences. In fact, there is no custom code whatsoever in the DSServerModule.

Assigning a value to this parameter is demonstrated in the IPDataSnapParametersClient application. The main form of this application is shown in Figure 15-1.

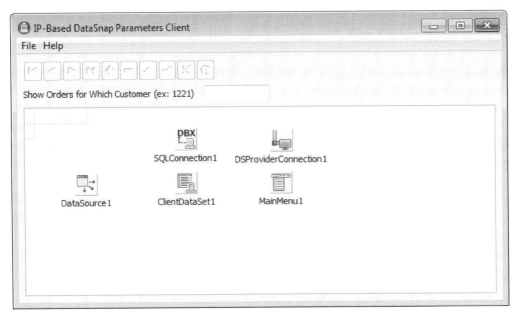

Figure 15-1: The main form of the IPDataSnapParametersClient application

The primary difference between this project and the IPDataSnapClient project shown in Chapter 14, *ClientDataSets and DataSnap Clients,* is the presence of the Edit, named CustNoEdit, and the code that appears on the OnClick handler for the Open menu item. This event handler is shown here:

```
procedure TForm1.Open1Click(Sender: TObject);
var
  CustNo: Integer;
begin
  if not ClientDataSet1.Active then
  begin
    if CustNoEdit.Text = '' then
      raise Exception.Create('Please supply a customer number');
    if not TryStrToInt(CustNoEdit.Text, CustNo) then
      raise Exception.Create('Customer number must be a number');
    //Good to go
    ClientDataSet1.Params[0].AsInteger := CustNo;
    ClientDataSet1.Active := True;
    Open1.Caption := 'Close';
    ShowMessage(IntToStr(ClientDataSet1.RecordCount) +
      ' records were found for customer ' + IntToStr(CustNo));
  end
  else
  begin
    ClientDataSet1.Active := False;
    SQLConnection1.Close;
    Open1.Caption := 'Open';
    ApplyUpdates1.Enabled := False;
```

```
    end;
end;
```

In order for this code to work, you must have first added a Param to the Params property of the ClientDataSet. To do this, select the Params property and then click the ellipsis that appears to display the Params collection editor. Click the Add New button in the Params collection editor to create one Param.

Next, select the added Param in the Params collection editor. Using the Object Inspector, you must set the DataType and Name properties. You can also set the ParamType property to indicate if it is an input or an output parameter. It is also possible to set a default value for the parameter. A ClientDataSet's Param is shown here in the Object Inspector:

Figure 15-2 shows how this project looks when it is running. A customer number has been entered, and File | Open has been selected. Of course, since this is an IP-based DataSnap client, this will only work if the IPDataSnapParametersServer is also running.

When File | Open was selected from the running form shown in Figure 15-2, the value 1356 was passed as the single Param from the ClientDataSet to the DataSetProvider. In response, the DataSetProvider bound this value to the :cust parameter of the Query on the DSServerModule. Then, when the DataSetProvider on this DSServerModule opened this Query, only records for customer 1356 were included in the result set. As a result, only those records were returned to the ClientDataSet in the DataSnap client.

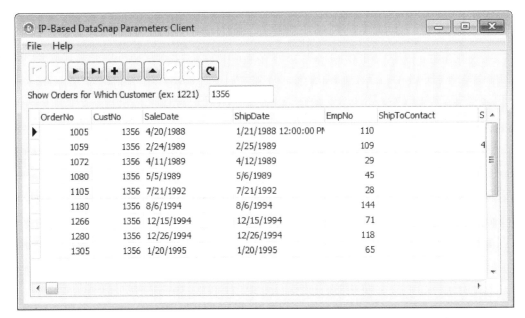

Figure 15-2: The running IPDataSnapParametersClient application has retrieved the orders for a single customer by passing a parameter to the DataSetProvider

Passing Commands to the DataSnap Server

While passing parameters between a ClientDataSet and its DataSetProvider gives you the ability to customize the data you retrieve from a DataSetProvider, it has its limits. Specifically, parameters can only be used in the predicates of a WHERE clause, or in the parameters of a stored procedure invocation. In other words, parameters can be used to specify what subset of records you want from a source, but it cannot change which source those records are retrieved from or change which columns are returned in the result set.

Fortunately, there is another option that is almost infinitely flexible. From the ClientDataSet you can define the entire command that is used by the DataSet to which the DataSetProvider points.

Note: The code for the client and server applications for this example can be found in the IPDataSnapCommandText folder of the code download. The COM-based version of these projects can be found in the COMDataSnapCommandText folder. See Appendix A.

You use the CommandText property of a ClientDataSet to define the query, stored procedure call, or table that will be used by a DataSet on the DataSnap server when the ClientDataSet requests records. Of course, this requires that this DataSet be one that accepts a SQL statement, executes a stored procedure, or opens a table. For example, a Query can accept into its SQL property a query passed by the ClientDataSet in CommandText. Similarly, a SQLDataSet will assign the ClientDataSet's CommandText value to the SQLDataSet's CommandText property. Even a Table component can accept a table name passed by a ClientDataSet's CommandText property to the Table's TableName property.

Once again, the example server is simple. In fact, it is so simple that it defines no SQL statement for the Query at all. The SQL that the Query executes will be defined entirely by the ClientDataSet.

There is one additional configuration that needs to be made in order to permit a ClientDataSet to pass commands to the DataSetProvider. You must add the poAllowCommandText flag to the DataSetProvider's Options property. You can do this using the Object Inspector by expanding the DataSetProvider's Options property, and then setting poAllowCommandText to True (the default value is False).

Passing a query from a ClientDataSet to a DataSetProvider is demonstrated in the IPDataSnapCommandTextClient application. The main form of this application is shown in Figure 15-3.

As you can see in Figure 15-3, the main form of this project includes two controls that you can use to define a query. The combo box can be used to select Custom SQL, in which case you must enter your own SQL query in the memo field below. Alternatively, the combo box also includes a list of tables known to be in the database associated with the Query in the DataSnap server. If you select one of these table names, a SELECT * query is constructed for you.

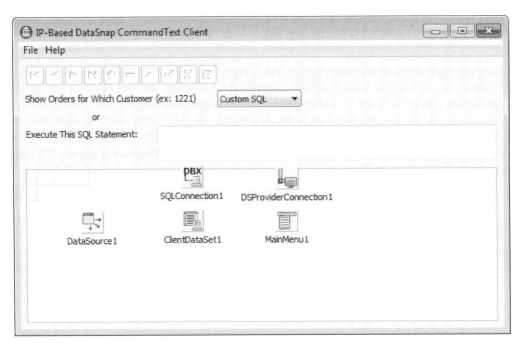

Figure 15-3: The main form of the IPDataSnapCommandTextClient project

The formation of the query and passing this query to the DataSetProvider on the DataSnap server is demonstrated from the OnClick event handler associated with the Open menu item. This event handler is shown in the following code. Otherwise, this project is identical to the IPDataSnapParametersClient project.

```
procedure TForm1.Open1Click(Sender: TObject);
var
  SQLStmt: String;
begin
  if not ClientDataSet1.Active then
  begin
    if TableNameComboBox.ItemIndex = 0 then
      if SQLMemo.Lines.Text = '' then
        raise Exception.Create('Please supply a SQL statement')
      else
        SQLStmt := SQLMemo.Lines.Text
    else
      SQLStmt := 'SELECT * FROM ' +
        TableNameComboBox.Text;
    //Good to go
    ClientDataSet1.CommandText := SQLStmt;
    ClientDataSet1.Active := True;
    Open1.Caption := 'Close';
    ShowMessage(IntToStr(ClientDataSet1.RecordCount) +
      ' records were found for query ' + SQLStmt);
  end
  else
```

```
begin
  ClientDataSet1.Active := False;
  SQLConnection1.Close;
  Open1.Caption := 'Open';
  ApplyUpdates1.Enabled := False;
end;
end;
```

Note: Permitting an end user to enter a SQL statement is dangerous. Allowing it is done in this example only because it emphasizes the incredible flexibility of CommandText. The problem is not that the end user might enter an invalid SQL statement. That will only cause an exception to be raised. The problem is that the end user could do real damage to the database if, for instance, they enter a DROP TABLE statement, a DELETE statement, or some other destructive command.

Figure 15-4 shows the IPDataSnapCommandTextClient in action. In this example, a custom query has been entered into the provided memo field, that query has been executed on the DataSnap server, and the results have been returned to the client.

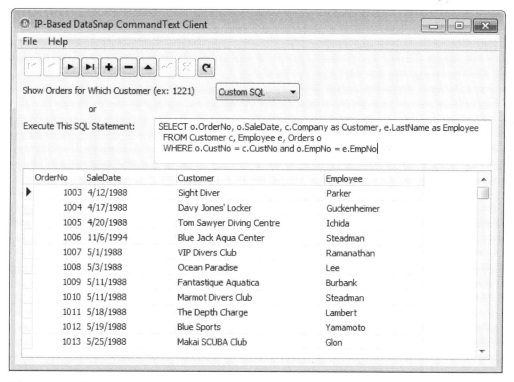

Figure 15-4: A custom query has been sent to the DataSnap server, which has returned the associated records

Note: Occasionally, a Delphi developer will see this example and come to the incorrect conclusion that a ClientDataSet can execute SQL. ClientDataSets do not posses a SQL engine, and do not process SQL statements. Using CommandText is pass-through SQL in its simplest form, and only works when the DataSet to which the DataSetProvider refers can execute the command.

Passing Data Between the DataSnap Server and Client

Although you cannot programmatically reach across from a DataSnap client and manipulate a DataSnap server, or visa versa, you can pass arbitrary data between the two applications. Your code on both sides of this interaction can then use this information to programmatically do something within their own process. For example, you could pass a string from a ClientDataSet in its request for data that includes a connection string. The receiving DataSetProvider could then use this connection string to connect to a database, after which it can use that database to perform the requested query.

Note: The term "arbitrary data" is not being used to imply some lack of importance to the data. I merely intend to imply that any data, for any purpose, can be passed between the ClientDataSet and the DataSetProvider.

While the preceding example demonstrates the additional flexibility that this feature enables, it fails to represent the complete arbitrariness of this data transfer. Specifically, the data that is passed between a ClientDataSet and its DataSetProvider might have nothing to do with the data request. For example, a ClientDataSet could use a MemoryStream instance to load a file from disk, and pass that file as well as the file name to the DataSetProvider. The DataSetProvider could be programmed to look for data in the request, and, having found some, save that file on the server using the file name that it was passed.

This interaction is two-way, in that a DataSetProvider can pass arbitrary data to the ClientDataSet. For example, having received a file from a ClientDataSet, the DataSetProvider may return some indication of success or failure of the save operation. Or, if the file already exists on the server, the DataSetProvider could return to the ClientDataSet the older version of the file before overwriting it.

You pass data between a ClientDataSet and a DataSetProvider by using one of several convenient event handlers that both classes posses. Examples of these event handlers are BeforeGetRecords and AfterGetRecords.

Which event handler you use depends on when in the request cycle the data is available on the sender, at what point in the request cycle the data is needed by the receiver, and what interaction is executing between the ClientDataSet and the DataSetProvider. For example, if the data sent by the ClientDataSet is needed before the DataSetProvider can load its data, like in the example where the connection string is passed by the ClientDataSet, then you will use one of the Before event handlers, such as BeforeGetRecords.

Similarly, if the data returned by the DataSetProvider can only be known after the data has been loaded, you will use one of the After event handlers, such as AfterGetRecords. Be aware, however, that whichever of these event handlers you choose on the sender, you may only retrieve that data from the corresponding event handler on the receiver. For example, if you send data from a ClientDataSet to a DataSetProvider from the ClientDataSet's BeforeGetRecords event handler, the DataSetProvider must also have a BeforeGetRecords event handler; Otherwise it will not be able to retrieve the data.

It is also important to note that not all Before or After event handlers execute every time there is a request-response cycle. For example, if you do not pass parameters to the DataSetProvider from a ClientDataSet using the Params property, the BeforeGetParams event handler will not fire.

One characteristic of each of these event handlers is that they include an OleVariant parameter named OwnerData. This can be seen in the following, empty BeforeGetRecords event handler:

```
procedure TForm1.ClientDataSet1BeforeGetRecords(Sender: TObject;
  var OwnerData: OleVariant);
begin

end;
```

If you want to pass a single value in OwnerData, you can use a simple assignment statement, such as the following:

```
OwnerData := SpecialMessageEdit.Text;
```

When receiving data from OwnerData where a single value is passed, you might need to convert the OleVariant to a value of the appropriate type. For example, from an event handler on the receiving end, the previously passed owner data can be read using code similar to the following:

```
var
  Msg: String;
begin
  if not VarIsEmpty(OwnerData) then
    Msg := VarToStr(OwnerData);
```

Note: The code for the client and server applications for this example can be found in the project IPDataSnapOwnerData folder of the code disk. The COM-based version of these projects can be found in the COMDataSnapOwnerData folder. See Appendix A.

If you need to pass two or more pieces of information you must initialize OwnerData as a variant array. There are a number of ways to do this and you should initialize OwnerData in a way that best suits the data you are passing.

The following code appears on the IPDataSnapOwnerDataClient project. When the OpenDialog that appears in this project has been used to select a file, the name of the file and the file's contents are passed to the DataSnap server from the ClientDataSet's BeforeGetRecords event handler.

```
procedure TForm1.ClientDataSet1BeforeGetRecords(Sender: TObject;
  var OwnerData: OleVariant);
var
  ms: TMemoryStream;
  TheFile: OleVariant;
  TheFilePointer : Pointer;
begin
  if FileExists(OpenDialog1.FileName) then
  begin
    ms := TMemoryStream.Create;
    try
      ms.LoadFromFile(OpenDialog1.FileName);
      TheFile := VarArrayCreate([0, ms.Size - 1], VarByte);
      TheFilePointer := VarArrayLock(TheFile);
      try
        ms.ReadBuffer(TheFilePointer^, ms.Size);
      finally
        VarArrayUnlock(TheFile);
      end;
      OwnerData := VarArrayCreate([0,1],VarVariant);
      OwnerData[0] := ExtractFileName(OpenDialog1.FileName);
      OwnerData[1] := TheFile;
    finally
      ms.Free;
    end;
    OpenDialog1.FileName := '';
  end;
end;
```

The name of the file as well as the file contents are retrieved by the DataSnap server defined in the IPDataSnapOwnerDataServer project. This can

be seen in the following BeforeGetRecords event handler of the
DataSetProvider:

```
procedure TServerMethods1.DataSetProvider1BeforeGetRecords(
  Sender: TObject; var OwnerData: OleVariant);
var
  ms: TMemoryStream;
  TheFile: OleVariant;
  TheFilePointer: Pointer;
  TheFileName: String;
begin
  if not VarIsEmpty(OwnerData) then
  begin
    TheFileName := VarToStr(OwnerData[0]);
    TheFile := OwnerData[1];
    ms := TMemoryStream.Create;
    try
      TheFilePointer := VarArrayLock(TheFile);
      try
        ms.Write(TheFilePointer ^, VarArrayHighBound(TheFile, 1));
      finally
        VarArrayUnlock(TheFile);
      end;
      ms.Position := 0;
      ms.SaveToFile(TheFileName);
    finally
      ms.Free;
    end;
  end;
end;
```

The IPDataSnapOwnerDataClient project includes a second interaction
between the ClientDataSet and the DataSetProvider. In this case, the
DataSetProvider returns information about the Query to the ClientDataSet.
Specifically, whether or not the query that was executed is editable.

A query is only editable if its records have a one-to-one correspondence
between the records returned and those in the underlying database. A side effect
of this is that it might not make sense to permit the user to edit the result set if
the query is not editable. In those cases where you will not permit the user to
edit the data, the Apply Updates menu item should not be enabled.

Note: Actually, it might make sense to permit a user to edit a result set when the query
that returns it is not editable. An example of this was shown in Chapter 3, Saving Data
with ClientDataSets and DataSetProviders, in the section "Writing Custom Updates
Using BeforeUpdateRecord."

The DataSetProvider reports whether the newly executed query is editable or
not using the AfterGetRecords event handler. The AfterGetRecords event

handler is used because only after the DataSetProvider has executed the Query can it accurately determine the Query's CanModify property. This event handler is shown in the following code segment:

```
procedure TServerMethods1.DataSetProvider1AfterGetRecords(
  Sender: Object; var OwnerData: OleVariant);
begin
  OwnerData := not Query1.CanModify;
end;
```

The ClientDataSet, if it is to read this information, must also implement an AfterGetRecords event handler. This event handler is shown in this code segment:

```
procedure TForm1.ClientDataSet1AfterGetRecords(Sender: TObject;
  var OwnerData: OleVariant);
begin
  if not VarIsEmpty(OwnerData) then
  begin
    //FTitle was initialized in the OnCreate event handler
    ClientDataSet1.ReadOnly := OwnerData;
    if ClientDataSet 1.ReadOnly then
      Self.Caption := FTitle + ' - ReadOnly'
    else
      Self.Caption := FTitle
  end;
end;
```

The IPDataSnapOwnerDataClient project is shown in Figure 15-5. In this figure, a custom query that produces a readonly query result has been executed. In response, the code on the ClientDataSet's AfterGetRecords event handler has made the ClientDataSet readonly, and has updated the title that appears on the main form.

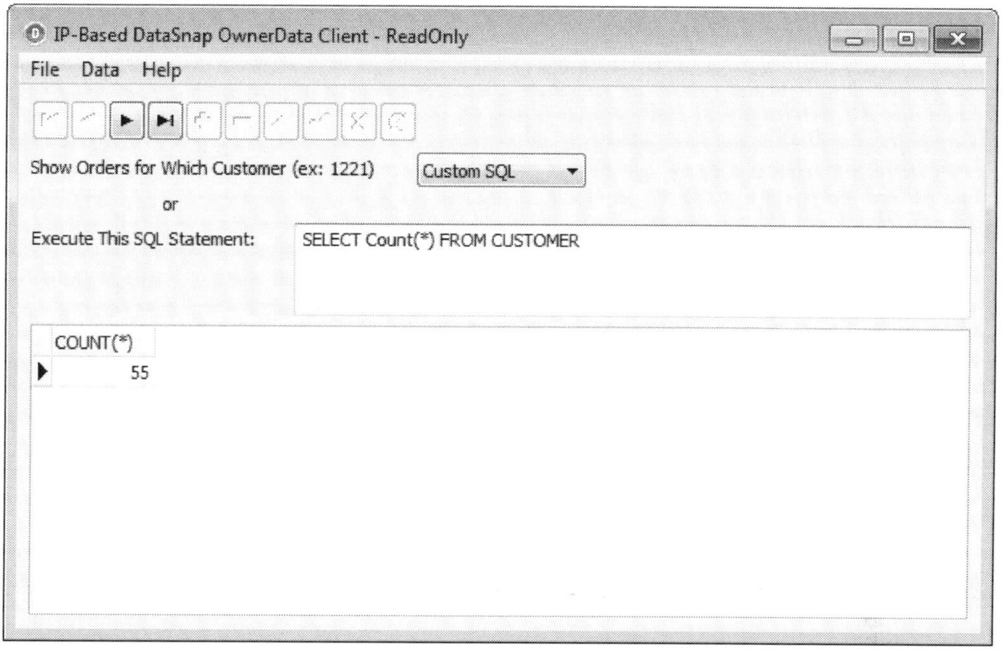

Figure 15-5: The ClientDataSet in the client application is notified about the CanModify property of the recently executed Query on the DataSnap server

Appendix A
Web Page for the Delphi in Depth: ClientDataSets Book

This appendix provides you with a brief discussion of downloading the sample database and code samples for this book

Web Page for the Advantage 10 Book

The Web page for this book is:

```
http://www.jensendatasystems.com/cdsbook/
```

Here you will find information about where to download the code samples, along with links for sites where you can purchase this book.

Code Samples

The examples described throughout this book are included in the code download. You will see notes throughout the text referring to either the project or folder that contains the project file. The code download is a compressed file named cdsbookcode.zip.

Note: When you download this compressed file, save it to a location on your hard disk. Do not just save the Web page link to the download as this page location may change in the future.

Once you download the appropriate file, extract its contents to a directory of your choice, for example, **c:\cdsbook**.

An errata contains a list of known errors and their corrections associated with a book that has been printed before the errors were found. And although I've tried to take care to ensure the accuracy of the information in this book, there is always the possibility that I will discover one or more errors after the book has gone to press. If errors are discovered, they will be reported with this book's errata, providing you with corrected information.

You will find a link to the errata on this book's Web page at http://JensenDataSystems.com/cdsbook. You can also submit suspected errors from this page. I regret that I cannot provide free technical support on this book. For information about consulting or training on Delphi, please visit http://www.JensenDataSystems.com/.

Index

speed. *See also* performance
    ClientDataSets and, 176
    scanning, 158
    searching, 156
SQL
    ClientDataSet to pass through
        executed, 307
SQL Server
    data source, 261
SQLConnection, 46, 292, 297
SQLDataSet, 11, 307
SQLResolver, 52, 59
StatusBar, 145, 156
StatusFilter property, 134
    Delta property versus, 135
StringGrid, 168
structure
    calculated virtual field, adding,
        87
    creating at runtime using Fields,
        89
    creating FieldDefs at design time,
        73–76
    creating FieldDefs at runtime,
        78–80
    creating Fields at design time,
        82–86
    creating manually, 71
    defined, ClientDataSet, 71
    defining, mechanisms for, 73
    example using Fields at runtime,
        92
SUM, 198
Table, 11, 307
TCP/IP. *See also* IP-based
    DataSnap client; IP-based
    DataSnap server
    DataSnap and, 263
    support for ClientDataSet-
        DataSetProvider
    communication over, 11

temporary index, 97, 99, 103
    persistent index versus, 103
    searching and, 159
Test Connection, 295
thin clients, 11, 262
Threading model, 270
TickGetTick Windows API call,
    156
TimeGetTime function, 155
Transaction Data Module Wizard,
    272
TRegSvr.exe, 269
UndoLastChange, 130, 219, 220
uninstalling
    IP-based DataSnap server as
        Windows service, 281
unique index, 96
UpdateMode property, 59
UpdateStatus method, 131
upWhereAll, 60
upWhereChanged, 60
upWhereKeyOnly, 60
Value List Editor, 298
VarArrayCreate, 167
VarArrayOf, 167
variant array, 25
    metadata, 25
VCL Forms application
    COM-based DataSnap client, 287
    converting to Windows service,
        279
    DataSnap server, 279
VideoLibrary project, 93
virtual fields, 86
VisibleButtons, 139
WebBroker, 272
WebConnection, 286
Windows services
    DataSnap servers, 279
XML file
    saving data to, 118, 121

MARCO CANTÙ
DELPHI 2010
HANDBOOK

Get up to speed with new versions of Delphi with the books by **Marco Cantù**, the best-selling author of the Mastering Delphi series. HIs new books are:

- Delphi 2007 Hanbook
- Delphi 2009 Hanbook
- Delphi 2010 Hanbook

You can buy individual Delphi Handbooks on paper (via Amazon) or in PDF format.

Looking for the complete set?

MARCO CANTÙ
DELPHI 2007
HANDBOOK

The PDF of the "**Delphi Handbooks Collection**" has almost 1,000 pages covering recent features of Delphi, in a single easy-to-search PDF file.

More information and links on **www.marcocantu.com**.

Delphi Services from Jensen Data Systems, Inc.

Cary Jensen is available for training, consulting, mentoring, and development. With more than 20 years experience in professional software development, he has helped his clients deploy a wide range of applications, including client/server applications, browser-based applications (ASP.NET Web forms and CGI/ISAPI), Web service clients and servers, Windows services, and batch applications.

Cary helps companies migrate their existing Delphi applications, oversees new development, and provides ongoing support and advise to development teams, and he can do the same for you. Whether you need only a few days or an extended commitment, Cary can help you either at your site or remotely.

For training, Cary provides both lecture-style and hands-on training. Classes can be customized to meet your exact needs, or you can select from Cary's prepared courseware.

Cary is also an Advantage Database Server expert. He can assist you in all stages of development, from configuring your Advantage databases and designing your data models to implementing stored procedures, triggers, notifications, replication, and more.

For more information, visit http://www.JensenDataSystems.com

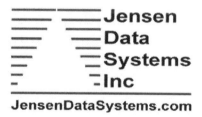

JensenDataSystems.com

www.DelphiDeveloperDays.com

Delphi Developer Days
Featuring Marco Cantù & Cary Jensen

Marco Cantù and Cary Jensen jointly offer Delphi Developer Days. Their annual Delphi Developer Days tours in 2009 - 2011 visited cities in the United States and Europe. Delphi Developer Days are multi-day live events and include both joint sessions, presented by Marco and Cary together, as well as simultaneous tracks in which Marco and Cary break out into separate rooms and present individual sessions on Delphi.

All attendees receive very detailed seminar books, which cover all topics presented by Cary and Marco, plus all of the source code. Attendance is limited to keep the event intimate so that you'll have the opportunity to ask them about any of the topics that they covered, as well explore other Delphi questions that you might have. Whether you are using the latest version of Delphi, or are developing with an older version, you will come away with information that will improve your development and make you more productive.

Future Dates for Delphi Developer Days
To be notified once additional tour dates are announced, please visit: http://www.DelphiDeveloperDays.com/NotifyMe.html

Brought to you by:

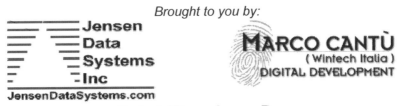

www.DelphiDeveloperDays.com